THE CHURCH AT WORK
IN THE MODERN WORLD

THE UNIVERSITY OF CHICAGO PRESS · CHICAGO

THE BAKER & TAYLOR COMPANY, NEW YORK; THE CAMBRIDGE UNIVERSITY
PRESS, LONDON; THE MARUZEN-KABUSHIKI-KAISHA, TOKYO, OSAKA,
KYOTO, FUKUOKA, SENDAI; THE COMMERCIAL PRESS, LIMITED, SHANGHAI

THE CHURCH AT WORK IN THE MODERN WORLD

WRITTEN IN COLLABORATION

BY

WILLIAM CLAYTON BOWER · EDITOR

EDWARD SCRIBNER AMES
ARCHIBALD GILLIES BAKER
SHIRLEY JACKSON CASE
WINFRED ERNEST GARRISON
CHARLES THOMAS HOLMAN
SAMUEL C. KINCHELOE
SHAILER MATHEWS

THE UNIVERSITY OF CHICAGO PRESS
CHICAGO · ILLINOIS

PREFACE

MOST of the separate activities of the church have been treated in introductions to the fields which they represent. These activities have been analyzed for the ideas that are operative in them, for the ends which they seek to achieve, for the techniques which they employ, and for the institutional arrangements which they have created. It is the conviction of the authors that the time has come to give attention to the operation of Christianity as a total movement in contemporary culture. From this viewpoint, what one actually sees when one considers this movement in its relation to current culture is the interaction of many activities in a total unified operation.

The authors have sought to make a beginning in this direction by undertaking to view the Protestant churches in America as operative in the modern world. They view the churches in action as constituting, in their collective aspect, the growing-point of a long historical process which at the same time adapts its ideas and methods of work to the demands of the ever changing social situation. They conceive the task of Protestantism in its relation to society to be creative. Its work is not only to be carried on in the present changing social scene, but if it is to exert an effective spiritual influence upon society, it must relate itself in a dynamic and creative way to the other social forces that are at work in the modern world.

The contemporary scene is one of rapid and fundamental change. In such a changing situation, the church, while utilizing to the fullest extent the resources of its past experience as a continuing community, cannot rely upon precedent to determine either its specific objectives, its procedures, or its institutional arrangements. The church at work in the modern world should face the future in terms of the possibilities of that world—empirically, and with insight, inventiveness, and experimentation.

The purview of this book is limited to Protestantism in America. Furthermore, its field is narrowed to the consideration of the practical operations of the Protestant churches. It is contemplated that the phases of Protestantism in America which involve its theology, its use of the Bible, its historical development, and its efforts in theological education will be treated in other volumes in a series of which the present book is the first to be published. These very important aspects of the church's life are not, therefore, dealt with in this book, except incidentally.

The difficulties of dealing with the Protestant church in America are very great. The difficulties arise in part from the fact that Protestantism in America presents no such corporateness as, for example, the Roman Catholic church presents. Moreover, endless varieties of belief, practice, and ecclesiastical organization exist among the Protestant churches. In order to present anything like a complete picture of the Protestant churches, it would be necessary to describe many varying types of belief, practice, and polity. Notwithstanding the endless variety of thought and action which the Protestant churches present, there is a certain inclusive identity of Protestantism which characterizes it as a movement. What, therefore, the authors have attempted to do is to select, interpret, and appraise certain types of activity which seem to them to indicate trends in the direction of the more effective functioning of the Protestant churches in contemporary American life. The authors have attempted to present these selected activities against their broad historic backgrounds, to analyze these activities for the assumptions and values that are operative in them, and to appraise them in the light of the new demands upon the church arising out of the changed social situation. The point of view from which the authors approach their task is perhaps quite as significant as the selection, the description, and the appraisal of the work of the church in the modern world.

It does not fall within the scope of this book to deal with the details of the several activities of the church, such as church organization and the techniques of religious education, personal counseling, missions, preaching, or the use of symbols. For such details the reader is referred to the considerable literature in these several fields. It is its purpose, rather, to bring these various activities of the church at work into a comprehensive view of their interrelatedness in a total operation, to interpret them, and to indicate the more significant directions in which operative Christianity, at least as represented by the American Protestant churches, is moving.

In the preparation of the text the authors have held

frequent conferences. As a result, while no attempt has been made on their part to secure unanimity of opinion on specific details, the discussion in the following chapters represents, on the whole, a common viewpoint and a common body of ideas.

The author of chapter ii expresses his indebtedness to Mrs. Marion Giersbach for draftsmanship of the maps used in that chapter.

THE AUTHORS

UNIVERSITY OF CHICAGO

TABLE OF CONTENTS

CHAPTER   PAGE

   I. THE GROWING-POINT OF CHRISTIANITY 1
      William Clayton Bower

  II. THE LOCAL CHURCH AND ITS COMMUNITY 19
      Samuel C. Kincheloe

 III. THE CO-OPERATION OF THE CHURCHES 53
      Shailer Mathews

 IV. RELIGIOUS CEREMONIALS AND THEIR SYMBOLISM . . 80
      Edward Scribner Ames

  V. THE CHURCH AS EDUCATOR 107
      William Clayton Bower

 VI. THE CHURCH'S WORK WITH INDIVIDUALS 134
      Charles Thomas Holman

VII. THE CHURCH AS A MISSIONARY AGENCY 160
      Archibald Gillies Baker

VIII. THE CHURCH AND THE SOCIAL ORDER 185
      Shailer Mathews

 IX. THE TASK OF THE PREACHER 210
      Shirley Jackson Case

  X. PRINT AND PROPAGANDA 236
      Winfred Ernest Garrison

 XI. FACING THE FUTURE 264
      William Clayton Bower

INDEX 295

xi

CHAPTER I

THE GROWING-POINT OF CHRISTIANITY

CHRISTIANITY A SOCIAL MOVEMENT

CHRISTIANITY is best understood in its essential character when it is viewed as a social movement. To think of Christianity as a social movement is to cast it in terms of process. Christianity is not something given. Its course on the field of history has not followed a pre-existent pattern. It is not now static. The future toward which it moves is not predetermined. It is a continual becoming in which change is united with continuity. Its outlook is in two directions—toward the past, in which are to be found its antecedents, and toward the future, in which are enfolded its consequents and its possibilities.

The Christian movement, however, is not an abstraction. It is an affair of persons, bound together in an associated life. It is, in its deepest sense, a continuing community. Under observation it appears as a group of persons behaving in characteristic ways. These behaviors are concrete and specific, and always with reference to concrete and describable situations. Its ideas are the ideas which people hold in regard to the meaning of their experience. Its techniques are procedures which people employ for the achievement of the ends which they seek.   Its institutions are the social structures which people evolve for making their collective purposes effective.

In its contemporary aspects the continuing Christian community is a vastly extended company of living persons who share a common body of ideas, values, and purposes.   It involves many races and many cultures widely separated by geographical distribution.   This cultural and geographical distribution has been greatly extended in the last two centuries. Christianity is for these persons a quality of life, real and present, and growing directly out of their immediate interaction with their objective physical and social world. In the going experience of this community beliefs are not remote and abstract theological structures; they are instruments for interpreting the present experience of living human beings and for rendering it manageable. Its rituals, ceremonials, sacraments, and symbols are not detached and self-consistent entities; they are techniques for expressing and reproducing appreciations that well up out of cherished values and for establishing effective relations with the spiritual forces that are resident in and beyond the group. It is only as Christian concepts, behaviors, and social structures become detached from the going experience of the continuing Christian community that as the products of past Christian experience they become external, formal, and authoritative. In their organized and abstracted form these cumulative products of a past Christian experience become Christianity in a generalized and abstract sense. In their vital and functional relations to the going experience of the contemporary

Christian community they are phases of the total behavior of a living human group.

But the Christian community has a still more vast
extension in time. As a continuing community it extends
over many centuries. As a historic movement it consists
of a succession of many generations of Christians. Each
of these living generations has sought to interpret its
interaction with its objective world under the conditions
under which it lived in terms of a body of values that
have come to be identified as Christian because they
have been cherished by the continuing Christian community. These ideas and values have not invaded the
life of the community from some remote and supernatural realm; they have grown up within the stream of the
experience of Christians through many changing historic
periods. This temporally extended community compre-
hends a great company of saints, prophets, teachers,
sages, and martyrs who have achieved immortality in
the continuing community. This was the insight of the
author of Hebrews who sought to hearten his contemporaries by reminding them that they were sur-
rounded by an innumerable company of the immortal
dead whose hopes and achievements lived on in the
undying aspirations and achievements of the living
members of the continuing community.[1]

Living Christians in their associated life constitute
the forward-moving present moment of the Christian
community. They are Christianity in its contemporary
aspects as a movement. The past of the movement lives
in them. They are the inheritors of its aspirations,

[1] Heb. 11:1—12:2.

ideals, and achievements. They are also the inheritors of its unfinished task. But they are more than the inheritors of the precious traditions that have arisen within the growing Christian community. As the living representatives of the historic Christian movement, they stand at that moment in history where the growing-point of the movement thrusts its uncertain way into the future. Within the moving stream of their experience in interacting with a changing world new functions are arising, new insights into the nature of the world and man are being acquired, and new values are emerging in the unending quest for the more abundant life.

CONTEMPORARY CHRISTIANITY IS CONDITIONED BY THE PAST

It is within this frame of ideas that it becomes clear not only that contemporary Christianity is continuous with its historic past but that it is conditioned by its past. History in its deepest aspects is a living tissue of antecedent and consequent.[2] This linkage of events is not something given and static. The present is the resultant of the interplay of social forces that are operative in the depths of the social process—often beyond man's conscious and intentional control. The present is not an isolated moment in time. It is in large part the outworking and the summation of factors that have been operative through long periods of history. Consequently, it is impossible to understand or appreciate contemporary Christianity at work in the modern world

[2] The concept of antecedent and consequent as here used does not connote causal relations.

except as it is viewed in the context of history. To remove the current Christian movement from its genetic past is not only to render it superficial and to rob it of its significance, but it is to lose all sense of its direction. To tear it from its past is not only to rend the living tissue that sustains it, but to mutilate the pattern of the whole, so that the fragment has no meaning.

But from the point of view of a social movement, contemporary Christianity is more than the resultant and summation of the antecedents of its past. As a movement it unites within itself change and continuity. The element of change is as important a characteristic of a movement, conceived as process, as is continuity. The living Christian community, like all its predecessors, is interacting with a changing objective world. New social forces play upon it. New situations, involving new issues, arise. These changing social situations make new demands upon the continuing community at the same time that they open up new possibilities to it. What the observer actually sees, therefore, when he contemplates the Christian movement from a historical point of view is a continuing community of like-minded human beings maintaining its identity through continuity with its past, but always undergoing change through fresh interactions with new phases of its present physical and social environment. What he sees when he contemplates contemporary Christianity is the growing-point of a long historical process which is at the moment of its forward movement undergoing still further change in response to the demands of the present changing social situation.

As a movement Christianity is a very complex process.

It presents the aspects of many interacting phases. These particular phases have a way of emerging within the process, of becoming relatively active—perhaps even dominant—with reference to other phases, and often of becoming recessive. As phases they may even entirely disappear. There are thus nuances within the process—even discontinuity in certain phases of it—but the continuity of the process is never broken. These nuances and these emergent and recessive phases of the movement are somewhat analogous to the mutations that occur in biological development, or to the growth of the several parts of the human body. In this way a cross-section of the Christian movement shows great unevenness. It is dynamic in certain phases and static in others. Some groups are creative, while others are reactionary. Groups within the movement show different attitudes at different times. Often these types of thought and attitude have been in conflict within the movement.

Moreover, the thrust that gives movement to Christianity is by no means always in the general direction of progress. At times it has quite definitely been in directions which deflected Christianity from ends that would make it progressive; sometimes the movement on the whole has been opposed to progress.

It is in this element of change that the possibility of creativity in the movement lies. Indispensable as continuity is to the movement, continuity alone would quickly come to rest in a static condition. This would yield only a survival of the past into the present. As a mere survival it would cease to be a movement. It would then be withdrawn from the dynamic interplay of social forces in which it is conditioned by these forces and in turn exercises an influence upon them. It would then become a subject only of antiquarian interest, not a force to be taken account of in the formation of the modern world. This is the Nemesis that has overtaken many one-time movements that have sacrificed change to continuity. Such a fate will overtake the Christian movement in the modern world, as it sometimes has in the past, if it becomes more concerned with recovering and reproducing its past than with utilizing the resources of its past in exploring its possibilities at the point where the edge of the movement cuts into the future. It is at the point where the movement is poised upon the concrete conditions of the present moment that new directions present themselves, that new possibilities open up before the movement, and that new achievements are glimpsed by the imagination. It is at this point of reconstruction that intelligence, appraisal, inventiveness, choice, and experimentation come into play. These factors of fresh insight and achievement constitute the creative phase of the Christian movement. They alone redeem it from being overtaken by institutionalism and traditionalism—qualities that inevitably destine it to become an exhibit in the museum that contains the survivals of man's dead past. But the creativeness of the present moment does vastly more than redeem the past from sinking to the level of a vestigial survival; it perpetuates the creativeness that has made Christianity in its truest sense a significant social movement throughout the successive periods of its historic development.

THE CHRISTIAN PAST LIVES IN THE PRESENT

It is this setting of the past in the context of the continuing Christian community that makes possible the insight that the Christian past lives in contemporary Christianity. This is not only true of its documents and institutions, but of its growing body of concepts and beliefs, its developing attitudes, its expanding outlook upon the world and man, and its enlarging values. Only, it should be observed, this living-on of the Christian past in contemporary Christianity is a differential process. Ideas, beliefs, techniques, and values are always relevant to the social situation. Change in the social scene always raises the question of the relevancy of the ideas and procedures by which the interaction of the living community with its objective world is instrumented. Ideas and procedures must, therefore, always be judged in the light of their functional relation to concrete and specific historical situations. Though vital and effective instruments in the social situations that evoked them, they may become dead and ineffectual in situations of another order. Thus it happens that certain concepts and practices that had their rise in the living experience of an earlier generation of Christians have become mere survivals in our changed world, and are no longer operative influences in it. On the other hand, certain ideas and values are of fundamental and enduring character. Their exterior forms may change with cultural shifts, but their essential validity survives the change that marks many of our most cherished concepts and formulas for decay. Effective functioning is the basis of this living-on of the past. When any part of the inheritance of the Christian past ceases to serve the ends of current living, it falls into *désuétude* and gradually loses its hold upon the attention of living men face to face with the realities of a going world. On the other hand, those parts of the inheritance that continue to serve the enduring needs of man not only live on but grow in clarity, in depth, and in their self-authenticating validity.

HISTORICAL CHRISTIANITY AT ONE TIME
CONTEMPORARY

Not only does the Christian past live on in contemporary Christianity, but contemporary Christianity makes it possible for living Christians better to understand historic Christianity. This comes about through the insight that what is now historic Christianity was at one time contemporary Christianity. Furthermore, in its contemporary phase it was practical. The outcomes which history records were at the time of their occurrence outcomes of situations as concrete and specific as those which the present generation of Christians faces. So true is this that it is impossible to understand the issue of events until the historian has reconstructed in intelligible detail the social situation within which the events assumed their form. The perspective of time creates an illusion of definiteness and finality which these outcomes did not possess when through much uncertainty they were arrived at. The washing-out of the concrete context of these outcomes leaves them stark and sharp upon the horizon of the distant past. But they were not so when our Christian progenitors muddled through many of their situations to outcomes that were just as clouded by uncertainty as are our own.

For the same reason the organization of these products of a past Christian experience into rational and logical systems seems to endow them with an intellectual quality that does not appear to attach to the present practical operations of Christianity. This accounts for the split that has not infrequently occurred between the "intellectual" quality of historic Christianity and the "practical" aspects of contemporary Christianity. This, too, is an illusion due to the warping influence of time. At the point of origin, the intellectual and the practical are inseparably united in an undifferentiated end-seeking act. Intelligence is the directive factor in purposive behavior, while the practical procedure consists of measures for making the act effective. Both originally arise when the free flow of end-seeking activity is blocked by frustration or uncertainty in the face of actual and immediate situations. It is only when ideas become abstracted from their concrete setting in experience and when action becomes irrational that ideas and action move in disparate planes. When the issues that eventuated in the historic creeds, the inclusion and exclusion of books from the canon, or the adoption of policies in regard to the relation of the church to the state, were present issues, they involved critical thought with reference to the factors involved in the practical situation and to their practical outcomes for the growing Christian movement. No less does effective dealing with the present issues which confront contemporary Christianity demand searching critical thought, competent judgment, and a command of tested knowledge than did the issues of any once present period in Christian experience. Neither is the demand upon intelligence less exacting in dealing effectively with these practical issues than in dealing with the products of a past Christian experience.

It was out of this stream of once current experience that the Christian community derived its ideology that, as time went on, became logically organized into the church's massive systems of theology. It was out of that stream of experience that there were deposited those bodies of literature that in time became its sacred Scripture. It was out of that stream of end-seeking activity that techniques arose for securing ends that would satisfy the spiritual needs of the group that in time have been formalized into ritual, ceremony, and sacrament. It was out of that stream of Christian experience that institutional structures emerged that have become the institutions of Christianity as a social movement.

RECONSTRUCTION IN CONTEMPORARY CHRISTIANITY

In the same way, and for the same reason, contemporary Christianity is reconstructing its theology, revising its techniques, and re-creating its institutions in the light of the demands of the present social situation. This contemporary reconstruction of inherited beliefs and practices and this creation of new ones are the direct outgrowths of the present interaction of the living Christian community with the changing modern world. In this the present generation is doing precisely what every preceding generation of Christians has done, and

what every succeeding generation of Christians will continue to do. Our own is not the first or only period of
change through which the Christian church has lived.
Some of these periods have been characterized by
greater rates of change than others. Our own happens
to be one of the periods of unusually fundamental and
rapid change. Nor is the reconstruction of Christian beliefs and procedures peculiar to the generation in which
we live. Other authors of this book have shown how
profound these reconstructions have been in relation to
shifts in the content and pattern of culture through successive Christian centuries.[3] One cannot overlook the
rise of Christian theology as a result of the impact of
Greek philosophic thought upon the practical way of
life of the early Christians which begins to appear in
Colossians and the Fourth Gospel in the New Testament
itself, or the effect of the Roman genius for organization
and institutions upon the transformation of the informal
early Christian churches into the Roman Catholic
church. Neither can one forget the influence of the
Renaissance as it swept northward in Europe to effect
the Reformation. No less can one neglect the influence
of the American frontier upon the ideology and structure
of American Protestantism.

It is, of course, inevitable that there should be a lag
in reconstruction behind the effective changes in culture
arising from the operation of forces that lie deeply imbedded in the social process. Interpretation follows ex-

[3] See esp. Shirley Jackson Case, *The Social Origins of Christianity*, *The
Experience with the Supernatural in Early Christian Times*, and *The Social
Triumph of the Ancient Church*; Shailer Mathews, *The Growth of the Idea of
God* and *The Atonement and the Social Process*.

perience—sometimes at a considerable distance after the event that occasions the reconstruction of ideas and procedures. This lag is not peculiar to Christian thought. It is signally true of art and philosophy. Science and technology alone of the various phases of culture show a more instant response to cultural change. In some instances they initiate it. This phenomenon of the gap between social change and the adaptation of ideas and institutions is what the sociologist calls "cultural lag."[4] The differential response of different phases of culture to social change accounts for the uneven character of current culture.[5] Ideas and behaviors operate under the inertia of tradition and habit. Religion, because it is concerned with the fundamental and comprehending values by which men live, has tended to be more conservative than most other phases of culture, and therefore slowest in its adaptation to social change.

THE PRESENT PERIOD ONE OF GREAT CHANGE

At any rate, the period through which we are passing is one of profound and swift change. These changes are the cumulative result of the interplay of many social forces that since the Renaissance have entered into the making of the modern world. In no period of the historic career of Christianity have changes been so profound in their effect upon human life. These changes are transforming not only the practical methods of living and the processes of production and distribution but the very

4 W. F. Ogburn, *Recent Social Trends* (1-vol. ed.), pp. 125, 166.

5 *Ibid.*, pp. xii ff.

structure of society and our intellectual outlook upon reality itself.

President Hoover's Research Committee on Social Trends has presented the results of its analysis of these changes in *Recent Social Trends*. This undertaking—the first of its kind in history—was an attempt to bring critical human intelligence to bear upon the movement of events in our time. It goes beyond description into analysis of the forces that have been and are at work in producing these changes. It seeks to interpret these forces and the changes which they are producing in terms of their meaning and value for human living. The study is cast in terms of trends, which points attention to the future and to practical programs of action in terms of social planning and social invention. In such an enterprise as this there is evidence that society as an association of living human beings is becoming aware of itself and of its responsibility for the application of scientific intelligence and collective purpose in discerning the ways in which our experience is moving and in giving direction to it.

Culture, like the Christian movement which it includes, is an exceedingly complex process. It, too, presents many phases, each, like Christianity, complex in itself. Its rate of growth and change is differential. It, too, like every other social process, when viewed in its inclusive totality, has its growing-point, or points, in the present. In this way various phases of culture, each having its own growing-point, may lag behind other phases which are developing more rapidly at any given time.

THE CREATIVE FUNCTION OF CONTEMPORARY
CHRISTIANITY

It is in this modern world of social change, with its science, its technology, its machines, its industry, its cities, its experiments in political organization, and its international and intercultural relations, that Christianity is to function as a spiritual force if it is to function at all. In such a changed and changing world it is the function of Christianity not to recover and reproduce the cumulative products of a past Christian experience but to discover the religious significance of the experience of the contemporary scene. It must discover the spiritual possibilities of the culture in which our common life is upborne and by which its attitudes are shaped and its ends determined. But the task of Christianity in the modern world is more than that of discovery. In so far as the living Christian community is true to its best tradition and to its unfinished task, its attitude toward the culture of the modern world must be creative. It must subject the ends we seek and the processes by which we attempt to realize them to critical analysis and appraisal in terms of the growing fundamental and enduring values which the Christian community cherishes as giving worth and dignity to human living. Its relation to contemporary culture should, therefore, be twofold. On the one hand, it should discover and give appropriate expression to the Christian values that are operative in the modern world—not in spite of its science, technology, art, and social arrangements, but in and through them. On the other hand, it should challenge the ends and procedures of modern culture by placing them in the context of man's deepest and most enduring spiritual needs and by judging the effects of both ends and means upon human values according as they defeat or further the achievement of the good life.

In order to fulfil its creative function in the modern world it is necessary that the church as the institutional expression of the contemporary phase of the continuing Christian community shall redefine its function. This function, which at the beginning of the modern period and well on into it seemed to be quite definite and clear, has become confused. In this respect the church is not differently situated from any other social institution. One of the striking characteristics of this period of cultural change is the redistribution of the functions of all our social institutions. Some of them are rapidly giving off functions that under earlier conditions clearly belonged to them. This giving-off of functions is particularly true of the family, the church, and the local community. On the other hand, certain institutions are rapidly taking on functions. This is notably true of industry and the state. This lays upon each institution, as well as upon society as a total organic unit, the necessity of redefining its functions under the changed and changing conditions of our time.

These changes of our time require not only the reorientation of the church to the total culture but the reconstruction of the ideology, the techniques, and the organizations by which it implements its functioning as a creative force in the world of today. With the emergence of new functions it is under the necessity of creating new ideas and new methods. It is increasingly clear that the church is attempting to carry on its work in the modern world with an equipment of ideas, procedures, and institutions that arose out of a past from which we are rapidly moving away. However valid and effective this equipment may have been for meeting the demands of the conditions under which it arose, it no longer corresponds to the reality of the present scene or meets the new demands of the present. That this reconstruction of the church's ideology and techniques has for some time been under way should not be an occasion for disquiet. There would be genuine cause for alarm if the church should prove incapable of reconstructing its ideas and approaches to the changed issues of the modern world. That would mean that Christianity had ceased to be a movement and had become a survival.

As the growing-point of a historical movement the living Christian community, set in the midst of the changing modern world, bears a grave responsibility. It is not only the carrier of the great inheritance of the insights, the aspirations, and the achievements of its past; upon it also rests the responsibility of facing the issues of human values in contemporary culture. In facing these issues with competence it will not only discover and fulfil its spiritual function in the modern world, but it will thereby re-create its past in a living and continuing Christian community.

SELECTED BIBLIOGRAPHY

CASE, S. J. *Evolution of Early Christianity*. Chicago: University of Chicago Press, 1914.
———. *Social Origins of Christianity*. Chicago: University of Chicago Press, 1923.

Stress the social approach in the study of history and the importance of viewing and estimating the past in terms of the situations, interests, and activities of real people.

DEWEY, JOHN. *Our Common Faith.* New Haven: Yale University Press, 1934.

Makes a clear distinction between the religious as a quality of man's experience and religion as the organization of the products of a past religious experience.

GRAHAM, WILLIAM CREIGHTON. *The Prophets and Israel's Culture.* Chicago: University of Chicago Press, 1934.

A presentation of the religion of the Hebrews as a form of social behavior.

MEAD, GEORGE HERBERT. *The Philosophy of the Present.* Chicago: Open Court, 1932.

Presents the thesis that the present is the *locus* of reality. The past exists only as it survives in the present, and is reconstructed in the light of the operative values of the present.

MATHEWS, SHAILER. *The Atonement and the Social Process.* New York: Macmillan, 1930.

―――. *Christianity and the Social Process.* New York: Harper, 1934.

―――. *The Growth of the Idea of God.* New York: Macmillan, 1931.

Present religion as a phase of culture, and therefore as a type of social behavior. Show the effect of social forces upon the development of religious concepts and practices.

Recent Social Trends. Report of President Hoover's Commission. New York: McGraw-Hill, 1933.

An analysis of the trends in contemporary American culture, with appraisal and suggestions for social planning.

WALLIS, LOUIS. *God and the Social Process.* Chicago: University of Chicago Press, 1935.

Presents the religion of the Hebrews as the outgrowth of the conflict of the Mishpat-Jahweh culture and the Baal-Amorite culture.

WHITEHEAD, W. N. *Process and Reality.* New York: Macmillan, 1929.

The application of the concept of process to the nature of reality. Reality itself is a becoming.

CHAPTER II

THE LOCAL CHURCH AND ITS COMMUNITY

THE LOCAL CHURCH

THE local church conceives that it has a parish. The word "parish" has geographical connotations. Occasionally a church speaks of the world as its parish. It is only with a sense of humor that a church can speak of itself as "the church of the indeterminate boundary." The struggle of churches to remake communities is significant as indicating that there is a relationship of the church to its community. Many churches hold that they must penetrate the community in which they are located. The revival service, the preaching mission, the great sermon, the church forum, the recreational hour, fellowship at the table, and the pastoral visit are means of making an outreach for members and for influence within certain geographical limits.

The local church is a continuing and a self-renewing group both by the addition of the children of its own members and of converts outside the church group. It also counts on the addition of members from other churches of its fellowship as they move into its community. All the major means for the continuation of institutions are used by local churches. These include the historic location, blood relationship, membership in a significant group, a continued leadership, and the momentum of community life.

Protestant churches are located in clusters in towns and cities and are often in competition with one another. This clustering of churches may be seen on the map of the white churches of eight early American Protestant denominations in Chicago.[1] (The term "early American Protestant churches" is used to indicate the Baptist, Congregational, Disciple, Episcopal, Evangelical, Methodist Episcopal, Presbyterian, and United Presbyterian churches.) This fact of competition has been one of the most determinative factors for the nature of the local church. It has often made for a kind of specialization and an accentuation of differences. The competitive nature of Protestant churches has kept the number of members per church relatively small and the salaries of ministers low. The average size of rural Protestant churches is about one hundred, while the average size of urban Protestant churches is three hundred.

Most churches emphasize membership and the sense of "belonging." Church groups often conceive that they are not only different from the larger community but also from the other churches of their vicinity. In this manner there is always a kind of subtle, if not overt, control over the conduct of the membership. It is conceived that the local church stands for something and that its members are in sympathy with its principles.

The significance of fellowship has been accentuated and magnified in Protestant churches. The member ex-

[1] See map, p. 22.

pects a degree of cultural and social homogeneity which the Catholic church member does not. Protestant people continually remark that they do or do not go to a certain church because they do or do not like the people who are there. While this human attitude may operate with Catholic people, it undoubtedly does not do so to the same degree. This is not to say that the fellowship of a Catholic church is not important. It may be much more important than their own members' theories regarding it would tend to indicate.

The local church usually has annual and monthly events, but its basic round of activities is weekly. The Sunday services at which preaching takes place are the events from which time is marked. Most churches have subsidiary organizations and activities but regard the main preaching or worship service as that which crowns the work of the week. The so-called "activities" of local churches are sometimes magnified, but are more often thought of as subordinate to the main task of the church—the utterance and inculcation of a significant message.

The organization of churches varies with denominational groups and with the size of the church. The church organization in many of the smallest parishes is exceedingly simple and informal. This is true in both rural and urban churches. Large churches often develop very complex organizations, with their highly specialized staffs and committees. The church school has many classes with specialized teaching and literature for each group. Some large churches have extensive welfare work and relationships with the community at large and with

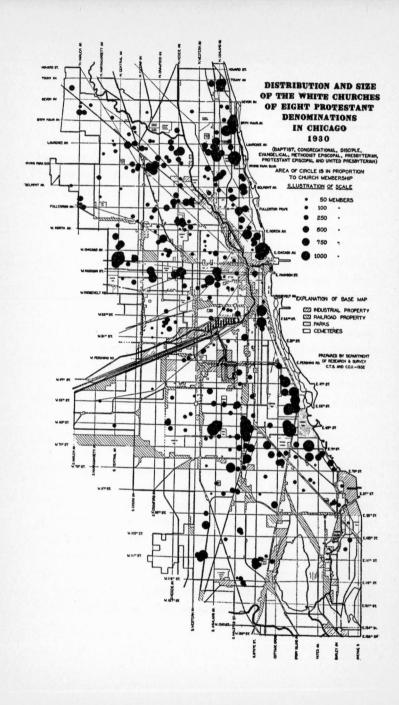

**DISTRIBUTION AND SIZE
OF THE WHITE CHURCHES
OF EIGHT PROTESTANT
DENOMINATIONS
IN CHICAGO
1930**

(BAPTIST, CONGREGATIONAL, DISCIPLE,
EVANGELICAL, METHODIST EPISCOPAL, PRESBYTERIAN,
PROTESTANT EPISCOPAL AND UNITED PRESBYTERIAN)

AREA OF CIRCLE IS IN PROPORTION
TO CHURCH MEMBERSHIP

ILLUSTRATION OF SCALE

- 50 MEMBERS
- 100 "
- 250 "
- 500 "
- 750 "
- 1000 "

EXPLANATION OF BASE MAP

- INDUSTRIAL PROPERTY
- RAILROAD PROPERTY
- PARKS
- CEMETERIES

PREPARED BY DEPARTMENT
OF RESEARCH & SURVEY
C.T.S. AND C.C.U.—1932

home and foreign missionary boards. Much committee work is necessary to keep contact with the overhead machinery. The study classes and forums have many different experts as speakers and deal with a great variety of topics. These large churches often have elaborate social and recreational facilities. The wealth and financial arrangements of churches which provide these organizations also vary. The financial ability of churches is related to the willingness to give and to the economic income of the communities in which they are located.

The nature of the programs of local churches is very definitely related to the vigor of denominational organizations. There are many forms of service which the individual church cannot create for itself but which must be supplied on a co-operative denominational or church-federation basis. Certain overhead services which denominational organizations offer, such as religious education and research and survey, may make for vital changes in the history of the local church.

THE PRIMARY WORK OF CHURCHES

Every Christian church group assumes that it has that which every human being needs. It has been said many times that it is not the work of the church to adapt itself to the world, to any local community in particular, or to any of the special conditions of humankind, but that it is the purpose of the church to transform the world into its own likeness. It is true that churches have certain broad purposes which may be very similar for all men. It is the task of the church everywhere to orient the human being to the cosmic order, to orient him to his fellows in terms of his own conception of his rôle in his group, to build a world-wide "fellowship of believers," to provide opportunities for "worshipful problem-solving," and thus to bring serenity to persons in a perplexed world and to produce prophetic messages describing the kind of world which we should have. These great tasks do not vary from community to community. They have a universality in both time and space. While it is true that these major purposes exist, very few would fail to recognize that communities are in very different phases of development and that the methods by which these great goals are to be achieved must be related to the conditions in which the various communities are. The language and program of churches vary from community to community. By modification for the needs of a local community is not meant the forsaking of principles but the interpretation of the church's message in such a fashion that it will be understood and used.

CHURCHES AND LOCAL CULTURE

It is clear that church groups, whether they will to do so or not, find themselves imbedded in and modified by the general culture of which they are a most fundamental part. The major denominations are related to the great cultural areas of the United States.[2] One of the most obvious economic, social, and cultural divisions in the United States is that between the North and the

[2] C. Luther Fry, *The U.S. Looks at Its Churches*. New York: Institute of Social and Religious Research, 1930.

South. Equally obvious is the distinction in the beliefs and practices of church groups in these two sections. Any one of the grand divisions within the United States, such as New England or the southern Appalachian mountain states, the cotton-raising states, the corn and wheat states, the Southwest or the Pacific Coast, has great variety within it. At the same time the predominance of different denominations in the grand divisions of the United States is clear evidence that so far as religion is concerned the beliefs and practices vary greatly from region to region. The French in Canada furnish a clear illustration of a natural region in which religion, language, and culture in general are coterminous. This very much abbreviated statement must call to mind the fact that even though people state the purposes of churches in some general fashion, there is a great variety in the way in which these churches behave in different regions.

Even though in our time in America cultural interpenetration, speeded up by all the modern means of communication, has gone on at a rapid rate, church people reflect the opinions and attitudes of local areas. The voting at the times of our elections is clear evidence of how church people take very different positions on political issues. It seems impossible and inhuman for a minister to be working with coal-mining groups and not to feel the struggle which those groups are making against the other groups with which they are in competition. The identification of church groups with local needs may be a form of colloquialism, but it is one that is difficult to condemn. It is true that in certain regions and in some denominations there is little relationship between the church life of many of the religious groups and the social problems which exist. It is often said that there is always a "cultural lag" of the position of churches with reference to the social, political, and economic problems, but very few maintain that there is no relationship between church and human need. Church people are always at the same time citizens and members of various other community groups. Human beings are unable to compartmentalize completely their attitudes and opinions.

A community is composed of a number of interrelated and communicating institutions which have a relationship to a locality. This might be illustrated from such a community as South Holland in the Chicago region. Here is a community which has life as a community. The observer finds a unity in it and a differentiation from surrounding territory and groups. When the community is examined it is found to have its life in its families, its churches, its schools, its nationality and language, its traditions, its background and unity, and its occupational homogeneity. Each one of its institutions is interwoven with the others, and all the relationships which people have through these institutions constitute the community unity. The community is not simply an area; it is an area in which people have some things in common and whose chief basis is communication.

While it is true that church groups are modified by local culture, it must also be kept in mind that denominational and religious groups afford a basis for a church group to be something apart from its local community and to act as a selective group in the local community, and hence to seek to bring that community into harmony with the general principles of a particular denominational group. It is at this point that we may see the working and growing edge of church groups. It is also at this place that modification and adaptation of method take place in order to accomplish the purposes of the institution. Effective churches in various types of communities are characterized by the fact that they make special plans to meet particular and peculiar local needs. Efforts to adapt a general position to local needs may not mean the relinquishment of principles but the growth and development of a new and more vital approach.

THE ADAPTATION OF CHURCHES

Some of the modification which churches have made has been "unconscious," a kind of biological adaptation, but in many instances a large part of it has been consciously planned. Groups have met and have asked themselves what they could do to meet the needs of their communities. These modifications have been in idea and structure—the two phases of any institution. They have been in the form of the modification of the content of messages, the manner in which these messages have been given, and the organization of the institution. The most obvious but perhaps not the most important modification has been in the subsidiary organizations in terms of clubs, classes, and activities which the church has used to give form and organization to its purposes.

It is clear that different churches in the same community are related to different cultural groupings in that community. There is a kind of competition going on among the churches in any local community by which process these churches take on certain forms which better fit them to meet the needs of particular groups. In urban communities there may be sharper contrasts between the different groups. In many small towns today a contrast is furnished by the Pentecostal, Nazarene, or Bible churches. In certain rural communities there is variety, but it may be on a very different basis from the variety of urban communities. There is competition without adjustment and accommodation. The main viewpoint may be very similar but some aspect of worship and practice is different. This might be illustrated by the Methodist and Baptist churches of the southern Appalachian mountain region where the main viewpoints of life are similar in all the religious groups, yet there are eleven Baptist bodies and nine Methodist bodies. The basis for the division seems very small to people outside the specific groups. These differences are something like the differences in the seventeen or eighteen kinds of Mennonites.

The urban aspect of this specialization and differentiation is illustrated excellently in one Chicago community where definite accommodation has taken place. One of the churches specializes on the beauty of ritual and the use of the best ritualistic forms to give expression to the life of its group. Its minister holds that the various aspects of life as represented by vocational groups should be brought into the church and hallowed there. A second church in this community has a very liberal theological point of view. This church maintains that religious values are always at the same time other kinds of values. It also specializes on a free and liberal recreational program for its people. A third church near by has worked harder than any other in the community to bring the different strata of the community into its membership and into its church school, clubs, and activities. This church has at times had the rather sharp problem of integrating people of very different cultural and educational backgrounds. Some of the other churches have been more selective of their membership by virtue of their more specialized appeals. A fourth church in this same community has taken the lead in organizing and maintaining a men's club for the whole community. None of the other churches has given much attention to this. This men's club has members from all the different faiths in the community. This church also maintains a pulpit with an emphasis on theology and at the same time on a social gospel. It represents an interdenominational or united-church approach in an effort to eliminate competition and to gain added strength and momentum. While each of these churches maintains its uniqueness and its own genius, all of them share the characteristics of the larger community in which they are located. Nearly all of them are willing to experiment in religious education, which is what one would expect in this type of community.

A religious succession is taking place in our time in those groups which have been impoverished and are unable to pay for highly trained ministers. The more emotionally expressive preachers often volunteer their services. The emotional fervor, energy, avowed sincerity, demand for social solidarity, reliance upon the proof texts of scripture, and promise of heavenly rewards catch the attention of uneducated people and enable these preachers to build a religious institution for the economically and culturally disinherited.

The established denominations tend to become formal, sophisticated, and secular in their approach. Many of them lose the sense of great causes and the sense of crisis and urgency. Many religious movements arise with great power and vigor, at least with much enthusiasm and the sense of absoluteness. They evidence sectarian attitudes toward their causes. As time goes on they tend to lose some of this sense of absoluteness and exclusiveness and are more willing to have dealings with other religious groups.[3] The newer group arising out of the hardships and sufferings can easily have the sense that its causes are great and urgent. Such causes are not only contagious but they give the adherents a sense of urgency and of mission which makes life worth while for them.

In many communities some of the older churches remain while a certain portion of the population accept the tenets of the newer, more zealous, and emotional preaching. The churches thus come to be related to the cultural groupings which have developed within the community.

[3] See Robert E. Park and Ernest W. Burgess, *Introduction to the Science of Sociology* (Chicago: University of Chicago Press, 1924), chap. xiii.

IN RURAL AREAS

From many studies which have been made, and from general observation, it would seem that the adaptation of local churches to the special problems of rural people has gone on at a slower pace than has the modification in urban communities. The general life in rural communities has had less stimulation for change in church forms or programs. In many cases there has been the tendency to emphasize the traditional aspects of each denomination. Rural churches seem to go to one of two extremes. They are either completely identified with the culture of the area in which they are or, because of language or a distinctive ritual, are quite apart from it. Language groups maintain their own distinctiveness with greater firmness than other groups.

The "larger parish movement" was at one time hailed as a kind of savior for rural religious life. It is operating today in very few places. There are still many churches with part-time preaching where more adequate organization is necessary. In these areas the larger parish would permit a region to develop unity in contrast with the one-day-a-week or one-day-a-month approach.

During the depression there have been some efforts on the part of rural groups in various parts of the country, but especially in Michigan, Indiana, and Illinois, to organize Christian self-help through community organization. These have been led for the most part by ministers. Some of these groups have gone in for classes and forums on economic conditions and several of them have taken their cues from the farmers' co-operatives. For the most part the participation has been in terms of

credit or consumers' co-operatives and very little in
terms of producers' co-operatives. While the co-operative idea is growing and seems to be breaking forth in
various groups, its relationship to church groups is still
very slight and is not growing at a rapid rate. It seems
to be a movement which is cutting across communities
outside the churches and making for community solidarity more rapidly than the churches wish to move.
Some ministers and churches are giving aid and lending
their forces to strengthening the farm bureau. The
various farm organizations take on different activities
and programs in the different communities in which
they are located.

In population shifts in both rural and city areas individual churches may die, but some at least of the
people move on to attend other churches. It is generally
agreed that the radio has very great significance for
churches, but it is not so clear just what effect it is
having on the redistribution of church populations.
Both rural and city people remain at home to enjoy the
gospel at their own firesides. In rural districts, owing to
good roads and automobiles, the village and town
churches have been gaining at the expense of the rural
churches. This has made for the mutual understanding
of country and town people. Often it has been the more
vigorous and wealthy people who have gone to the
towns. The shift has been to the very great disad-
vantage of the rural churches. In some cases the rural
church has had its parish greatly diminished, and the
village church has not yet learned how to think of its
relation to the larger community. The village has several churches which are selective out of the larger com-

munity but fail to see its unity. Instead of giving unity and self-determination to the local community, the churches in their denominational zeal are effective means of keeping the community divided.

It seems fairly clear that the newspaper, the movie, the radio, and most of all the automobile, are playing a significant part in changing the relationship of rural churches to their local communities. It is also clear that for the most part the more significant adaptation of the message and program of these churches is due to the local ministers. There are very few local communities which will not respond to a minister who has insight and some program of action by which the church may be related to the local community conditions and need.

Certain groups of foreign-language background may really constitute a society within the larger community. In many of these cases the minister is a significant leader for his part of the community. In fact, church and community are practically one. In some instances these ministers confine themselves to the narrow practice of religion and the church as such is not integrated with the community at large.

ADAPTATION IN URBAN COMMUNITIES

The city has a structure of which the churches and church populations are an important part. The churches are influenced by and in turn influence this structure. There are in most cities characteristic concentric zones within the urban area to which can be related types and conditions of churches.[4]

[4] Robert E. Park and Ernest W. Burgess, *The City* (Chicago, 1925), and T. V. Smith and Leonard D. White (edd.), *Chicago*, chaps. viii and ix by Dr. Ernest W. Burgess.

There are also in the large city, especially one into which there has been heavy foreign migration, sectors extending out from the heart of the city. These great population sectors have their linguistic, cultural, religious, and occupational characteristics. In Chicago the great early American populations from the East and Middle South and the North-Central states flow out in three great population ridges to the north, the west, and the south. A half-dozen other significant groups have started near the center and have moved out, taking their cultural and religious institutions with them.

One other important aspect of the structure of the urban community must be mentioned to give completeness to the frame of reference of the city, namely, cultural and population islands.[5] Neither the zones nor the sectors operate without resistance on the part of certain population groups. When one of these resisting population groups is able to compel the incoming population flow to pass around or to one side of it and is able to preserve its character for a time, the religious institutions of that community have an extended lease on life.

Very often the cultural islands are in the form of a string out from the center of the city along the main sectors. Occasionally, however, they stand out in relative isolation from the rest of the community. These separate islands have their sharp differentiation from the surrounding territory in respect to housing, economic income, language, religion, delinquency rates, and many other factors. The early American population islands have a number of Protestant churches near their

[5] See map, p. 35 for illustration of sectors and cultural islands.

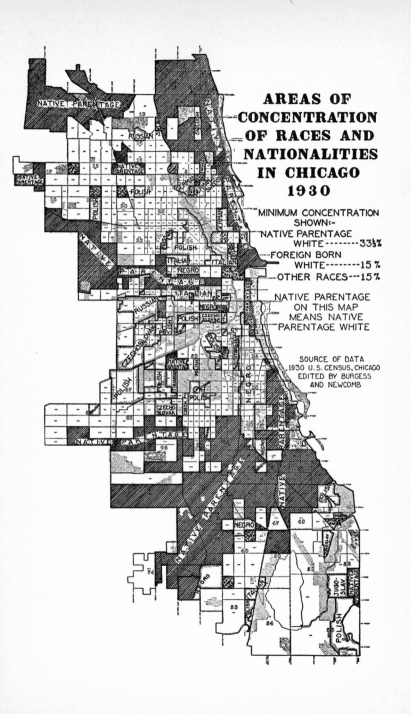

AREAS OF
CONCENTRATION
OF RACES AND
NATIONALITIES
IN CHICAGO
1930

MINIMUM CONCENTRATION
SHOWN:-
NATIVE PARENTAGE
WHITE -------- 33½%
FOREIGN BORN
WHITE -------- 15 %
OTHER RACES --- 15 %

NATIVE PARENTAGE
ON THIS MAP
MEANS NATIVE
PARENTAGE WHITE

SOURCE OF DATA
1930 U.S. CENSUS, CHICAGO
EDITED BY BURGESS
AND NEWCOMB

centers. Outside the cultural islands in the large city the churches are more widely spaced.

While it is more difficult to observe the local community in the great urban center, it is very easy to see sharp contrasts in the physical and social characteristics of local areas. The modification and adaptation of urban churches to their local communities also stand out sharply. There are certain major reactions which urban churches have made to the natural areas of the city. These major reactions are moving, federating or uniting, institutionalizing, turning to stricter religious faith and practice, dying, becoming downtown or inner-city churches. There are many gradations and special variations within these general types of reactions.

It is quite obvious that a downtown church in the center of a great metropolitan area does not have an immediate local neighborhood to which it ministers. Its adaptation is to the region from which its audience comes. The truly downtown church of the large urban area specializes in the voices of great preachers and great musicians. The themes have to do with the more general topics with which the larger community is concerned.

The church which is part way downtown and is a kind of sectional downtown church also tends to specialize in great preaching, splendid music, lectureships, and forums. This inner-city area—the great area about the heart of the city—has lost many Protestant people. It is in the so-called "changing community" from which churches move or in which they die, federate, or become institutional churches or neighborhood houses. Some of them make the adaptation of turning to a more strictly religious viewpoint. Some of them come to have an easier time because so many of their competing churches die. Occasionally a church in the great inner-city area becomes a community church in truth simply by right of survival. All these churches ask how they can become all things to all men in order to save some out of the great multitude that passes by and that their own lives may continue. The early American churches which have sought to maintain themselves in the great inner-city region have had to make adaptation to the changes in land usage which have come with people of different cultural and economic status. They have also had to make special adaptations to the major nationality and language groups. The more or less conventional adaptation among immigrant groups has been that of the institutional church and the neighborhood house. Modifications have come in where the conventional or historical Protestant church has been unable to live by virtue of an incoming group which has been largely Catholic or Jewish. Catholic churches prosper where there are many people of their own background and tradition. The same is true of Protestant churches and Jewish synagogues and temples. The only significant Protestant churches of the inner-city region which have maintained their earlier character have had generous support from a few large givers. Some of these churches have received large endowments.

The historical Protestant church in the city working-man's area has with few exceptions been unable to maintain itself on the basis of its conventional program.

Many industrial communities, especially in the North, have been composed largely of Catholics. Often the Protestant groups have turned to secular means, to the programs commonly used by settlements, namely, clubs, classes, recreation and various kinds of activities, and to the offering of personal help and counsel. These programs are costly and the people who receive the ministries either cannot or will not pay for them. This means that the support comes very largely from groups living outside the area. The Protestant churches have on the whole received few converts from these Catholic or Jewish constituencies. The adaptation, therefore, has been that of collecting money from the wealthier churches and citizens and from missionary and extension societies to maintain programs designed to do good to the great number of immigrants who came into the great American cities during the latter part of the last and the first part of the present century.

It is difficult for churches to plan for new conditions. It is especially difficult for such planning to take place where the incoming groups are of a different cultural background from the people who constitute the church group. Even now, as the second and third generations of incoming European population move farther out into the northwest and the southwest areas of Chicago, church groups are not in agreement as to the way in which they should meet the increasing problems of delinquency, social disorganization, and personnel demoralization. Should they foster neighborhood houses in these areas? Should they give their funds to the establishment of institutional churches in their regularly organized churches? Should they preserve their mission churches in the areas which are heavily Catholic or Jewish? Should the early American church groups, such as the Baptist, Congregational, Methodist, Presbyterian, Disciple, and Protestant Episcopal, encourage Continental European groups, such as the Lutheran, the Reformed groups, and others, to do the work in these areas? Perhaps the time has come for a more complete comity arrangement among these various groups. In many communities where the nationality background is mainly of northern Continental European origin the Lutheran churches find a ready response. It might be well for them in such cases to be given less competition by the so-called early American Protestant denominations.

The religious ministry to homeless men in the great city has specialized in messages of individual salvation of an orthodox and evangelistic type and also in supplying relief to the hungry, the naked, and the unsheltered. In some cities, notably Minneapolis, work in the open is provided and a program of reorientation is maintained. There are a few attempts to cultivate a fellowship in which the new-found life may grow.

The church in the rooming-house area has had a difficult time to remain alive. The people to whom it ministers need much time for personal counseling and problem-solving and many social affairs, yet the group to whom the ministries are made have low incomes to support the church. Churches in rooming-house areas have specialized and have spent much money in gaining contact with the dwellers in single rooms and small apartments. These regions have been characterized by great anonymity and high turnover. Moreover, many people in these areas find themselves taking attitudes which the conventional church cannot sanction and therefore purposely avoid contact with the people who want to make or keep them "good." Not only the church but practically all local community institutions have great difficulty in maintaining themselves in these areas. The need is very great for societies and fellowships in which young people in rooming-house areas may talk out their experiences and problems in an atmosphere of freedom and creativity, instead of cynicism.

Perhaps no part of the city has been more baffling to churches than the great apartment-house areas. It is disturbing to church workers to find so many people within short distances and yet to find it so difficult to support churches. The inhabitants of these areas have developed the attitude of unconcern for local conditions and local institutions. They seem powerless to change political corruption and to meet many other social problems. They do not know their neighbors. They do not own their own homes and can move when they wish. The high turnover rate of the population in the apartment-house area makes church work difficult and expensive. When the weather is good, people escape, if they can afford it; and when it is bad, they prefer to sit at home with the Sunday papers and the radio. The movies come as a means of emotional outlet and catharsis. Many churches in these areas lose from one-fourth to one-third of their old members each year. These must be replaced if the church is to survive. The families are small in these areas, which means that the group is not replenishing itself.

Churches in apartment-house areas have used a great variety of programs and devices to penetrate their communities. It is here perhaps more than elsewhere that churches need to be large and strong. They need to lift themselves up above the level of the three- or four-story building. They must have a momentum sufficient to swing community attention their way if they are to survive. Here is where the significant personality with strength, vividness, efficiency, and capacity for organization is demanded. The churches which succeed best in apartment-house areas have vivid preachers, have efficient follow-up organizations, develop great facility for communication and publicity, and offer fellowship to those who wish it, and, above all, have sufficient size and momentum to withstand the drift and movement of city life.

The churches in the non-industrial suburbs are best able to maintain the historical and conventional Protestant church programs. It is taken for granted that there is variety in the suburban towns. Many of them, however, are characterized by a normal distribution of the sexes and by a high percentage of people from thirty to fifty years of age. There is a goodly number of small children, but the college age and beyond is lacking. The men are away through the daytime. It is a return to the matriarchal dominance of family life. Church life prospers through the winter months but the great outdoors is popular in spring, summer, and early autumn. There are ample funds for adequate church buildings and capable ministers and often for additional staff. The wealthier suburbs tend to be very well organized, and the church often finds itself in competition with the extra-curricular activities of the schools and other activities for the time of the young people. In many instances the leaders of the town are in great demand. A few people are greatly overworked, but in many instances there are a great number who are not participating in significant group life.

Protestant churches in industrial suburbs have many of the same problems which they have in the region of workingmen's homes in the city proper. These suburbs, especially in the North, have a high percentage of Catholic church members. The morale of these communities is often low. The resources of the people are not great. Their churches are often drab and without real life and vigor. Just as in the city, the working people often need many kinds of help. The minister who succeeds is often the man who can find various ways of dramatizing in action the meaning of the Christian church. He does not depend on preaching and teaching alone.

All the foregoing types of adaptation of churches to local communities cannot be illustrated in detail. Perhaps a case of a church which is digging into its local community will help to make more vivid the principle and the process.

There is an early American Protestant church in an area of many laboring people in Chicago which impresses one as having a character which fits it to the needs of its area. It is an area in which many early

American churches have died and from which several have moved. This church has taken advantage of all the fatalities which have occurred to others. It does not call itself a community church but has all the other characteristics which community churches have. It is a church of the people. Its members are not very denominationally conscious but they are church conscious. If this church were on a foreign mission field it would be called "indigenous." Its local and neighborhood character is shown first of all by the distribution of its members, many of whom live in the area in which the church is located. The church building is very similar to other buildings in the community. Every part of it is used. Great pains have been taken to make it churchly inside. There is generous participation in the life and work of the church by the members. The people treat the church as they would a home. This is especially true of the children who come and go often. The music is by local talent and consists of a large choir of young people but with much participation on the part of the audience. The service is conducted in a beautiful and dignified manner. The sermon always deals with some of the great themes of life and of the church, but is filled with illustrations which are readily understood by the audience. The minister in various ways has identified himself with the life of the community. While the minister does not neglect the great work of a Protestant church—that of giving utterance to a significant message—he has become a symbol in the community of the Christian way of life in the good deed. Where there is trouble or difficulty he is present. He seems to sense the places and

times when he is needed. The building has been re-
modeled at small cost, and the general expenses of the
church are kept on a basis which is very little above
what the community can support.

COMMUNITY CHURCHES

One would expect the community church to be
adapted to its local community. E. S. Ames says that a
church is a community church to the extent that it is
available for the community in which it is located. Some
churches, however, have gone so far as to label themselves community churches. There are the denominational community churches where the advertising value
of the term "community" is sought but where the people
are warned that the church is related to some particular
denomination.   There are denominational community
churches where the denominational label is left off but
where the church is really a denominational community
church. There are union or federated churches where
the church seeks to become stronger and larger and to
eliminate competition by union or federation.   These
churches often quite frankly carry the names of the
uniting churches. Sometimes they represent so many
groups that it is impracticable or of no merit to carry a
list of names. Some of these churches have the spirit of
a true community church. Occasionally churches which
have turned from their denominational relationships to
become community churches have received a new sense
of their obligations to their local communities.

There is the community church which began as a community church and which has a zeal to live up to its

name. Very often its first step is to free itself as much as possible from any denominational emphasis. Its basis of missionary and philanthropic contributions is determined by the congregation without undue pressure for one denomination out of proportion to the membership and strength of that particular group. If a church has a community right-of-way, it has the great advantage of offering itself to its community for all sorts of needs in a way that would embarrass any one of a number of denominational churches with the other denominational churches in the community. It may offer itself without seeming to be indulging in unfair competition. The community church has a clear charter for thinking in terms of all the needs of the local community. This is only true when there are no other local churches. There are very few churches which are community in this more restricted use of the term.

JOINING FORCES WITH COMMUNITY ORGANIZATIONS

An important major adaptation of churches to many modern social problems in either rural or urban areas is that of joining forces with each other and with other community organizations and institutions. The complex nature of community needs is such that the individual attack of the local church does not succeed in getting results. This fact has been especially obvious with reference to the great problems of modern cities. The corruption of political life has been pronounced. Business graft has been present in great abundance. Much of the commercialized recreation demoralizes. The rates of juvenile delinquency have been high. Some church groups are beginning to realize that an intensive community-wide attack involving many groups and institutions must be made if delinquency is to be reduced. Modern urban community life is so complex that fragmentary or isolated attempts for improvement are certain of defeat.

There has been in Hyde Park and Kenwood in Chicago for years a rather significant co-operation on the part of the churches. They have had good fellowship and the usual participation in union meetings. During the earlier years of the depression they united in conducting a leisure-time institute for which they raised special funds and employed a director. Some members of the group conceived a plan for a community-wide attempt to meet local needs. The plan in general is that of a community council, but it is a more thoroughgoing organization of the resources of the community than usually takes place. The statement of the purpose of this group is as follows:

It will be the purpose of the Hyde Park–Kenwood–Oakland Community Council to look for the needs of these communities and to seek to have them met by various agencies, institutions and persons now existing, or to encourage new work that will meet those demands.

It is the hope of this group to eliminate wasteful overlapping and to use the energy of all groups to care for those tasks which remain undone.

The needs of these communities and of the entire area are to be interpreted in the widest sense; wholesome social, civic, economic, religious, cultural, family and personal life will be included.

The Council will make use of research and survey material and of common knowledge as it seeks to meet the new problems as they arise. It hopes that many of the older, more chronic problems of our life can be met with the new energy and thought which will come out of our united effort.

The enterprise has been characterized by unusual community interest and participation. This is a case of church people realizing that many groups other than the churches must be enlisted if the real advancement of the community is to be attained. This does not mean that any of the religious institutions will have less to do. They will have much more to do.

SOME GENERAL COMMUNITY NEEDS

Just as the primary work of the church may be stated in general terms, so the needs which are common to many communities may be outlined in broad terms. Some illustrations of these general needs are here outlined.

There are very few communities in which there is not an urgent need for the cultivation of unity within the organizations which seek the general public good. In many local communities there is wasteful overlapping, on the one hand, and neglect of special problems, on the other. The church is a kind of mother to the whole community, and a group which has the vision to conceive of all men as brothers may well lead in the coordinating and planning of the use of all community resources to build the good local community. This is especially urgent in the city in view of the fact that urban areas tend to be organized on the basis of associations rather than geographical units. Social control operates within special groups, but urban areas are often "nondescript" and lacking in unity and social control.

There is the need for a definition of public issues in practically every community, both rural and urban. In many communities individuals are unable to know the right or wrong of public questions. In many cases there is no absolute right or wrong but only a better or poorer position. In American communities today the assumption cannot be made that all people are working for the good of the order. There is great need for the clarification of the merits of the various positions which may be taken. This can very often be done without the church entering into partisan politics.

There is the challenge to the church today of family disorganization and personal demoralization. The task is not simply one of meeting the problems of divorce and desertion but also that of meeting the many subtle forms of discord and unhappiness. Undoubtedly changes are taking place in the mores of family life. The church and the family have stood together for centuries. The church has properly taken the position that the welfare of the individual is tied up with his relationship to his family. This aspect of our community work has been taken care of by specialized family welfare workers where the family has been on relief. Wealthier families have been able to get expert advice and help. There are many middle-class families where these problems receive no special help. A minister with insight into these problems may help make adjustments before the process of disorganization has gone so far that it can never be solved. There are also many people on the margin of personal disorganization for whom the word of the minister at the proper time may be the means of readjustment.

There are in many urban communities a great many delinquents. The problem of delinquency is a baffling one. It is so complex and has so many related factors which if not causal at least go along with it. Up to the present time churches have played a very small rôle in the reorientation of the delinquent. No one today, however, can adequately state the rôle of prevention which the church has played by keeping people attached to a group "in whose eyes they wish to appear well." The prevention of delinquency at the present time seems to be in terms of the use of time, especially in terms of recreation. This approach means that all the institutions of a local community must be engaged in the enterprise if delinquency is to be reduced.

There is a special appeal for church groups to participate in the set-up of recreational programs by and in a community as a community enterprise under the guidance of citizens and church members, as versus unorganized gang life, on the one hand, and commercialized recreation, on the other. For centuries the church has preached against vice, especially as found in recreation. There is now a need for leadership in a positive program in the use of leisure time.

The widespread presence of race and class conflict requires an understanding of these problems in terms of the unity of the human race and of the problems of human nature involved in such issues.

There are very few communities today in either urban or rural areas where political corruption in one form or another does not exist.

The church has, from time to time, taken a definite responsibility in educational work. While the state has taken over the work of education, the church may still find much room for the determination of the goals of our educational process and for working on the special forms of religious education and in the clarification of public issues by means of forums and adult education. These problems are especially acute in view of the fact that many high-school graduates have been unable to go on to college and are, at the same time, unable to secure employment.

These needs and many others are found in varying degrees and combinations in different communities. The program of the local church grows out of an understanding of the needs of the particular local community. Some churches are now using the research and survey methods of the social sciences to build up a picture of community conditions and to make them vivid for the members of the church and of the community.

In its effort to keep abreast of the times the church need not forget its main work or its own genius. While the church looks to the general public welfare of its community and realizes that experiences at work, at play, or in the home may break down or build up the so-called "spiritual life" of the member, it keeps ever before itself its great purpose—that of giving to the person a sense of the rôle which he must take with reference to the great goals of life and a sense of purpose and destiny.

SELECTED BIBLIOGRAPHY

BLUMENTHAL, ALBERT. *Small Town Stuff*. Chicago: University of Chicago Press, 1932.
Presents a description of the intimate life of a small town.

DOUGLASS, H. PAUL. *The Church in the Changing City: Case Studies Illustrating Adaptations*. New York: Doran, 1927.

DOUGLASS, H. PAUL, and BRUNNER, EDMUND DE S. *The Protestant Church as a Social Institution*. New York: Harper, 1935.

A volume which presents a comprehensive picture of both rural and urban Protestant churches in America today. It brings together the results of the studies made by the Institute of Social and Religious Research over the last thirteen years.

FRY, C. LUTHER. *The United States Looks at Its Churches*. New York: Institute of Social and Religious Research, 1930.

An analysis of the 1926 religious census. Reveals the regional distribution of religion in the United States.

HERTZER, JOYCE O. *Social Institutions*. New York: McGraw-Hill, 1929.

A sociological discussion of the nature of institutions.

HOLT, ARTHUR E. *Social Work in the Churches*. Boston: Pilgrim Press, 1922.

A study in the practice of fellowship; see especially chap. viii, "The Church and the Immediate Geographical Community."

HOOKER, ELIZABETH R. *Hinterlands of the Church: A Study of Areas with a Low Proportion of Church Members*. New York: Institute of Social and Religious Research, 1931.

LYND, ROBERT S. and HELEN MERRILL. *Middletown*. New York: Harcourt, Brace, 1929.

Section V deals with the religious practices of a typical midwest city of twenty-five thousand. One of the best recent community studies.

MORSE, H. N., and BRUNNER, EDMUND DE S. *The Town and Country Church in the United States*. New York: Doran, 1923.

OGBURN, WILLIAM FIELDING. *Social Change: With Respect to Culture and Original Nature*. New York: Viking Press, 1927.

PARK, R. E., and BURGESS, E. W. *Introduction to the Science of Sociology*. Chicago: University of Chicago Press, 1924.

See especially chaps. xii and xiii and Index for institution and community.

PARK, R. E., BURGESS, E. W., MCKENZIE, R. D., *et al. The City*. Chicago: University of Chicago Press, 1925.

This is not a textbook but a series of very valuable articles on the city. The volume also contains a Bibliography.

SANDERSON, ROSS. *The Strategy of City Church Planning.* New York: Institute of Social and Religious Research, 1932.

"Like Community like Church" is the theme of this book.

SHAW, CLIFFORD R., and McKAY, HENRY D. *Social Factors in Juvenile Delinquency: A Report on the Causes of Crime for the National Commission on Law Observance and Enforcement.* For sale by the Superintendent of Documents, Washington, D.C.

This is a study of the community, the family, and the gang in relation to delinquent behavior. It contains materials on the distribution of delinquency within the urban community and case-study materials on the factors involved in the process by which delinquency comes to be.

WIRTH, LOUIS. *The Ghetto.* Chicago: University of Chicago Press, 1928.

Presents a historical statement of the Ghetto and a description of a modern one.

WISSLER, CLARK. *Man and Culture.* New York: Crowell, 1923.

Presents a picture of the culture area.

WOOD, ARTHUR EVANS. *Community Problems.* New York: Century, 1928.

Presents a discussion of problems which are found in many communities.

ZORBAUGH, H. W. *The Gold Coast and the Slum.* Chicago: University of Chicago Press, 1929.

See for sharply contrasting areas within the city.

CHAPTER III

THE CO-OPERATION OF THE CHURCHES

HISTORICALLY considered, organized Christianity is an aspect of Western civilization. To be understood it must not be regarded as a philosophy or even a mass of doctrines. The human element is as strongly marked in the history of the church as in the history of the state. The same people that built Western civilization developed the Christian religion. A group of Jews carried their faith in Jesus as the expected savior of their nation to those who were not Jews who accepted him as the savior from death. The Jewish terminology was kept, but the Christians themselves were not Jews. The increase in the number and wealth of the Christians gave the church a political influence. And, conversely, the habits of the accepted theories and institutional organization furnished the patterns for the organization of the church. As the solidarity of the movement was kept by the adoption of certain tests of membership or creeds, orthodoxy was born. It was the belief of the victorious party. The differentiation which such a process was to accomplish in modern times was prevented by the state. The division between the Eastern and Western Christians was due to the division of the empire and the ethnic and cultural differences between the peoples of the East and the West.

Thus the ecclesiastics of both sections of Christians

regarded their views as truly catholic and orthodox. In consequence there developed two main types of Christianity. Both alike accepted the Nicene Creed and regarded the Bible as furnishing the material and authority for doctrines. Their theological differences were over such matters as the date of Easter and whether the Holy Ghost proceeded from the Father or from the Father and the Son; the real basis for the differences lay within the social structure itself. The Christianity of the West was to share in the collapse of a classical civilization in Europe, and to share in the evolution of a social order with characteristics quite its own. The area within which Western civilization developed was that of Latin Christianity. It was that development that is reflected in the history of organized Christianity. Eastern Christianity was static because civilization within the area of the Eastern Empire was to pass out of the control of Christians into that of Mohammedans. Arabians and Jews became the custodians of progressive culture. Christianity was the religion of depressed or unprogressive groups.

THE SOCIAL ORIGIN OF DENOMINATIONS

As a movement conserving religious and moral values, Western Christianity reflected the social minds of successive periods of European culture. Its history was one of differentiation of groups that attempted to give new emphasis or different interpretations to these values. The church as an organization became a replica of the Roman Empire, and in consequence looked upon such differentiation as treason or rebellion. Unity was maintained by crushing groups who proposed dissent from established religious formulas or organization. The state became the instrument of an attempt to build up a totalitarian church. The Holy Roman Empire in which the pope and emperor were regarded as the two vice-gerents of Christ was for centuries a theoretical unity although in practice it became a breeding-ground of bitter political struggles. The unity of the church became increasingly closely knit. It controlled the education, the family, and to a large extent the individual life of Western Europe. It was the religious institution of a developing civilization utilizing the classical heritage to give unity to its administration and its thought. By the thirteenth century the Roman Catholic church had become the representative of the cultural life of Western Europe, the organizer of political theory and the director of diplomacy and the mistress of social customs. Only in the field of economics and politics was its influence not absolute.

With the rise of the new nationalism in Europe there came a struggle within the church. Those governmental units of lands which had never been thoroughly Romanized broke from the Roman church and established churches under their own control. At one time a large portion of Western Europe had seceded ecclesiastically from the pope. The development of politics, however, left the pope in control of the areas that had been included in the old Roman Empire. State churches which arose from this Protestant revolution preserved the doctrines of Latin Christianity except as they insisted that justification was by faith alone and rejected the Catholic teachings as to sacraments, priesthood, and the papacy. Political and economic as well as theological forces combined to produce divergencies between the state churches. German and Scandinavian Protestants were Lutheran; those of Switzerland, France, Holland, the Rhine provinces, Scotland, and, in a modified way, England and Wales were Calvinist. These state churches used the powers of the state to maintain uniformity in doctrine and organization. But this conformity did not have the dogmatic basis of the Roman Catholic church, and for this reason as well as for the economic and political trends found difficulty in maintaining religious conformity. If their leaders conceived of a Protestant unity as over against the Catholic, such expectations were never fulfilled. Nationalism prevented ecclesiastical union.

English religious life was to differentiate farther than that of other Protestant countries. This was due in part to the rise of capitalism, which was particularly strong in England, as well as to the conflict between an unconstitutional monarchy and democracy. Not only were non-Episcopalian groups formed like the Presbyterian, who for a while controlled the state church, but separatist groups which were democratic in structure and came out from the state church. This may, with considerable accuracy, be said to mark the differentiation in Protestantism which we call "denominationalism," but the ground upon which these tendencies were most completely developed was Colonial America.

The colonies of America were the outcome both of economic expansion and of the pressure brought upon

religious minorities by the state churches. The migration from Europe to America during the seventeenth
century was due to both these causes. The colonists included groups who came from the state churches as well
as persecuted minorities. As a result, by the middle of
the eighteenth century the Atlantic Seaboard of America
was peopled by a number of groups of different Protestant origins. Maryland was the only colony founded
by Catholics, and Puritans early gained control there.
Congregationalists, Presbyterians, Episcopalians, Lutherans, Friends, and German Moravians maintained
with considerable precision their group solidarity, although they were in different colonies. Among them,
however, were developing still other non-conformist
groups like the Baptists and Methodists. Such a variety
of organized religious groupings existed nowhere in
Europe.

When the Constitution of the United States was
adopted, this variety of religious bodies led inevitably to
the abandonment of the idea of a state church. While it
is true that in some of the separate states the relationship of the church and state temporarily continued, the
federal government was prevented by the first sentence
of the first article to the first amendment to the Constitution from making laws "respecting the establishment
of religion or prohibiting the free exercise thereof." Thus
religious liberty was born of ecclesiastical variety. As
the means of communication developed, these various
groups of similar polity and doctrine coalesced, and the
denominations in the modern sense of the word resulted,
each with its own characteristic agencies of group action.

As the continent began to fill with its new inhabitants, the denominational groups all felt the responsibility for carrying Christian influence into the new territory. The consequent frontier life has been repeatedly described. It produced types of religious life which were less conventional than the parent-bodies of the Atlantic sea coast and led to a more or less unrestricted competition among the different denominations. Each was moved, not only with the common desire to extend the gospel, but also with the hope that their respective churches would share in the expansion of the American life. Doubtless because of the optimistic conviction that new settlements would expand into municipalities, denominational expansion was greater than later events justified. But, wherever and whenever the religious life furnished the chief, if not the only, opportunity for social life, it was natural that there should have been competition between the various types of Protestant life. Thus America became the home of denominationalism. The development of Protestantism became a competitive expansion of Christianity not only at home but abroad. It was a natural outcome of the application of democracy to religious life. Outside the English-speaking world denominations were numerically weak and in most cases the outcome of missions. On the continent of Europe Protestantism is largely limited to state churches. It is only in comparatively recent times that non-conformist groups have been legally permissible.

Paradoxically a perception of the dangers that lay in sectarianism has served to increase the number of denominations. The movement inaugurated by Thomas and Alexander Campbell in the first half of the nineteenth century sought the "restoration of primitive Christianity in order to the union of Christians and the conversion of the world." Groups under other leaders sought the same ends. Several of these united. Organization for maintenance of evangelism, education, and foreign missions followed, and since the middle of the nineteenth century the Disciples of Christ have made the movement for Christian unity a basis for noteworthy denominational activity. They have furnished not a few outstanding leaders in movements looking toward Christian union.

The development of strong denominational organization, despite the disappearance of the original ground for separation, still prevents the union of the northern and southern branches of the Baptists, Methodists, and Presbyterians in the United States. Such a persistence of disunion is due not only to corporate history but to social conditions and difference in theological attitudes. But these denominations respectively find a certain degree of denominational co-operation in international conferences which possess no actual jurisdiction but serve as a means of developing a sense of denominational solidarity. Such bodies are the Lambeth Conference (first meeting in 1867), the World Alliance of the Reform Churches (holding the Presbyterian system, first meeting in 1877), the Ecumenical Methodist Conference (first meeting in 1881, representing twenty-eight different branches of Methodism), the International Congregational Council (first meeting held in 1891), the Baptist World Alliance (organized in 1905; meeting every five years), the Lutheran World Conference (formed in 1923 from representatives from twenty-two nations).

Such organizations while conserving denominational loyalties also serve to lessen sectarianism in that they emphasize the need of co-operation. Particularly was the need of joint action felt after the World War when the Protestants of the United States undertook to assist the Protestants on the continent of Europe. Federations have been organized in France, Switzerland, Great Britain, and Germany. These organizations resulted in an increasing fellowship between the Protestant groups of the different countries. The National Lutheran Council has rendered much service to the Lutherans in various European countries. Through its Commission on Relations with Religious Bodies in Europe the Federal Council was able to send large sums for the rebuilding of Protestant churches in France and Belgium, and to assist in other ways in the re-establishment of continental Protestantism.

NEW DENOMINATIONAL CO-OPERATION

It is apparent that denominations sprang from experienced need and are the outcome of economic and political conditions which have largely disappeared. The various religious bodies conserve a common religious faith and, with the exception of a few of the smaller bodies, all but identical theologies. The old motives for differentiation have been replaced by a more or less rationalized loyalty to the denomination itself. Group inertia has largely replaced the early enthusiasm born of a sense of possession of more truth than other groups.

The theological struggles which played so large a rôle in the sixteenth and seventeenth centuries are becoming anachronistic. Denominations are feeling the integrating process of our modern world. True, the extent to which denominationalism is becoming co-operative is not uniform. The Catholic churches refuse official co-operation with other religious groups, and some denominations like the Southern Baptists and the various Lutheran bodies recognize it only within explicit limits. Yet among them there is an increasing readiness to join with other religious groups in social service, local evangelism, and other activities which do not involve what seems to them ecclesiastical compromise. Thus group solidarity is coming to serve religious and social rather than ecclesiastical ends. Outside of small sects, differentiation within Protestantism is being replaced by co-operation, and denominationalism, like democracy, is passing from the individualistic to the social stage. There is, in fact, often wider difference between members of the same denomination than between denominations themselves. A century ago differences between the Fundamentalists and the Modernists would probably have resulted in the formation of new denominations. At the present time they generally find expression in conferences, the specification as to how gifts shall be appropriated and used by the denominational boards, and, in rare instances, in the organization of new missionary boards.

Indeed, it seems as if the movement toward interdenominational co-operation has been paralleled by a new emphasis upon denominational loyalty and efficiency.

But such tendency is not a reversion toward sectarianism. It is rather a means of conserving a religious heritage in the interests of common Christian ends. The revival of denominational loyalty is now almost uniformly made contributory to the forwarding of the Christian religion rather than theological controversy. The structure of Protestantism, and particularly of American Christianity, illustrates how groups which have the same function, while differing in details, may become efficient means of bringing about a common purpose. By them secondary loyalties may be made to serve a loyalty to the Kingdom of God. Denominations thus tend to become not ends but centers of organization of the Christian movement.

As the basis of all co-operation is the fact that denominations and churches have in common the permanent values of the Christian movement. While there is difference in doctrines, there is common acceptance of Jesus as savior, monotheism, and the Bible as the source of moral and religious teaching. While superficially the Christian movement seems to have been split into hundreds of rival sects, actually this common Christian faith demands that these divisions be regarded as mutations.

There are three general types of proposals for co-operation of the Protestant churches.

First, the representatives of Catholicism within non-Roman groups seek church unity on the ground that there should be one church based on the acceptance of the Nicene Creed, the historic episcopate order, and two sacraments. The Lausanne Conference on Faith and

Order was the outgrowth of this conception, but found that various denominations as well as the Eastern churches could not reach unity even on the basis of the Apostles' or the Nicene Creed. History was more influential than plans for the future. Yet, despite its tentative character, the Lausanne Conference was an advance upon the conditions it disclosed, and did result in the recognition of a common Christian heritage and task.

The second type of co-operation does not seek identity in doctrine or polity but joint action in activities and moral leadership. The Universal Conference on Christian Life and Work held in Stockholm in 1925 represents this type of co-operation. By its Continuation Committee and its secretariat it has maintained the interest aroused at Stockholm, and has served to develop a sense of unity, especially among the Protestant bodies of Europe and the Eastern churches.

This type of co-operation without ecclesiastical union is characteristic of the federative movements among the various Protestant denominations.

The third type is that of organic union. This does not propose to end denominations or interdenominational co-operation, but attempts a closer union than that represented by federation. There has been a union of certain denominations like the Congregationalists and the Christians, the Free Baptists and the Northern Baptists, the Cumberland Presbyterians and the Presbyterians, and the merging of several groups of Lutherans. There is also a tendency toward the union of the Southern and Northern Methodist churches in the United States. The most striking illustration of this union of denominations is to be seen in the United Church of Canada, which includes the Methodist and Congregational and the major portion of the Presbyterian bodies in that country.

Obviously there are in these various proposals for Christian co-operation two radically different conceptions of the church. The one is that of Catholicism. According to this view as set forth by the Bishop of Peterborough, "The church is one big union, one great family circle, in which all groups with gifts and idiosyncrasies, so far as they are in accordance with the mind of Christ, would find a place." This view looks to a visible unity—"a Catholic church holding to the same fundamentals of the faith administering the sacraments which were ordained by Christ acknowledging one universally agreed ministry."

As over against this Catholic view is the Protestant which seeks unity through practical co-operation between the Christian denominations and churches. Such a conception involves no unity of ecclesiastical administration or of doctrine or affirmation of error on the part of others. It asks neither Catholics nor Protestants to yield fundamental convictions.

One prerequisite of Christian unity, in both its Catholic and federative form, is a common spirit of sacrificial love, and this is growing in evidence. Ancient issues which gave rise to opposing groups of Christians are sinking into true perspective. Protestants are getting together by working together. The outcome is as would be expected. Jesus Christ and his gospel are the center of the Christian movement. As those on different

ecclesiastical radii move toward that center, the nearer
they get to it the nearer they get to each other.

Present movements toward the co-operation of
churches are an illustration of a fact constantly recurring in Christian history, namely, that action has
been justified rather than caused by ecclesiastical and
theological formulas. As Christian communities ante-
dated the New Testament, ecclesiastical practices preceded the doctrine of the sacraments, and non-conformity preceded religious tolerance, so it is in the new
centripetal development of Protestant groups. Paradoxically, a denominational organization has become an
agency for interdenominational activity, and denominational loyalty is contributing to Christian unity.

The forerunners of this movement, however, were not
denominations but individuals belonging to various
denominations who joined in a number of organizations
and movements. Such voluntary unofficial groups developed a sense of common tasks outside of denominational activities. Their aims were practical rather than
theological. The past century has been marked by a
development of this type of co-operation. In most cases
it reaches across the national boundaries and serves to
develop a sense of unity of the Christian movement.
Chief among these non-ecclesiastical movements are the
Young Men's Christian Association, the Young Women's
Christian Association, and the Young People's Society
of Christian Endeavor. These organizations sprang from

the evangelical churches, and active membership in them has been conditioned by theological orthodoxy. The religious aspects of the Associations have become less characteristic than their social service through education, hostels, gymnasiums, and summer camps. They have thus become one type of agency through which Christians may co-operate in some form of social service.

The Young People's Society of Christian Endeavor, founded in a Congregational church, immediately assumed interdenominational character. In fact, its success in this regard was so great that the various denominations found it desirable to establish similar institutions limited to their own groups. Thus sprang up the Epworth League among the Methodists and the Young People's Union among the Baptists. The Young People's Society of Christian Endeavor, however, has not been entirely displaced by such denominational agencies.

Another youth movement was born in the latter part of the nineteenth century. The Student Volunteer Movement, while regardful of denominational organization, by its great conventions served to develop among college men and women a feeling that Christianity was greater than any denomination. At the present time many of those most active in interdenominational work shared the missionary enthusiasm as student volunteers or participants in the movement's conventions. It is not difficult to see the significance of the fact that the youth movement in America and Great Britain was evangelically religious. Its motto was "The Evangelization of the World in This Generation." Until 1914 social and political problems were only indirectly brought within its field. As the mood and interests of college students began to center around problems of the social order, the original interest in missions lessened, but it was the generation trained in this co-operative Christianity that furnished the leaders in the co-operative movements among the denominations.

The Evangelical Alliance, formed during the middle of the nineteenth century, brought together leaders of Protestant denominations from various countries. It had no official relation with denominations but served to unify forward-looking Protestants. It was a forerunner of other and more effective interdenominational bodies. As these developed the Evangelical Alliance found its field of influence narrowed and finally absorbed in new organizations.

Bible societies in various countries have been less interdenominational than distinct organizations which emphasize the common interest of Protestantism in the Bible. They have served as a non-denominational influence by circulating vast numbers of the Scriptures either in whole or in part.

Various reform movements accustomed the members of different denominations to common activity. These are almost innumerable, especially in the field of temperance.

The interest of the churches in international peace, especially since the founding of the Church Peace Union by Andrew Carnegie, has been expressed in many resolutions and in movements which represent not only Protestant denominations but Roman Catholics and

Jews. Probably the most active of this body is the World Alliance for International Friendship through the Churches which has constituent groups throughout Europe as well as America.

There are many other religious groups, composed of individuals drawn from various denominations, which serve as agencies for co-operative action. The effect, so far as Protestantism is concerned, has been to develop a new sense of unity. Co-operation of individuals has showed how wasteful and anachronistic is competitive denominationalism in the face of needs springing from the social order itself.

CO-OPERATION AMONG LOCAL CHURCHES

A result of this co-operation of individuals is to be seen in the new fellowship between denominations, the rise of federated and community churches, particularly in new towns and suburbs where the maintenance of a number of small denominational churches has been impracticable. Union ministers' meetings have become general, as has also the co-operation of local churches in evangelistic campaigns and in more or less short-lived movements against political or social evils. Church federations have been organized in a number of cities. Several of them have paid secretaries; others depend more upon volunteer work in which the union ministers' meeting is particularly active. As important as any of these city federations are those of New York, Rochester, Chicago, and St. Louis. These federations maintain workers in charitable institutions, organize religious education through the church schools, establish general

programs of comity and church extension, support undenominational churches among foreigners, establish
co-operative evangelism, and more or less systematically
tend to build up moral reserve for citizenship. In the
development of these federations is clearly to be seen
the growing conviction that while denominations conserve historic loyalties, differences in doctrine and polity
are less significant than a common responsibility to extend the influence of the Christian religion. The executive secretaries of state and local federations have organized an association which serves as a clearing house for
discussion and planning.

CO-OPERATION IN RELIGIOUS EDUCATION

In the field of religious education there has been a
distinct growth of co-operation. This will be described
in chapter v, "The Church as Educator," and it is
necessary at present only to call attention to the outstanding facts in the history of this development during
the last three-quarters of a century. While Sunday
schools had been in existence for a number of years, it
was not until 1872 that the attempt was made to develop
uniform lesson series. From this new interest developed
the International Sunday School Association. The financial dependence of this organization upon various
publishing houses led at last to the organization of the
Sunday School Council of Evangelical Denominations
in 1910. At the same time there developed a World Sunday School Association which endeavored to unify religious education in the various countries. The world-

wide organization, however, did not lead to such thorough co-operation as was developing in America. In 1922 the two bodies above mentioned, which had been more or less rivals, merged in the International Council of Religious Education, which represents forty-three leading evangelical Protestant denominations in the United States and Canada. Through this Council the various denominations are enabled to utilize the new efficiencies which have developed within the field of religious education and reorganize their curriculums and methods.

The interest in the religious education of the rising generation appears also in the co-operation of nineteen church boards of education, in the Council of Church Boards of Education. The purposes of this body are stated as "to promote the interest of Christian education as conducted by the boards represented through the interchange of ideas, the establishing of fundamental educational principles held in common, and co-operation upon the field wherever practicable." The Council, through its constituent boards of education, has connection with the work of 278 colleges, 71 junior colleges, 227 secondary schools, 93 theological schools and departments, and 30 training schools. While it has no actual authority, it is an agent for co-operation, and in its publications is an organ of communication between various workers in educational institutions. Theological seminaries have formed a conference for the discussion of theological education. It initiated an investigation which was carried forward by the Institute for Social and Religious Research. The resulting study has been issued in a series of four volumes: "The Education of American Ministers."

CO-OPERATION OF MISSIONARY BOARDS

The co-operative spirit among the denominations is especially to be seen in the committees and conferences composed of representatives of various mission boards.

The Home Missions Council represents 26 denominational boards and affiliated relationship with 10 interdenominational bodies, 19 state home-mission councils, 15 state councils of churches, and 45 city church federations. Through its committees on church building and architecture, rural church work, city work, comity, and publicity, it endeavors to prevent duplication of work in new fields; and, in co-operation with the Council of Women for Home Missions and the Federal Council of the Churches of Christ in America, it carries on work among the Indians and immigrants and foreign-speaking persons. The Home Missions Council has been especially active in the various regions of the West, and has established a joint department of co-operating boards on the Christian approach to the Jews. It issues tracts and other forms of publications looking toward the development of co-operative action.

The Council of Women for Home Missions represents twenty-three women's home mission boards of the United States and Canada. This Council publishes books for the study of home and foreign missions and also holds conferences and institutes for the study of missions. It works in close co-operation with the Federation of Women's Boards of Foreign Missions, and in developing an inclusive program does not make the conventional sharp distinctions between home and foreign missions.

In foreign missions there has been a marked development in co-operation during recent years. Its cause lies not only in the new co-operative spirit of denominationalism but in a recognition of the responsibility for self-direction which is being taken over by the new churches in mission areas. In this particular the missionary movement is being affected by the new national spirit which developed in China and India. The denominational differences which have grown up in America and Europe seem out of place in the lands where no historical basis for such distinctive bodies exists. Confronting common tasks, the various missions have tended, during recent years, to allocate the areas of denominational responsibility and at the same time to transfer responsibility to native churches. In South India definite steps have been taken toward the organization of an inclusive church. In other mission fields there is co-operation between the various denominations in the maintenance of schools, colleges, and theological seminaries. In these regards not a few of the mission fields are in advance of their supporting denominations in America. Asiatic Christians find increasing difficulty in the maintenance of denominational competition, and among the missions themselves co-operation is being furthered by national and local councils.

The Foreign Missions Conference of North America at the present time represents 118 foreign-mission boards and societies. Its purpose is the establishment of general plans which may be put into operation by the respective mission boards. It endeavors to prevent overlapping of work, to develop friendly relations between denominational leaders, to hold conferences on special problems, and in general to face the new conditions which are so rapidly developing on the foreign field. It also furthers research. This Conference and its Committee of Reference and Counsel are purely advisory, but constitute an important means for the consideration of administrative and other problems which arise in the foreign missionary undertaking. It also unites with the national missionary organizations of other countries in the support of the International Missionary Council which was an outgrowth of the World Missionary Conference held in Edinburgh in 1910. Under the auspices of this latter body a Council of 250 Christians from all parts of the world met at Jerusalem and sought to define more accurately a common task of foreign missions. Altogether, as might be expected, co-operative Christian effort is being decisively furthered by the foreign missionary movement.[1]

The importance of such co-operation is obvious. It, however, like all co-operative movements, is exposed to dangers. On the one hand, the action of a co-operative body will always be retarded by the desire not to break with its most conservative elements. On the other hand, policies and methods tend to become static and are in constant need of readjustment as conditions which vary greatly in different areas and peoples are better understood. The transfer of detailed control to interdenomi-

[1] See, for further discussion, chap. vii.

national groups of missionaries and nationals serves in considerable measure to void these difficulties. But many mission boards are sensitive to any criticism which seems to affect the doctrinal or ecclesiastical presuppositions upon which they are based.

THE FEDERAL COUNCIL OF THE CHURCHES OF CHRIST IN AMERICA

The Evangelical Alliance proved to be the beginning of a federative movement far greater than itself. In 1893, at a meeting of the Alliance in Chicago, Dr. Philip Schaff proposed there should be some sort of federal government in which various denominations should cooperate in the "spread of the gospel at home and abroad, the defense of the faith against infidelity, elevation of the poor and neglected classes of society, works of philanthropy and charity, and moral reform." There followed the development of the Open and Institutional Church League, the National Federation of Churches and Christian Workers, the Interchurch Conference on Federation in 1905, and in 1908 the great meeting in Philadelphia at which was organized the Federal Council of the Churches of Christ in America. The action leading to its organization was taken by a body largely composed of delegates chosen from various denominations which had adopted the plan of federation which had been proposed by the Interchurch Conference on Federation. While non-evangelical bodies had participated in that Conference, the organizers of the Federal Council found it advisable to make evangelicalism a basis for membership in the new organization. The preamble to its constitution states the purpose of the Federal Council "to manifest the essential oneness of the Christian churches of America in Jesus Christ as their divine Lord and Saviour." Several city and state federations have no such theological basis of membership, but it is probably true that the experiment made by the Federal Council could hardly have been successful had the doctrinal test been absent. As it was, doctrinal sensitiveness prevents membership on the part of several religious bodies, among them the American Protestant Episcopal church, Lutheran bodies, and the Southern Baptist Convention. At the present time 23 denominations, with approximately 22,000,000 communicants, send delegates to the Council, and the Episcopal and the United Lutheran churches have co-operative or consultative relationship.

In order to keep the denominations in closer contact with its activities, the Council now meets biennially rather than every four years. As its name indicates, it is a body of delegates chosen by the constituent religious bodies. Each is entitled to three members and one additional member for every 100,000 of its communicants or major fraction thereof. The Federal Council has no authority over its constituent bodies, and its province is limited to the expression of its counsel and the recommending of a course of action in matters of common interest to the churches, local councils, and individual Christians. It has no authority to draw up a common creed or form of government or of worship, or in any way to limit the full autonomy of the Christian bodies adhering to it. Its object as stated in the constitution is:

(1) to express the fellowship and catholic unity of the Christian church; (2) to bring the Christian bodies of America into united service for Christ and the world; (3) to encourage devotional fellowship and mutual counsel concerning the spiritual life and religious activities of the churches; (4) to secure a larger combined influence for the churches of Christ in all matters affecting the moral and social condition of the people, so as to promote the application of the law of Christ in every relation of human life; (5) to assist in the organization of local branches of the Federal Council to promote its aims in their communities.

There has been a steady growth in the influence of the Federal Council as a means of expressing the general feeling of the Protestant bodies. Since it has no authority, its actions cannot be regarded as binding, and hardly a year passes in which some of its constituent bodies do not find it necessary to reconsider its membership because of displeasure at some public expression of the Federal Council or some of its commissions. The actual withdrawals, however, have been few. The opinion has been expressed that there should be relationship in the Federal Council analogous to that of the states to the federal government of the United States. These proposals have not met with general acceptance.

The efficiency of the Federal Council has been due largely to its general secretary and Executive Committee. In its earlier stages there was danger lest the public announcements of its commissions might be in advance of the sympathies of its constituent bodies, but as the Council became better organized, much of the criticism was avoided. At the same time it is to the credit of the Council that it has had a great share in the organization of Christian attitudes toward war and economic changes. In this regard probably its most significant act has been the publication of what came to be known as the *Social Creed of the Churches*, which states in distinct form what may be regarded as social idealism.[2]

In other respects the Federal Council has been an agent of Christian public opinion. As the Roman Catholic church embodies the principles of imperialism, so the Federal Council embodies the principles of federative democracy. It illustrates how in religion it is possible to find unity in attitude without coercion in organization.

The sense of a common task is forcing Protestantism to a community of feeling and purpose. It is growing clear that if Christians are to have their desired influence, they must abandon their ancient hostilities and devote themselves co-operatively to the salvage of individuals and a distracted world. However great may be the economic and political elements in the present world-tension, the human element is certainly supreme. Disarmament, industrial justice, and international hatred are ultimately problems of personality. Men must gain the attitude of good will if they are to organize a better world. To develop good will, to energize it with faith in God and love for man, is indisputably the function of a church. The problems of the individual are too similar to permit interchurch hostility. A common

---

[2] The creed in its present form, adopted in the session of 1932, is printed in chap. viii.

effort for a common cause, a sense of the Christian needs of society and individuals, alike serve to emphasize beliefs in which Christian bodies agree rather than doctrines in which they differ.

SELECTED BIBLIOGRAPHY

Annual Reports of the Federal Council of the Churches of Christ in America.

These are indispensable for the understanding of the federation movement in the United States. The publications of the Federal Council not only cover actions of the successive meetings of the Council but discuss the relations of the church to social and political issues.

Annual Reports of the Foreign Missions Conference of North America.

Annual Reports of the Home Missions Council.

ATHEARN, CLARENCE R. *Inter-church Government.* New York: Century, 1925.

A summary of the various proposals and methods of federation up to 1925.

BROWN, WILLIAM ADAMS. *The Church in America.* New York: Macmillan, 1922.

DOUGLAS, HARLAN PAUL. *Church Unity Movements in the United States.* New York: Institute of Social and Religious Research, 1934.

A scientific comprehensive study of church movements made by the Institute of Social and Religious Research.

MACFARLAND, CHARLES S. *The Progress of the Church Federation.* New York: Revell, 1921.

Especially valuable as an account of the federation movement by one of the most efficient leaders.

MATHEWS, SHAILER (ed.). *Outline of Christianity.* New York: Dodd, Mead, 1926. Vol. III.

A presentation of the positions of different Christian bodies by their representatives, accompanied by a socio-historical interpretation of such movements.

NIEBUHR, H. R. *The Social Sources of Denominationalism*. New York: Holt, 1929.

A historical treatment of social, economic, and geographical influences in the development of denominationalism.

SHEDD, CLARENCE P. *Two Centuries of Student Christian Movements*. New York: Association Press, 1934.

A full presentation of the various movements among students with particular reference to the Young Men's Christian Association and the Young Women's Christian Association, the Student Volunteer Movement, and the World's Student Christian Federation.

SWEET, WILLIAM WARREN. *The Story of Religions in America*. New York: Harper, 1930.

A very readable presentation of the history of the various religious movements in America.

CHAPTER IV

RELIGIOUS CEREMONIALS AND THEIR SYMBOLISM

THE difficulties experienced in the transition from the traditional to the newer forms of religious expression are nowhere more acutely felt than in the use of liturgical symbols. Ceremonial usage tends to persist after the ideas and customs with which it arose have changed. Naturally, that older usage still carries in its familiar words and scenes emotional tones that belong to its whole background and cannot be evoked at will from new systems. It is not uncommon to see ministers whose fashions of thought have changed endeavoring "to enrich the service" by appropriating elements from old liturgies. The results are usually disappointing and incongruous. The difficulty may be illustrated in terms of any important factor of the complex religious tradition. It may be seen in the observance of the Sabbath; in the attitude toward church attendance; in the use, or neglect, of the Bible; in the recession and remoteness of all the divine personages whose halos were once so bright.

NEED OF A RESTATEMENT OF RELIGIOUS EXPERIENCE

What is needed is a restatement of the nature and objectives of religious experience, and the development of ceremonials and symbols in keeping with this restatement. Many churches are earnestly trying to make religion a vital and appealing aid to the fullest and richest living. They seek to discover the depths of human need and aspiration from which it springs. They realize that any routine or merely formal cultivation of it is fruitless, no matter how ardently and persistently people may be exhorted to support it. Unless religion has the quality of spontaneity and affords genuine satisfaction of real needs it is destined to languish and be neglected. The demand is for an interpretation of religion that brings it within the human scene, shows it as one that ministers rather than is ministered to, demonstrates that it carries its own weight and more, and proves that it can speak the language of enlightened men without apology or compromise. The tendency is toward a more humanistic, naturalistic, experimental religion, but all these terms are damaged by the battles through which they have come and are not adequate to designate the warmth, fulness, and beauty which the wisest and noblest souls feel.

Religion has come to be understood as an expression of the out-reaching, forward striving of the human spirit toward the freest and highest development. It is an experience of individuals, but it involves an associated life with other persons; its task is never completed, for it recognizes that the chief end of man is to grow; it takes account of the long experience through which the race has come, but it finds in that tradition no final authority to preclude further effort; it views man as a child of nature, but of a nature within which are processes and conditions which sustain man's aspiration toward a "spiritual" life of intelligence and love. There is here no vestige of the idea of original sin, or of the helpless passivity of totally depraved beings. Therefore, the drama of human life thus suggested is that of a striving toward ever new goals. Sometimes the goals sought prove disastrous. Often the efforts fall short of complete realization. Men are not infrequently diverted from the good quest. They lose their way at times and wander far, but often they recover the path and arrive home again.

The religious life is well represented as a pilgrimage, but now the pilgrims have no finished highway ahead. They make their own roads into unexplored regions. They travel in companies and have the joy of understanding companionship. They converse together about the way they take and about those who are laggard or weak or discouraged. There are marching songs for the day and songs of remembrance for the night. There are laughter and pain, but there are always hope and trust for the journey. What ceremonials would such a religion of pilgrimage develop? Would they not be recitals of the great achievements of the past, when some great bridge had to be built, or when the floods swept away work that had been done; when food fell short and heroic men found fresh supplies; when the plague attacked the pilgrims and wise men found remedies; when hatred and violence brought warfare and the hearts of the best were filled with fear; but when, nevertheless, there were undaunted spirits who believed in the pilgrimage, and heartened others to renew the way of the open road? Such pilgrims might well have a vision of the great life of which they were a part, and by which they were sustained. Many would celebrate the wonder of that life. They would celebrate their highway, they would celebrate their happy comradeship, they would celebrate their great leaders, they would celebrate in anticipation the destinations toward which they moved, they would celebrate their sheer joy of immediate existence, and rest themselves for a time in deep peace. The ceremonials are thus the ritualized replicas of the common life, with such emphasis and idealization as arise from fond memories and hopeful anticipations. The patterns of the reproductions are unmistakably those of the basic experience with imaginative elaborations of their meaning and appeal. These patterns lose nothing of their wonder and mystery by being referred to the human actors in the scene. On the contrary, such reference enhances the understanding and the possibilities of the creative work of the associated life of man through the long processes of history.

THE CEREMONIALS OF SUPERNATURALISM

A fuller appreciation of this conception of religious ceremonials and their symbolism may be gained by placing in contrast here the traditional practices which rest upon a supernaturalistic conception. Supernaturalism exalts God as the supreme creator and governor of the world and the determiner of human destiny. Man, having fallen from his first estate, lies bound in sin, with no hope of deliverance except through the miraculous grace of the divine atonement and the mediation of the superhuman Savior. The ceremonials of traditional churches dramatize that atonement and the salvation which it offers. The cross is their central symbol, and the acts of worship repeat man's effort to appropriate its redemption. Because man in his weakness, and by his contacts with the world, is continually subjected to temptations and to compromise with the saintliness he seeks, it is necessary for him to return again and again to the mystic altar where he may find healing and new courage.

The drama re-enacted in the ceremonials of such churches has three main stages. The first is the recognition of the presence of God: "The Lord is in his holy temple; let all the earth keep silence before him." The second is the confession of sin "with an humble, lowly, penitent, and obedient heart." The third is the assurance of the absolution and remission of sins expressed in the "Gloria." In these attitudes is illustrated the original and essential meaning of "worship." It is the recognition of the exaltation and majesty of the divine being, all-perfect, infinite in power, goodness, and mercy. Before him, as before an almighty ruler, man prostrates himself, proclaims himself a miserable sinner in whom there is no health, and begs for divine mercy for the sake of the atonement made by the death of Christ. For this penitence and self-abasement man claims forgiveness, pardon, and deliverance. Whereupon he sings psalms of adoration and praise. This is the basic pattern of the Mass, of the services in the *Book of Common Prayer*, and of the less formal orders of Protestant churches. It is also the form of ascent to spiritual union with the divine as practiced in conventional mysticism.

It may be contended that the difficulties which arise for many people in this procedure are due to the fact that they take it all too literally, and without sufficient poetic license. But when all allowances are made, there still remains the impression of a Deity so transcendent and so autocratic that man is reduced to a passive suppliant and to a dependent recipient of divine favor. In such a frame there seems to be no place for human initiative and creativity in the realization of new dimensions of aspiration and achievement. All goodness and reality appear to be already embodied in divinity so that at most man only reproduces and copies what is eternally given in complete perfection. At best man can but repeat, generation after generation, his aspiration, failure, and renewed endeavor toward a goal infinitely beyond his reach, and beyond even his comprehension. Supernaturalism, in this form, affords merely the repetition of the same circular drama, with only illusion as to any real movement or eventuation. No wonder man's "good works" become only "filthy rags," and the supreme end of his endeavor a mystical union with the Infinite.

It is possible that a more constructive view of ceremonials should begin with a different statement of their fundamental attitude and intent. The very word "worship" implies the prostration of the worshiper before a supreme and self-sufficient divine ruler. Such a conception infects the very idea of divinity with a desire for praise and adulation from servile subjects. This is no longer in keeping with the highest moral character. The same limitation inheres in the characterization of religious ceremonials as "divine services." When a person reports that he has attended divine service, it seems to mean that he has paid his vows and has made offerings of prayer and praise with which the Deity is well pleased. For many people this is doubtless an ideal and meaningful experience, but just as certainly it is for others dangerously near to magic and the crudest superstition. The counterpart of it is the idea of a heaven in which throughout eternity the chief occupation of the redeemed is worshiping God with golden harps and endless hallelujahs. Quite a different attitude is felt when religious ceremonials are conceived as the imaginative representation of significant activities concerned with the creative and expanding life of mankind. Now they appear as contributory to the realization of that larger life and to its fuller appreciation and enjoyment.

HUMAN NATURE AND CEREMONIALS

But this attitude involves a view of man as changed as the idea of God. Unless genuine and worthy meaning can be given to the natural aspiration and striving of man for better and nobler life, he must remain utterly dependent upon an outside and transcendental Deity for every good impulse and every imagined plan for spiritual growth. It is as much the tranditional notion of the sinfulness of human nature as the familiar transcendental supernaturalism of the divine nature that has dominated the ideas and the practices of worship. Extensive studies of religion in various cultures has given support to the idea that man is naturally religious. Similar inquiries show that he is a moral being in the sense of having standards of conduct to which institutions, literature, and art witness in many ways. The fact that man has risen from lower levels makes his ascent all the more impressive.

It is the fact that human nature is ever in a process of development, and is in a mixed state of partial goods and evils, that gives man and his ceremonials significant character. His history is checkered. It is not a smooth and clear advance at every point, but in the long perspectives there have been gains in many things that make for larger consciousness and for control of the conditions of life. Language, tools, social organization, arts, and religions have deepened and elevated human existence. No catastrophes, such as pestilence or war, have yet been sufficient to destroy the will to live, or to thwart aspiration for better things to come. The fact that as men gain knowledge of themselves and the world apprehension, and even despair, possess the souls of some is to be taken together with the fact that this fear and despair act as incentives to others to find ways to conquer the dangers and attain some greater security. At least if the despair of human nature depicted in traditional religious rituals had been generally accepted and acted upon, it is hard to see why it would not have completely paralyzed any impulse of hope or endeavor. No wonder it has often been asserted that religion has tended to keep men subservient and slavish to rulers and other men of power who claimed deference as vicegerents of God. In view of these implications concerning God and man, which persist in the word "worship," it may be better to undertake a statement of the nature of religious ceremonials and symbols in other terms.

Nothing affords better opportunity to see this contrast than the celebration of the Lord's Supper, which holds a central place in the great majority of churches. In the doctrines of transubstantiation and of consubstantiation the supernaturalistic theory is dominant. But in the conception of the Last Supper as a memorial institution another idea emerges. It is the idea of the value of contemplating in loving and appreciative reflection the work and achievement of Christ. Remembrance of the life and spirit of Christ, his purity of soul, his loyalty to his vision even unto death, his appeal to his friends to follow in his way, stir the affection and the will to renewed devotion to his cause. When viewed as an entirely voluntary celebration of that great life, without magic or superstition, the Communion becomes an occasion of fellowship with Christ and with all who seek to share in his cause, and has measureless dynamic power for direction of effort and for ecstatic elation of spirit.

The ordinance of baptism has also been observed in very different moods. At one extreme it is a mysterious means of divine grace through which sin is washed away and spiritual regeneration accomplished. The tendency, however, is increasingly toward the observance of baptism as a symbolic rite in which the candidate is dedicated to a new life of Christian fellowship and service.

SYMBOLISM IN RELIGIOUS ASSEMBLIES

The gathering of people in churches on Sunday morning is itself part of the religious drama. They come in

very different states of mind and degrees of consciousness. Habit is a large influence. But if called upon to
give reasons for their presence, they would say they
wanted to get into a different atmosphere for an hour,
to hear good music, to listen to a sermon. If they spoke
from the depths, they might say they were lonely, they
were troubled and anxious, they wanted to bring someone else, they felt responsibility for the cause, they came
in loyalty to Christ, they came because a religion of intelligence and love is the hope of a distraught and suffering world. The assembling of a congregation symbolizes
all this and more to the mind of any sympathetic observer. Here are all these individuals from various
homes and occupations. They have some interest in this
place and in what it signifies. They give their time and
money to maintain it, and they find satisfactions since
they return week by week.

Any building exerts its influence upon those who enter
it. Churches have higher roofs and offer the impression
of upreach and spaciousness. If there are columns and
arches, these enhance the perspective and the sense of
security and support. The windows open out upon the
sky or carry in color and form some symbols of persons
or events which invite memory and imagination. The
whole converges upon the chancel and the altar, upon
the cross and candles. The quiet and peace of the place
relax the mind and tend to open it toward the meaning
of what is to be enacted. A churchly building, or a building used as a church, comes to have its own meaning
either through its structural intent or by association. It
influences all who are sensitive to its form and associa-

tion to feel that it is a house of aspiration, a refuge of security, a center of genuine companionship and of ideal intimations, a home of the soul offering hospitality and a touch of something vast and beautiful.

Everything about a church tends to emphasize the affirmation of life. The clear, sure notes of the organ, the swelling strains of the hymns, the message of comfort and instruction, express the buoyancy and uplift of an expanding life. It is this confidence in life, and in the possibilities within reach for all persons, which constitutes the major chord of all the religious symbolism. Here is asserted the will to live, to secure significant status, to lay hold of the deep-laid anchors of life, to possess those values which moth and rust do not destroy, and to invest in things that cannot be stolen, to form ideal friendships that can be trusted, and to work for a cause that cannot be defeated. This affirmation of life affords poise and serenity against the distractions and the false values which thrust forward their appeals. The concrete experiences of every day may wear upon the spirit, obscure the great certainties, and cloud man's vision until he is filled with doubt, and tempted to cynicism and despair. It is in its general tone of vibrant and expansive living that the universal religious note is struck. Religious people may be pessimistic about some specific things, but on the whole they believe in life and in its capacity for yielding larger and finer satisfactions. Some high days of the church year are so symbolic of this sense of life that they gain the deepest and heartiest response of all days of the year. Christmas and Easter Sundays reach the maximum enthusiasm. They mark the rebirth of the race and the renewal of the life of nature, and in them the joy of man overflows in festal celebration. It is the spirit of these days which moves at the heart of all church rituals through all the seasons. Since these are nature festivals in many cultures their use in Christianity illustrates the deep religious quality inherent in their original as well as in their adopted function.

While the dominant note of all church ceremonials is this affirmation of life, it is important to realize that this note is not easily or steadily maintained in the face of the world of actual experience. Men undergo frustration of their plans through many causes. They make errors of judgment, accidents befall them, illness supervenes, loyalties fail, courage lags, death comes near. The sermon is the most flexible and adaptable part of the ritual, and therefore its task is to set particular experiences in the light of the whole, to afford means for recovery of trust in life, to point the way to more enduring values, or to fortify the mind and heart to bear up under the blows of fate. This calls upon the minister for the widest resources of knowledge and sympathy. He needs to be able to bring forward out of the great religious tradition and out of history examples of brave souls who have suffered in similar ways and have met their misfortunes with unbroken faith and trust. There is place, too, for a philosophy of life which not only reveals the nature of the world in which we live and is able to remind men in reasonable ways and through long vistas of the perilous conditions of existence and of its pitfalls and tragedies, but also to reaffirm with equal assurance the rewarding experiences and the enduring values.

It is the sermon which fits the universal mood of the religious attitude to individual needs. Therefore the range of its themes is as great as the concerns of men, but its purpose is ever the same. The purpose of the sermon is to renew trust in life. The story of a new scientific discovery which promises to eradicate some dread disease becomes a religious subject by virtue of its contribution to health. The issues of a political election are religious because they pertain to the moral and spiritual welfare of the community. A new poem may have such moving and inspiring meaning that its interpretation may become a religious event. The celebration of the birthdays of great patriots, like Washington and Lincoln, are useful reminders of the debt always owing to wise and able leaders. It is noticeable that the sermon has thus broadened its scope, and fitted itself more directly into the living experience of human beings. But it is also true that the sermon keeps itself within the frame of a larger setting. It is one feature of a complex movement and has its significant function in contributing to the happy and courageous spirit in which religious men bear themselves in such a world as this.

Many things in a well-conducted church symbolize the long tradition within which it stands, but nothing does so more effectively than the sacred books. These writings have gathered sanctity by their use and by the important place they have held in shaping the conduct and sentiments of many generations. They are the records of the aspiring souls who clung to their visions and their dreams against many odds. Here are preserved the prayers and songs, the adventures and the triumphs of prophetic minds, and the annals of priestly rites whose performance lifted the burden of sin and restored peace to the heart. The preservation in these books, especially those of the New Testament, of the casual conversations of Jesus, and the personal letters of Paul, together with other materials, rescued by seeming accident from oblivion, is almost as impressive evidence of their miraculous character as was the earlier claim of their direct inspiration.

It gives new meaning to these older scriptures when there is included with their use other readings from many sources. For then it may be seen that all scripture has its value and its authority in the message it conveys and in the appropriate form of words employed. It is important that men realize that they have a continuing revelation and that the sources of genuine inspiration have not been withdrawn or closed. The use of modern prose and poetry freshens the sense of a living faith and makes it articulate in new ideas and phrases. Compilations of suitable readings from general literature and from the sacred writings of other religions are becoming more available, and they deepen appreciation of the fact that witnesses to spiritual aspiration and insight have not been wanting in any people. Thus there is carried forward from the distant past into the living present a flowing and creative body of scripture which constitutes a growing Bible of religious thought and devotion.

The hymns of the church are also a cherished expression of this expanding religious life. Some of these embody new and rich applications of the expanding spirit of Christianity. Hymns of social aspiration and progress, like Chesterton's "O God of Earth and Altar" or Adler's "Hail the Glorious Golden City," sound new notes of faith and hope. William DeWitt Hyde has ventured to put into a hymn of thanksgiving his gratitude for a growing world: "Creation's Lord, we give thee thanks that this thy world is incomplete; that battle calls our marshalled ranks, that work awaits our hands and feet." A. S. Isaacs has given an index to the reality of practical religious living in these words: "A noble life, a simple faith, an open heart and hand—these are the lovely litanies which all men understand." The hymns afford almost the only opportunity which the congregations of the non-liturgical churches have to unite in audible expression of their faith and feeling, and therefore they invite the most careful consideration and cultivation. In them, as nowhere else, is attained a unified and mutually heartening release of conviction and devotion. It is in the hymns heartily sung by the whole congregation that is best symbolized the common purpose and spirit of the religious enterprise.

In some respects it is the organ which carries the unity and richness of the entire ceremonial. It is the first to greet the assembling congregation. Its voice strikes for everyone the notes of welcome and announces the mood of confidence and joy. From an aria by Bach, through the hymns and interludes, to Wagner's "Pilgrim's Chorus" as a postlude, it is the rich-toned organ, with its wide range of harmonies and volume, which pervades the whole assembly and flows through all the spaces and depths like an unseen but powerful presence. Just because it is inarticulate and all-enfolding, the organ music offers a common medium yet allows each mind to make its own response and its own interpretation. It is like a tide of life in which all are borne up and carried forward while each one feels it for himself alone. Perhaps nothing illustrates better the fact that the religious life is at once a common social experience and at the same time something unique and distinct for every individual participant.

"Prayer is the soul's sincere desire, unuttered or expressed." In a very real sense prayer is the inner movement of imagination, of meditation, and aspiration accompanying in the minds of all participants the action of the whole ceremonial. It is the more or less articulate, imaginative expression of what is felt by all members of the congregation. In the audible words of the pastoral prayer this hidden stream rises to explicit expression and gives unity through one mind and voice to the common need and aspiration. The reality and significance of prayer are most truly and adequately understood when it is regarded as the spontaneous outpouring of the hearts of men in thankfulness for the blessings of life, and of the hopes and strivings for wisdom and strength. Formal liturgical prayers may give dignity and beauty to these universal moods, but the informal, direct utterances of the soul have a quality of immediacy and living urgency which compensates for stylistic defects. Effective prayer rises from the depths of man's appreciative and out-reaching spirit. This is the ground of its genuineness and potency. It is a common experience of all thoughtful and sensitive minds, for all men have the same inner movements of joy and questing whether or not they know these to be the essence of prayer. It is a mistake to suppose that the act of prayer waits for theoretical conviction concerning proof of a listening Deity or of its objective efficaciousness. Prayer is an original and impulsive operation of imagination and desire. It does not depend upon evidence of its reasonableness any more than ordinary conversation implies understanding of the metaphysical nature of the person addressed. Conscious and considered prayer does have the value of elevating the mind to the level of an ideal companionship and of enabling one to think of one's self and one's life from the point of view of another and a better self. Such an experience is chastening and enlarging, and the consequences are very real and objective. They do not bring magical results, but they produce effects that are more significant and more powerful than magic.

Religious rites are practically universal in connection with the most crucial moments of human life—birth, puberty, marriage, and death. In all these events the rites are the affirmation and the celebration of life, of its mystery, wonder, and will to fulfil itself. Christening, observed in a wide variety of forms, is the recognition of a new soul born to the family and the group. In the infant centers new hope. Parents, sponsors, and friends are dedicated to the protection and guidance of this unfolding life as a serious and joyous duty.

Weddings are religious events in themselves. Their high emotional tone, owing to their felt importance for the individuals themselves and to the community to which they belong, makes them religious. In marriage the deepest forces of individual and racial concern are involved, and elicit the fullest and richest festivity and the most generous gifts of approval and affection. This moment of the consummation of mutual love and passionate devotion is the peak of human ecstasy and mystical fulfilment. It therefore calls out all possible forms of beauty and loveliness. Out of this human scene are created the patterns of the divinest aspirations. Spiritual marriage is the acme of mystical longing, and the church fondly contemplates herself as the bride of Christ.

Churches have the most living sense of the vitality of their mission when they gather into themselves new recruits. They are therefore keenly concerned to incorporate each rising generation as it grows up from childhood into self-conscious appreciation of the meaning and values of life. At puberty a transformation of the individual occurs which makes him susceptible to the appeal of social idealism and institutional organization. Churches are alert to meet this awakening with their claims of opportunity and obligation. They stand ready with instruction and persuasion to induct the youth into their fellowship and service. In the avowals of loyalty and dedication which these young people make, the churches feel their own life confirmed and their strength renewed and perpetuated.

It may seem at first sight that death is the defeat of religion especially when religion announces itself as the affirmation of life, but man's unconquerable will to live never shines with brighter light than when death comes. The generality of mankind have never believed that death ends all. They have imagined some kind of existence, usually a glorified form of that they know on earth, into which men pass when the breath goes out of the body. Often they have believed that the spirits of those who have gone live about their familiar haunts for the most part invisible and friendly. The doctrine of immortality came late in history, for the idea of eternity is not easily grasped. That doctrine of immortality was another magnificent evidence of faith in life. No more elaborate religious ceremonials have ever been created than those which the Egyptians built to sustain their souls in the journey to the after-world.

Christianity has held tenaciously to an immortal life beyond the grave. Its rituals have never wavered from that hope, and they have thrown about the darkness of the tomb the light of vivid expectation of resurrection and endless continuance hereafter. For many thoughtful Christians, however, there has come to be a firmer ground of faith in the power of life to conquer death. They find comfort in the idea that we live as long as we are remembered, or as long as the causes and institutions to which we give our life endure. In a very real way every man lives beyond his own death whenever in imagination he goes beyond it and pictures the world as it will be, or sets up plans with a time-fuse to become effective in a distant future. The ceremonials for the celebration of the death of a good man are ceremonials concerned with his life, with what was enduring in it and worthy to be continued. The greatest sources of comfort and inspiration are to be found in what he was, in the qualities that endeared him to friends and made him admirable in the way he met his changing fortunes and his significant opportunities. In these ceremonials is also voiced the deep sympathy of comrades and fellow-sufferers. Never do the hearts of men overflow with more genuine love and understanding. Out of their own grief and loss they bring gifts of courage and peace. There is healing in their words, as there is in the words of the prayers and hymns which sound out the notes of undaunted faith and assurance.

SYMBOLISM IN NON-LITURGICAL ACTIVITIES

In addition to the conduct of such ceremonials as have been indicated there are many activities of a less formal character which every church maintains. While the life of the institution centers in the recurring ceremonials, it has other relations with its members and the community which are important channels of its influence. One of these is co-operation with welfare agencies which seek to carry on the promotion of good citizenship, poor relief, public health, social reforms, and other related interests. Churches find themselves obliged to adopt some policy concerning them. Only an inclusive and sympathetic attitude is likely to be regarded as consistent. It is impossible longer to draw a line between the sacred and the secular in a way which limits the religious concern to the ceremonials themselves. Whatever affects the realization of the best life for men, women, and children must be taken into account. Every individual stands in the midst of a wide-reaching complex of social and physical conditions which affect his well-being, and which must be included within any serious attempt to help him realize his human possibilities. It is by virtue of their importance for the attainment of the main objectives of religion that they become in a real sense religious. It is partly to preserve appreciation of their religious character that the church is called upon to share in their work. Whenever a church holds itself aloof from participation in such causes, it tends to withdraw within itself and to be something apart from the full stream of reality and from the processes that are essential to the success of its cause. On the other hand, these enterprises are often in danger of separate cultivation of their special purposes until they obscure the unity and wholeness which religion seeks as a necessary and practical condition of the most adequate living. It is an important function of the minister to include the interpretation of these agencies within the broad scope of the religious life, and to recognize them as germane to the vision of the good life.

The public assemblies of churches are educative in their effect, but they are unable to cultivate the detailed and systematic programs of education that are necessary to the development of groups of different ages and special interests. While the conduct of classes may stress intellectual and cultural needs, this may still be done in a manner that keeps in view the larger setting within which the instruction is given. After all it is a church school, and this encompassing relationship to the larger whole gives a spirit and meaning to the class which it would not have in isolation or in some other kind of association.

There are activities which border upon direct educational processes which may be sponsored by the school or may draw upon its co-operation. The development of dramas and pageants and concerts is increasingly employed within the general church life, and they may contribute incalculably to the enrichment of interest and appreciation. They offer the possibility of engaging persons of all ages and of enlisting members of diverse groups in an active co-operation which enables all to share actively in expressing and promoting the common cause which often is only theoretically and formally recognized. It is desirable that all members achieve some kinesthetic sense of what their membership in the group signifies. Probably in no way is this so well done as in training for and presenting a pageant or dramatic performance.

Protestant churches have been described as deliberative assemblies rather than as worshiping bodies in the Roman Catholic sense. By this it is meant to emphasize the participation and the co-operation of individuals in a conscious social process as compared with the direct relation of each person to the priest or the altar alone. Where the forms of belief and the orders of worship are prescribed and authoritatively administered, there is little opportunity for the individual to do more than follow the indicated way and accept what is ordained. In Protestantism, on the other hand, there is emphasis upon changing and growing ideas, and upon "the priesthood of all believers." The local church is in many communions the final seat of authority, and this accordingly invites reflection and participation by all members.

Consistently with this conception, discussion in study classes and in open forums is encouraged, and in theory at least the minds of the group move freely toward some general agreement based upon the organized thought of all. Ideally this represents the growing and creative process of the church, and it may actually attain this significance when the procedure is guided by the right spirit and by a genuinely social and experimental attitude.

It has been a slow process for Protestants to comprehend within the religious life the interests of play and art. These seem to lack the serious and strenuous spirit which has been associated with militant and aggressive religion. But human beings need their periods of relaxation and of freedom from intense concentration. Gradually it is coming to be understood that in this natural rhythm of life these non-strenuous periods are times of the greatest plasticity and afford occasion for the freest adjustment of personal relations and of mental patterns. Those congregations are fortunate which have a church house for educational and recreational use. It brings a new atmosphere into the whole institution to have the members dine together, converse over the tables, play games, sing and dance, and share in the natural human-interest activities within the practices of the church. This does not turn the church into a club or a café or a public dance hall. But it keeps these interests within the influence and spirit of a vital and conscious religious ideal. Even if no specific word is said on such occasions about religion, there is no uncertainty about the situation, for here are the officials of the religious functions, and the same persons who on Sunday are sincere participants in the celebration of all that religion involves. This impression is greatly strengthened by the fusion of all age groups in the same activities. Too often churches permit for younger persons what they think improper for the elders and deacons of the congregation, and thus symbolize by this discrimination some question about the legitimacy of the activities themselves. It is a conviction with most thoughtful church people that religion should comprehend within its sanctions and practical arrangements the whole nature of man in a system of behavior permitting the expression and systematization of all interests in an organized personality pattern. A well-conducted church house, as a free meeting place for all members in a wealth of activities and associations, provides an ideal opportunity for the realization of that conviction.

There are certain operations basic to the practical life of religious organizations that are often as much obscured from the total picture as are the recreational activities. These are the financial and business concerns. Official boards often occupy a surprisingly large part of their time with financial matters, and they do not always succeed in bringing them to the congregation in ways that give to money problems their proper status in the life of the church. It yet remains for some church to discover how to secure a fair and adequate co-operation of religious people in this important feature. The average church member seems disposed to keep up the bargaining habits he has learned in business and in payment of his taxes. He is too willing to let the officials struggle with the problem as best they can. There is no system of equality that can be clearly administered. It is impossible by rule to define what the share of each should be, but there is something sadly lacking in the religious institution which fails to incorporate these practical matters within the spiritual meaning and atmosphere of its life.

CONSCIOUS PARTICIPATION IN THE DIVINE

The individual who thoughtfully and sympathetically participates in these ceremonials and in the less formal activities of a church easily feels himself sharing in a larger and a nobler life. It is a life continuous with his own best aspirations and endeavors. It is a life which others have experienced throughout human history, and have expressed in Scriptures and in symbolic acts of ritual and sacrament which responsive souls have cherished and preserved down to the present time. Religious ceremonials and symbolism, ever changing and ever seeking more fully to express the ideal hopes and deeds of the human will and heart, are manifestations of the living processes of the divine. Such symbols objectify the highest reaches of imagination and aspiration, flowering out of the actual experiences of the real world of man's striving and out of his chastened but undefeated hopes. These symbols preserve the best of life, and bring within sight of all men in the churches and in religious literature and celebrations visions of their own better selves and of their unfulfilled possibilities. The symbols hold a mirror up to nature, revealing what men might be by showing what in some moments they have been and what in other moments they have dearly imagined themselves to be. Sometimes the ideals have seemed so above and beyond the actual that men have ascribed them entirely to a supernatural realm and have felt themselves abased in sin and despair in contemplation of such high perfection. But again, and now more than ever, men conceive and with new faith believe, that these divine possibilities are not alien but akin to the life of the soul itself. It is this which gives new and deeper meaning to the life of Jesus Christ, for he is the symbol not only of the divine descending into the human but of the human ascending into the divine.

SELECTED BIBLIOGRAPHY

AMES, E. S. *Religion*, chap. vii, "Religion and Art." New York: Holt, 1929.

COE, G. A. *A Social Theory of Religious Education.* New York: Scribner, 1917.
Deals with problems of worship in relation to education.

COIT, STANTON. *Social Worship.* New York: Macmillan, 1913.
A remarkable compilation of meditations and lessons prepared for the furtherance of "humanistic religion."

HARTSHORNE, HUGH. *Manual for Worship.* New York: Scribner, 1915.
Practical suggestions for training in worship.

MELAND, B. E. *Modern Man's Worship.* New York: Harper, 1934.
A philosophical interpretation in terms of mystical naturalism; an original and constructive work.

PRATT, J. B. *The Religious Consciousness*, chap. xiv, "Objective and Subjective Worship." New York: Macmillan, 1920.

SPERRY, WILLARD L. *Reality in Worship.* New York: Macmillan, 1925.
A study of public worship and private religion.

VOGT, VON OGDEN. *Art and Religion*. New Haven. Yale University Press, 1921.

————. *Modern Worship*. New Haven: Yale University Press, 1927.

These works present all phases of religious art and liturgy with an interpretation of worship as "celebration."

WIEMAN, H. N. *Methods of Private Religious Living*, chap. vi, "Public Worship." New York: Macmillan, 1928.

CHAPTER V

THE CHURCH AS EDUCATOR

THE CHURCH AN EDUCATIONAL INSTITUTION

FROM the beginning of its career the church has been an educational institution. The church's educational function is deeply rooted in the method of Jesus, who thought of himself and was thought of by his contemporaries as being a teacher. His method was not so much a formal proclamation of a systematic message as that of starting with persons face to face with the specific and concrete situations of their everyday experience and of helping them to see the spiritual implications and possibilities of their experiences. The early church soon established schools for preparing converts for church membership and later schools for training church leaders. During the Middle Ages the Benedictine requirement of daily reading and the copying and collecting of manuscripts gave rise to the schools for monastic initiates, while the interest of the monks in serving the illiterate peoples among whom they lived led to the founding of schools for children outside the monasteries. Cathedral schools sprang up in various parts of Europe for the training of the clergy and the instruction of converts. The great medieval universities were the outgrowth of the intellectual interests of the church. The Reformation shared the enthusiasm of the

Renaissance for learning, centering its attention upon the biblical and patristic literature rather than upon the ancient classics, as in the south of Europe. The first efforts at education as a state function grew out of the Reformation, as in the universal and compulsory schools established in Saxony. The philanthropic and public schools in America were dominantly religious. Since the secularization of American education the church has definitely assumed education in religion as one of its major responsibilities. The earliest institutions of higher learning in America were church foundations. In recent years the church has shared with the state a growing dependence upon education as a method of furthering their respective ends.

An analysis of nineteen centuries of the church's educational work discloses the fact that the content and procedure of the church's educational program have been determined by cultural change. The profound reconstruction of the objectives, the curriculum, the method, and the organization of current religious education through which we are now passing is only the latest phase of this historic effort of the church to meet the demands of its changing world.

Within its historic educational tradition the educational function of the modern church assumes four forms: religious education for all age-groups in the local church and community, higher education in church colleges, religious foundations in connection with state universities, and the training of professional religious leaders in theological seminaries.

RELIGIOUS EDUCATION IN THE LOCAL CHURCH
AND COMMUNITY

The program by which the church attempts to provide religious education for all age-groups in the local church and community is the outgrowth of a long historical process involving changes in American culture.

The earliest schools in America were dominantly religious. In the northern colonies, particularly in Massachusetts, they were under the control of the church. Their supervisors were clergymen. The chief requirement of teachers was that they should be devout persons and orthodox members of the church. The sessions of the schools were opened with prayer, and a religious spirit was diffused throughout their entire program. The textbooks consisted of the hornbook, containing the Lord's Prayer, from which the children learned the alphabet, the Bible, and the catechism. The *New England Primer* was added later. At this stage general education and religious education were undifferentiated. Because the middle colonies were more heterogeneous in their religious affiliations, education assumed the parochial type. The schools of the southern colonies were permeated by the spirit of religion, after the pattern of their English models.

In time, however, through the co-operation of several factors, the American public school became secularized. This was due in part to the expanding frontier and the substitution of the school district, a geographical and civil unit, for the town meeting. It was due in part to the increasing demands of an expanding culture upon the curriculum. But more than to any other single factor it was due to the sectarianism of American Christianity and the competition of the various sects to control the schools. Gradually there grew up the doctrine of the separation of church and state. The practical outworking of this doctrine was the exclusion of religion from the public schools, which passed under state support and state control. In the deepest implication of this event, the doctrine of the separation of church and state did not then and does not now mean that religion in its universal and functional character has no place in the public school. It did mean and does mean that sectarian religious teaching can have no place in the American public-school system. This fact is of great importance in exploring the solution of the complicated problem which the secularization of public education has bequeathed to our generation—a problem which is reset under the changed conditions in which we find ourselves.

In attempting to discharge the responsibility for teaching religion which the secularization of public education thrust upon it, the church quite naturally seized upon the Sunday school, which had been imported from England near the end of the eighteenth century, though there had been some sporadic attempts to use Sunday for purposes of instruction in religion. The Sunday school was an alien institution. It arose in Great Britain as a phase of the philanthropic movement in European education. The Raikes schools had their origin in social conditions quite different from those which generally obtained in America, being designed for the dispossessed and the underprivileged.

Whether the ready accessibility of the Sunday school was a fortunate circumstance under the conditions in which the church of the eighteenth century found itself only a longer historical view will determine. Be that as it may, it typed the character of religious education in the vast majority of Protestant churches through the nineteenth century and continues to do so even yet. Those Protestant groups, such as the Lutheran churches, that maintain parochial systems are, of course, notable exceptions to this general trend.[1]

While public education developed along scientific lines, the Sunday school developed under the influence of philanthropic and evangelistic motives. It was looked upon as "the nursery of the church." It was imbued with a missionary passion. Many of the great churches in the Middle West owe their origin to the establishment of "mission" Sunday schools on what was then the great American frontier. The temper of the movement was pietistic rather than educational in any fundamental and scientific sense. It has throughout remained a lay movement, the teaching of religion having been committed to consecrated but untrained persons who were otherwise professionally or vocationally engaged.[2] Its educational objectives have for the most part been con-

[1] How greatly the parochial system has appealed to certain Protestant communions as a solution of the complicated problem created by the secularization of public education is suggested by the experiment in parochial education undertaken by the Presbyterian Church in the U.S.A. See Lewis J. Sherrill, *Presbyterian Parochial Schools, 1846–1870* (Yale University Press).

[2] Something of the effect of lay leadership in the movement may be suggested by the fact that when the International Lesson Committee projected the curriculum for the majority of the Protestant churches in 1872, the business man's ideal of mechanical uniformity in mass production prevailed

cerned with the teaching of the Bible as an authoritative revelation of divine truth. While the public school addressed itself to the total child population of the nation and to increasingly larger numbers of its youth, the Sunday school followed the sectarian organization of American Protestantism. As a result, it has ministered for the most part to the child and youth constituencies of the several denominations, leaving more than half of the total childhood and youth of the nation untouched.

The opening of the twentieth century witnessed a great awakening of interest in the educational function of the church. The elementary schools had been established by the states by 1850. By 1850 more than six thousand academies had been established throughout the nation. The latter half of the nineteenth century witnessed the rapid extension of state and city systems of education. The same period was prolific in the establishment of colleges. This period was characterized by the rapid development of state universities, which completed the full range of the development of public education. The period from 1870 to 1910 witnessed the rapid and continuous rise of normal schools and departments of education in universities, established for the purpose of training a professional body to carry on the functions of education.[3] The rise of the curve of teacher-training institutions was out of all proportion to the increase of population. The American people had be-

---

over the ideals of the educator. Had the work of the Sunday school been at that time projected on an educational rather than a big business ideal, its history might have been quite different.

[3] The curve for private as distinguished from public normal schools broke sharply in 1895 and has rapidly descended since that date.

come educationally minded. They had come to believe that education was a primary function of the state. They were convinced that it was society's most effective method of social control and its chief instrument for achieving social progress.

The church also had come to share this general enthusiasm for education as a method of religious advance. The rapid development of religious education as a movement within the church is one of the most striking phenomena of recent American Christianity. Popular courses of leadership training had a widespread vogue. Chairs and departments of religious education were established in church colleges and in independent universities and theological seminaries. Experiments in various types of curriculums were undertaken. The movement developed large-scale denominational and interdenominational organizations for promoting and administering the educational work of the church, the scope of these organizations culminating in the World's Sunday School Association. A very considerable body of literature devoted to religious education grew up. The educational efforts of the church were extended beyond Sunday in a program of week-day religious education in which the churches offered instruction in religion to pupils released from public-school time upon the request of parents, or after school hours. Its efforts were also extended into the summer vacation through the development of vacation religious education.

There can be little doubt that something of a messianic hope attached itself to the movement of religious education. Ministers, local churches, denominations, and the church in general saw in religious education the solution of most of their problems. This was, of course, an over-simplification of the problem and its solution, and was destined to be rectified by experience.

But the new interest in religious education was not simply an interest in more religious education. With the turn of the century there began to appear an intense interest in a new kind of religious education. The first datable event in this outreach of the church toward a more adequate educational program was the organization of the Religious Education Association in 1903, under the dynamic leadership of President William Rainey Harper. It represented a *rapprochement* of churchmen and public-school educators. A century of experience had demonstrated the incompleteness and weakness of a public education from which the idealism and motivation of religion had been excluded. It had also demonstrated the educational inadequacy of the traditional Sunday school. The Religious Education Association accordingly devoted its convention platforms and its magazine to the advocacy of the introduction of religion into education and of education into religion.

For some time movements of protest had been arising within the religious education movement itself. The teachers of young children felt most keenly the impossibility of achieving educational results from the use of the "International Uniform Lessons" which had been in vogue since 1872. Out of this protest grew the "International Graded Lessons" in 1908, in which religious instruction was graded to meet the interests and capacities of the several age-groups. Impatient with the conservatism of the International Sunday School Association, a group of educationally minded editors and religious leaders organized the Sunday School Council of Evangelical Denominations in 1910. In 1918 a Commission of Seven was appointed by the International Lesson Committee to make a comprehensive study of the whole curriculum problem in religious education. This Commission of Seven recommended that a special committee composed of trained religious educators be appointed to work out a curriculum in the light of the most approved educational theory and practice. This committee began its work in 1920. The committee added to its advisory membership some of the most outstanding educators in America.

In the meantime, the tension between the conservative International Sunday School Association and the more progressive Sunday School Council of Evangelical Denominations had reached the breaking-point. The religious educational movement was on the verge of dividing over whether the movement should follow its traditional policies or adopt a genuinely educational program. Fortunately, the issue was settled by the merging of the two bodies into the International Council of Religious Education in 1922.

This Council, representing the co-operation of forty-three of the leading evangelical Protestant denominations in the United States and Canada, has from the beginning organized its work upon a thoroughgoing educational basis, signalizing its educational ideals by calling to its general secretaryship the general secretary of the National Education Association, by setting up an

Educational Commission, and by establishing a Bureau of Research. The Council is committed in its ideals and procedures to the philosophy and techniques of progressive education, though it makes provision for wide variations in educational ideals and standards among the constituent denominations. Its departments are staffed by educators trained in the leading American universities. Through it the co-operating denominations are at work reconstructing curriculums, standards, method, and leadership education. In these processes it is attempting to base its procedures upon research and experimentation.

In the earlier stages of the reconstruction of religious education it was quite natural that those who were attempting to improve the educational work of the church should look to public education for its models. One has facetiously but quite truly remarked that in its early modern phase religious education was little more than public education dressed up in a Prince Albert coat. But as religious education has become more mature it has come to feel that it must work out its objectives, its curriculum, its techniques, and its organization in terms of its own subject matter—the nature of religion and its functional relation to the experience of growing persons. As a consequence, religious educators have turned more and more to the psychology and philosophy and history of religion and to the fields of the psychological and social sciences and less and less to the formal and subject-matter-centered schools of the state. It is needless to remark that in a field so new, only the barest beginnings have been made. But it is a matter of great significance that the church is on its way to an understanding of its educational function in terms of the creative function of religion in personal and social experience.

In this temper modern religious education conceives its objective to be not the transmission of the cumulative products of a past Christian experience but the assisting of growing persons to achieve a Christian adjustment to their world with the help of such resources as are available in historic Christian experience. It is less concerned with the teaching of religion than with providing conditions and resources by which growing persons may achieve a religious quality in every phase of the experience by which they realize themselves. In this way religion becomes not an isolated and specialized department of experience but a potential quality that attaches to every relation and function of normal human living.

The school of religion thus becomes a laboratory set up in the midst of experience into which are brought the fundamental issues of personal and social living for analysis, interpretation, evaluation, and experimental reconstruction in the light of Christian values. Its curriculum becomes the experience of growing persons as that experience undergoes analysis, appraisal, and redirection toward Christian ends. Its method becomes that of creative experience—an actual facing of life's issues under mature and competent Christian guidance. The burden of education shifts from teaching to learning. Learning to live as Christians becomes inner, self-reliant, responsible, releasing—an achievement of self-realizing persons rather than a result imposed by the adult members of the Christian community upon its immature members. It is more concerned with the acquisition of attitudes and methods of dealing with life-situations intelligently and effectively than with giving ready-made patterns of belief and conduct predetermined by adult experience. The school of religion becomes an inclusive fellowship in which the young assume responsible participation in keeping with their growing capacities.

So conceived, religious education in the modern church is coming to be not an isolated function but a method and a spirit that pervade the entire unified parish as a total religious operation. So conceived it moves out from the cloister into the community where life-situations are actually being met—in the family, in the church, in vocation, in leisure-time activities—and where attitudes and character are actually being formed. In this outdoors the modern church through its religious education is beginning consciously to relate itself to the other agencies which affect character, seeking through co-operation with them to help growing persons to achieve a well-rounded, complete, and satisfying life on its highest levels.

The greatest task which now confronts the church in the reconstruction of its educational program is to bridge the gap between the theory and practice of its leaders and the stereotyped practice in the great mass of local churches. The church, with all other educational agencies, stands on the frontier of an educational venture in American culture that requires the utmost intelligence and resourcefulness in meeting the demands of a social situation that outruns all the precedents of its past experience.

THE CHURCH COLLEGE

The earliest colleges in America, including Yale, Harvard, and Columbia, were church foundations. They were established primarily for training ministers, "dreading," as the inscription over the Harvard gate has it, "to leave an illiterate ministry to the churches when our present ministers shall lie in the dust." Consequently, the earliest college curriculums were chiefly concerned with the classics and religion.

The period from 1825 to 1900 was characterized by the rapid and widespread founding of denominational colleges. By 1900, 494 colleges had been established. Of these, 15 were state universities and 9 were colonial colleges. This reveals vividly the leadership of the church in founding institutions of higher learning.

In view of its religious purpose, mention should be made of the academy, which was the precursor of the public high school. The academy had its rise around 1750 and reached its peak in 1850. Thereafter the academy as a semipublic but religious institution rapidly declined, practically ceasing to exist after 1916. It was displaced in American education by the public high school, which had its beginning around 1810 and rose after 1875 by an almost perpendicular curve.

Many of the denominational colleges were founded without regard to the needs of their respective constituencies. Many of them were unwisely located. Many were inadequately financed. Their number being in excess of need, there arose sharp competition among them.

In many cases the educational standards of equipment, library and laboratory facilities, and teaching personnel were poor or indifferent. Their institutional mortality was high.

The motives back of the founding of these colleges were deeply religious, with a strong tincture of sectarian propaganda. In their truest genius they attempted to give a liberal education to the youth of the denomination, in a genuinely religious atmosphere, and with definite instruction in the Bible and religion. In many cases courses in the Bible were required by charter for graduation. Attendance at regular religious exercises was required. Voluntary religious organizations, such as the Y.M.C.A. and Y.W.C.A. and the Student Volunteer Band, gave further stimulus and expression to religious attitudes and purposes.

The denominational college has been variously administered. In some instances the college has been under the direct control of the denomination which determines its faculty personnel, its program of study, and its educational policies. In other cases the college, while ministering to a denominational constituency and deriving its moral and financial support from it, is under the direct administration of a self-perpetuating board.

Financially, the church college has chiefly derived its support from its church constituency, largely, if not chiefly, in the form of current contributions from churches and individuals. The more fortunate colleges have been able to build up endowment funds derived usually from individuals of wealth in the communion or from other interested citizens. More recently the funds available from current contributions and endowments have been supplemented by grants from such sources as the General Education Board and the Carnegie Fund for the Advancement of Teaching, gifts from the latter being used for providing retirement allowances for teachers.

Since 1900 profound changes have occurred in the American educational scene which have had far-reaching effects upon the church college. The period since 1900 has witnessed the rapid extension of state universities, not only in number, but in the development of the diversified educational programs which they offer. Beginning around 1720, there has been a steady rise of state normal schools. Recently there has been a pronounced tendency for these to develop into four-year standard colleges. With a declining interest in denominational differences is united an increasing tendency for students to attend accredited institutions nearest their residence. While some colleges continue to draw students from great distances, most colleges tend to draw about one-half of their enrolment from within a radius of approximately fifty miles. Since 1929 the tendency has been for more than one-half to be drawn from this radius. As a result of superior educational opportunities, economy, and convenience, at the present time there are more young people from the churches in state institutions than in church colleges.

At the same time the isolated four-year college of liberal arts has been greatly involved in fundamental shifts in the structural organization of education. One of these shifts has been the rapid extension of city high schools to a junior college level—a nation-wide movement. Another has been the rapid development of municipal colleges or universities—a movement that is affecting unfavorably state universities as well as church colleges, especially by diverting the most wealthy sources of tax income. Still another has been the growing tendency to divide the four-year liberal-arts program into two sections—the junior college, frequently growing out of or attached to superior high schools, and the senior college, attached to the university with its professional schools, as at Johns Hopkins and in the divisional organization of the University of Chicago.

These trends have effected great changes in the status and function of the church college. The first notable fact is that few church colleges have been established since 1900. Furthermore, the function and atmosphere of the church college have materially changed. This result has arisen in large part out of the fact that the clientèle of the church college has changed. Its student personnel is recruited largely from the contiguous territory under the operation of the fifty-mile-radius trend. The effect of this factor, together with the pressure to offer opportunities comparable with those in state institutions in order to hold its church young people, has led the church college to adopt a program of study, such as is possible with its shrinking resources, as little as possible differentiated from that in state institutions. The operation of the economic motive has led many to seek education at less expense at the church college, with the result that the student body is increasingly drawn from the lower-income groups.

In the meantime, the requirements of standardizing agencies as respects endowments, equipment, library and laboratory facilities, and teaching personnel have become more and more exacting. Under this pressure the problem of the church college largely resolves itself into one of finance. Some church colleges in order to avail themselves of funds from the General Education Board and the Carnegie Fund have declared themselves non-sectarian and have receded to the status of church-related colleges. Some of the stronger colleges have severed their connection with their denominations entirely in order to finance themselves from a wider constituency. The weaker colleges, unable to meet the standardizing requirements, have become junior colleges. The weakest ones have closed their doors. Some church colleges located in cities have become municipal universities.

The church's educational function as regards higher education is at present involved in much confusion and great difficulty. The church needs to think through its function on the college level in the light of the changed educational scene. That there is need for the Christian ideal in higher education no one in the church will deny. That the traditional program of the church college is inadequate to satisfy this need few would question.

Five possibilities present themselves as ways in which the church college may most effectively meet this need. One is the utilization of the educational value of the small, compact, and homogeneous group. The possibilities in this direction are suggested by the new experiments in large universities where the student body is being divided into small residential groups that carry on their work in face-to-face social units, as at Yale and Harvard. This compact group the church college already has.

Another possibility lies in the direction of cultivating in the church college the more distinctive cultural aspects of education as contrasted with the emphasis which the universities place upon research and professional education.

A third possibility lies in the direction of organizing the church college upon a functional basis by which the first two years would constitute a junior college in which the objectives would be those of orienting the student to and of developing appreciation of the various phases of contemporary and historical culture, while the last two years would be devoted to pre-professional education. In that case the college would make much of vocational guidance. The possibilities of this plan are enlarged if the final year can be taken in a professional school and counted toward the baccalaureate degree, as is now done in some church-related colleges.

If the more adequate church-related college can command the financial resources, a great possibility is open to it in experimenting with newer types of education—a function in which public institutions have not generally shown much initiative.

In its truest tradition, there is the possibility of the church college organizing itself as a vital religious community. In such a fellowship religion might not only be studied as an integral phase of culture but itself be subjected to critical analysis with a view to understanding it in the light of the results of the scientific study of religion. In these ways religion would again become the specialty of the church-related college. By some such means the present somewhat anomalous religious character of the church college might be transformed into an adventure of discovery and creative religious living.

CHURCH FOUNDATIONS AT STATE UNIVERSITIES

With the shift of student personnel from church colleges to state universities there has grown up in recent years an increasing sense of responsibility on the part of the church for carrying on religious work with students in state universities and for offering courses in religion that would be available to them. From this initial interest in caring for its own young people the church has felt a growing responsibility for making the resources of religious instruction and fellowship available to all students in the state universities irrespective of church affiliation. Under the impulsion of this motive the church has made several gestures in this direction.

The earliest form of this movement consisted of the establishment of Bible chairs contiguous to several state universities, as at the University of Virginia, Indiana University, and the University of Kansas. Courses in religion are offered for which credit may or may not be received in the university. In other cases several denominations unite in a co-operative school of religion in which courses are open to students in the university and for which university credit may be received, as in the case of the Bible College of Missouri in connection with the University of Missouri and the Oklahoma School of

Religion in connection with the University of Oklahoma, or, in more informal ways, as in the case of the Association of Religious Teachers at the University of Texas. The School of Religion at the University of Iowa is both a union school of religion involving Protestants, Catholics, and Jews, and operates as an integral department of the university. In other instances foundations have been established by the several denominations with a view to providing Christian fellowship and personal counseling, as in the case of the Wesley foundations at the University of Illinois, the University of Ohio, Pennsylvania State College, and the Iowa State Teachers College. In still other instances various denominations have united in a joint religious fellowship, as at Cornell University and the University of Pennsylvania. Some churches maintain at the seats of state universities a university pastor, sometimes in charge of a church in the university community. In 76 per cent of 79 tax-supported schools studied by Hartshorne, Stearns, and Uphaus in 1932, courses in religion were offered, with a marked tendency to increase the number of courses.

Of these various approaches it may be said that they are yet in their initial and tentative stages. As yet the distance between these foundations and the university has only been partially bridged. As yet no sufficient appeal has been made to the interest and imagination of the student bodies.

For a long time, of course, religious work among the students in state universities has been carried on with varying degrees of success by voluntary religious organizations such as the Y.M.C.A. and the Y.W.C.A. It is a matter of great significance that in recent years there has appeared a tendency on the part of universities to absorb these extra-institutional religious functions into the regular educational operations of the university itself. It is also not without significance that in some state universities there is a freer, more spontaneous, and in some respects a more vital religious atmosphere than in some church colleges, where religion has become official, external, and authoritative, and where a too direct attack upon the imposition of religious beliefs and practices has led to a negative reaction on the part of the students.

That there are great possibilities in this new field for the constructive functioning of a vital religious influence among students there can be no doubt. The problems are difficult and their solution is far from clear. They present themselves as problems worthy of the church's best intelligence and experimental exploration.

THE THEOLOGICAL SEMINARY

The church, like all other social institutions, must assume responsibility for training its own professional leaders—ministers, religious educators, missionaries, administrators, teachers, and journalists. This the church has undertaken to do through its theological seminaries.[4]

At first these seminaries were for the most part maintained, like the church colleges, by their respective denominations for the preparation of their own profession-

---

[4] Inasmuch as another volume on theological education in this series is contemplated, this phase of the church's task as educator is not elaborated here, only a brief and general statement being made.

al leaders. As time has gone on, however, the tendency has been for the theological seminary to become non-denominational and to serve the needs of the wider Christian community. In many instances the seminary has become a professional school in the large university where the function of research has been added to that of teaching.

On the whole, in the past the education which the seminary has given the prospective leaders of the church has been dominated chiefly by linguistic, literary, theological, and historical interests. These were the fields in which competency was demanded by the earlier social conditions in America. Of late the seminaries have begun to be influenced by functional ideas with a view to preparing young men and women for helping persons and religious groups to discover the religious significance of their experience in the contemporary world and to bring to bear upon its issues the reconstructive forces of Christian values and ideals. In this creative task the seminary is seeking to utilize the wealth of historical Christian experience as a resource. It seeks to develop a leadership that is not dependent upon precedent, but has developed a competency to face the concrete facts of contemporary situations and to deal with them creatively.

Under the influence of these trends theological seminaries have in recent years been subjecting their objectives, curriculums, and methods to analysis with a view to bringing their programs into vital and realistic relations with the functional needs of the future leaders of the church.

From this survey of the work of the church as educator it is clear that its educational function, while having continuity throughout the historic development of the Christian community, is far from being something given and static. It has changed again and again as the church has faced changes in the social situation and sought to reconstruct its methods and means in response to the demands of changing conditions. This is the meaning of the current transition through which the educational function of the church is passing. If the issue is confused and the church seems to be uncertain of its way, it is because the problem is exceedingly complex and the church has no precedents that fit the present situation. The church is, therefore, thrown back upon a fresh analysis of a new situation and upon an experimental exploration of its possibilities.

Fundamentally, the church's educational problem is not greatly different from the educational problem of the state. The seeming perfection of the public school is somewhat illusory. Public education, too, is undergoing profound reconstruction as to the ends it seeks and the character of the educational process by which it seeks to achieve them. The issues are constantly becoming more sharply drawn between the concept of education as the transmission of knowledge or the molding of the young into the existing institutions and behaviors of society and a creative type of education that will use the great cultural inheritances of the past as resources for helping the present generation to discover and to face the issues of contemporary life with inventive intelligence and a sense of responsibility for a better social order. The question is becoming increasingly acute as to whether the state in its rôle as sovereign is competent to perform the rôle of educator, if education is to be free to criticize the ends and processes of the *status quo* and to assume a reconstructive attitude toward it.

Certainly a bifurcated education in which the state attempts to meet only in part the intellectual, moral, and spiritual needs of the childhood and youth of the nation, and in which the church also attempts to meet their moral and spiritual needs apart from other educational experiences of the nation's childhood and youth, is an intolerable situation which cannot permanently endure. To the degree in which education becomes a function on the part of the mature members of society in assisting its immature members to achieve an intelligent, effective, and social adjustment to their world, education of all types whatsoever finds itself under the necessity of achieving some sort of co-operation the procedures of which shall be determined by the needs of growing persons and of society. Uncertain as the form which that co-operation may assume may now appear, the necessity of arriving at it is scarcely open to question. This apparently means the exploration of many possibilities by which American education may be brought into some functional integration.

It is our conviction that the church has the capacity to undertake the reconstruction of its own educational program in the light of these new demands and in relation to the other agencies that in one way or another contribute to the education of American childhood and youth. We base this conviction not only upon the reconstructions in the church's educational program that have been achieved in the past in response to changing conditions but even more upon the significant reconstructions of the church's program of education that are now under way.

SELECTED BIBLIOGRAPHY

ON RELIGIOUS EDUCATION FOR AGE-GROUPS

BETTS, GEORGE H. *Teaching Religion Today*. New York: Abingdon Press, 1934.

An interpretation of the more recent ideals of religious education.

BOWER, W. C. *Character through Creative Experience*. Chicago: University of Chicago Press, 1930.

———. *The Curriculum of Religious Education*. New York: Scribner, 1925.

———. *Religious Education in the Modern Church*. St. Louis: Bethany Press, 1929.

The third title deals with the way in which a modern church sets up its program of religious education. The second title presents the basic theory of curriculum. The first title deals particularly with method.

COE, GEORGE A. *What Is Christian Education?* New York: Scribner, 1929.

A critical analysis of present practice and suggestions as to improvement.

HARTSHORNE, HUGH, and EHRHART, EARLE V. *Church Schools of Today*. New Haven: Yale University Press, 1933.

HARTSHORNE, HUGH, and LOTZ, ELSA. *Case Studies of Present-Day Religious Education*. New Haven: Yale University Press, 1932.

HARTSHORNE, HUGH, and MILLER, J. QUINTER. *Community Organization in Religious Education*. New Haven: Yale University Press, 1932.

HARTSHORNE, HUGH, STEARNS, HELEN R., and UPHAUS, WILLARD E. *Standards and Trends in Religious Education*. New Haven: Yale University Press, 1933.

A series of studies conducted under the auspices of the Institute of Social and Religious Research, covering the organization and administration of religious education in ten outstanding churches, methods of classroom teaching, the standardizing efforts of overhead organizations in Sunday schools and colleges, and co-operative movements in local communities. Present a factual picture of current practice.

INTERNATIONAL COUNCIL OF RELIGIOUS EDUCATION. *The Curriculum Guide*, Books I–VII.

————. *The Development of a Curriculum of Religious Education*, Research Bull. 5.

The working-out of a practical procedure for the building of curriculums on the experience of the learning group and with the aid of resource material.

LOTZ, P. HENRY, and CRAWFORD, L. W. (edd.). *Studies in Religious Education*. Nashville, Tenn.: Cokesbury Press, 1931.

A fairly representative presentation of the various aspects of modern religious education by various authors.

SOARES, THEODORE G. *Religious Education*. Chicago: University of Chicago Press, 1928.

A comprehensive statement of the philosophy of religious education.

VIETH, PAUL H. *Objectives in Religious Education*. New York: Harper, 1930.

An analysis of the opinions of ten leading religious educators regarding the objectives of religious education. Of particular significance because this statement has been adopted as the working basis of the objectives of the International Council of Religious Education.

ON THE CHURCH COLLEGE

HITES, LAIRD T. *The Effective Christian College*. New York: Macmillan, 1929.

An interpretation of the church college from the point of view of its central religious function.

KELLY, ROBERT L. (ed.). *The Effective College*. New York: Association of American Colleges, 1928.

An analysis by several authors of the strength and weakness of the American college as these appear under the effects of social change.

KENT, RAYMOND A. *Higher Education in America*. Boston: Ginn, 1930.

LIMBERT, PAUL M. *Denominational Policies in the Support and Supervision of Higher Education.* New York: Teachers College, Columbia University, 1929.

LEONARD, R. J., EVENDEN, E. S., O'REAR, F. B., *et al. Survey of Higher Education for the United Lutheran Church in America,* Vols. I, II, and III. New York: Teachers College, Columbia University, 1929.

Needed Readjustments in Higher Education. Edited by WILLIAM S. GRAY. Chicago: University of Chicago Press, 1933.

Proceedings of the Institute for Administrative Officers of Higher Institutions, Vol. V.

REEVES, FLOYD W., and RUSSELL, JOHN D. *College Organization and Administration.* Indianapolis: Board of Education, Disciples of Christ, 1929.

Report of survey of Disciple colleges.

REEVES, FLOYD W., RUSSELL, JOHN D., *et al. The Liberal Arts College.* Chicago: University of Chicago Press, 1932.

Report of survey of Methodist colleges.

TOWNER, MILTON C. (ed.). *Religion in Higher Education.* Chicago: University of Chicago Press, 1931.

CHAPTER VI

THE CHURCH'S WORK WITH INDIVIDUALS

THE HISTORICAL DEVELOPMENT OF THE CHURCH'S WORK WITH INDIVIDUALS

THE cure of souls—the spiritual care of members of a congregation—is an ancient function of the Christian church and the Christian clergyman. Perhaps the most fundamental aspect of the minister's task has always been his work with individuals. In intimate personal contact with his people the pastor has sought to bring help to the tempted, spiritual renewal to the defeated, assurance of forgiveness to the penitent, comfort to the troubled, guidance to the perplexed, courage to the sick and the bereaved, and in a multitude of ways has sought to meet the peculiarly personal needs of the individuals who comprise his congregation.

The New Testament reveals how profound a concern for individuals characterized primitive Christianity. A very large part of our record of the life of Jesus depicts him dealing with individuals in a wide variety of intimate personal needs. The apostle Paul's letters are filled with evidences of deep pastoral concern for individuals whose lives he had touched. There are words of comfort, encouragement, friendly greeting, and rebuke. Various passages in the New Testament reveal the growth in the early church of such practices as house-to-house visitation, the rebuking and exhorting of individuals, and catechetical instruction—all of which indicate the church's highly individualistic emphasis, and the manner in which that emphasis determined its practices. The salvation of individual souls, in order that they might be ready for the blessed appearing of the Lord, which was believed to be imminent, was the overmastering passion of the primitive Christian community.

A major concern of the New Testament church was the maintenance of a high standard of personal morality on the part of members of the fellowship, and much of the church's dealing with individuals was of a disciplinary character.[1] The method of individual guidance and corrective discipline which soon became established was public confession of sin before the entire congregation, and action by the congregation forgiving or exacting penalty as the case might require. Gradually, with the passing of the years, the practice of public confession and discipline began to yield to a growing tendency to private confession to the pastor, now gaining status as a priest, who gave disciplinary direction. In Origen's time (182–251) the private direction of conscience was unofficially gaining importance, but confession and public humiliation for sin was still the general practice. It is not until we reach the Middle Ages that the private confessional reaches its complete development. Chiefly under the influence of the "Penitentials," a series of manuals for the guidance of confessors in prescribing the penance required for sins, uniformity of practice was achieved. Under the "seal of confession" the cure of souls was administered in intimate and highly elaborated

[1] Matt. 18:15–17; I Cor. 5; II Cor. 2:6; 13:2.

form. The sacrament of penance, as developed in scholastic doctrine, consists of contrition, confession, satisfaction, and absolution. It is believed to secure the remission of guilt and of eternal punishment for sin; the temporal punishment for sin is expiated by the sacramental penance which the priest imposes. In this form the sacrament is still administered in both the Roman Catholic and the Eastern Orthodox churches. Confession is an essential condition to receiving absolution.

One frequently hears it suggested that the Catholic practice of confession is of great value in relieving those tensions which arise from a sense of guilt and as an aid in making a new beginning. But there are Catholics who question its effectiveness in all cases. Dr. E. Boyd Barrett, a Roman Catholic, once a priest and now a practicing psychiatrist, on the basis of his experience in the confessional and in the psychiatric clinic, dissents from the view that confession, as a general rule, affords that healthy mode of self-revelation that psychologists regard as desirable. It is too fragmentary, too artificial, and too coercive in character to be a health-giving mode of release. "Legislation," he says, "has dehumanized confession, and made it, for perhaps the majority of Catholics, a burthen rather than a source of comfort."[2] For the Protestant who does not believe in sacramental absolution, such a form of confession can have little value; and, moreover, Protestants urge, such confession lessens the power of self-direction, destroys moral autonomy, and, where the priest gives the benefit of the ethical doubt, probably lowers ethical standards.

[2] *Journal of Religion*, VIII, No. 2 (1928), 188–203.

The Protestant reformers abolished sacramental penance, and with it the confessional in its Catholic form. Luther, while "disgusted, wearied, shamed and distressed by the endless chaos of superstitions" which had gathered about the confessional, did not wish entirely to discard it but rather to utilize it as an opportunity for a confidential interview in which the sinner might unburden himself and seek guidance from his pastor. Calvin, however, went farther, and abolished the old confessional outright. But the needs of sin-stricken or distressed individuals made it necessary to provide them some sort of guidance. Calvin therefore advised the individual suffering anguish of soul to "have recourse for relief to a private confession to his own pastor." Confession may, indeed, Calvin says, be made "to any member of the church who may seem most fit; yet as, for the most part, pastors are to be supposed better qualified than others, our choice ought chiefly to fall on them." But confession was to be entirely optional.

In the Anglican communion there has always been a Catholic element which has desired to maintain sacramental confession and absolution and to require it as a prerequisite to the Eucharist. But, while this element in the church has considerably increased its strength since the Oxford movement in the middle of the nineteenth century, the practice of sacramental confession and absolution is unauthorized, and the customary practice in all branches of Anglicanism conforms rather closely to that of Protestantism generally.

The care of souls in Protestantism has made use of

both private consultation and public confession. The pastoral work of the minister has never been viewed by those who have given the matter earnest attention as a mere business of making a round of calls. The many volumes dealing with pastoral theology that have been produced since the beginning of the Reformation reveal the deep concern of the minister to aid his parishioners to overcome their temptations, achieve a victorious Christian life, and bear their trials with fortitude. Some of the quite early books give an astonishing amount of attention to detailed instruction in the art of personal counseling. Preaching and public worship are to be supplemented by this painstaking work with individuals.

And public confession of sin, requests for the prayers of one's fellow-Christians, and personal testimony concerning one's experience in the Christian life have been prominent features of Protestantism in many communions. Until quite recently it was a vigorous feature of Protestant church life in America. In the Methodist class meeting, which has now fallen into pretty general disuse, there was a semipublic mutual confession and correction which, under the direction of a skilful class leader, sometimes probed pretty deeply into moral delinquencies.

A very definite set of theological presuppositions can be found to undergird this Protestant ministry for the cure of souls, just as these same presuppositions determine the message of the preacher. The awful picture of the lost state of man, the drama of redemption, and the availability of salvation through faith in Christ are constantly reiterated. And the task of the pastor as personal counselor is pre-eminently, by persuasion and appeal, to bring lost souls to conviction of sin and faith in Christ, in order to secure their eternal salvation. To this, of course, is added much common sense and good advice to persons perplexed and troubled as they face the baffling issues of life; but the central feature of the pastor's task is a religious ministry to lost or tempted souls, and the counsel which he gives is determined by the theological dogmas of the church.

It is necessary to linger here for a moment, for it is precisely at this point that the most significant shift is taking place at the present time. These theological pre-suppositions which were almost universally accepted fifty years ago, and upon which the pastor's counseling was predicated, are no longer considered tenable by many modern-minded ministers, and the whole task requires reorientation. The modern-minded minister is just as much concerned about his parishioner's soul's salvation as was his predecessor, but the basic assumptions upon which he operates have changed, and the very term "salvation," when used, has taken on new meaning.

The pattern of ideas to which we have referred, which underlay the pastor's counseling of a former generation, and which, of course, guides the counseling and preaching of many ministers today, was believed to be derived directly from the Bible, which was accepted as an authoritative revelation from God. All that the minister had to do was to interpret this revelation and administer this authoritative system. Of course a good deal of ingenuity went into the building-up of this doctrinal system on the basis of certain scriptural passages. According to this doctrinal system, all of mankind's failings were due to a fundamental defect of human nature, and that defect was the result of Adam's sin. Man's originally innocent nature had been corrupted by Adam's disobedience, and this depravity was now inherited by all Adam's descendants. Both by inheritance and by his own volition every man was a sinner; and the penalty of sin was death. But God had provided salvation for man in Christ, who bore the penalty of sin, in order that men, through faith in him, might be saved. Thus the cure of souls was the administering of this system. Little account was taken of the peculiarity of individual needs because, whatever might be the individual peculiarities, the fundamental difficulty was corrupt human nature. And the pastor's task was to bring the individual to repentance and faith.

But two things have happened. The historical study of the Bible has taken from that great book the kind of authority that was supposed to reside in it, so that we no longer look to it for a divine revelation upon anthropology, or for a divinely revealed exclusive "plan of salvation." At the same time the social and psychological sciences have had a great development, so that, while these sciences are still in their infancy, a sound understanding of human nature is gradually being achieved, and new light is being thrown upon the problems of human behavior and personality development.

This does not mean that the Bible has become valueless. It reveals how religion, in an amazing variety of situations, has functioned as an integrating and socializing force in personal and communal life; it shows how men and societies, under the influence of religion, have been spiritually renewed. Indeed, if one studies the Bible as a record of the way in which religious men have met their life-problems, one finds there a much more rewarding revelation of human nature and its remaking than is to be found in the theologizing that has been based upon the story of Adam.

The better understanding of human nature that has resulted from anthropological, sociological, and psychological investigation has greatly enriched the concept of salvation. The minister who has been affected by ideas current in the field of the social sciences no longer interprets salvation merely as post-mortem rescue from punishment for sin, but as release here and now from those forces within and without the individual that frustrate and defeat him, and his achievement of personal self-realization and fulfilment. This requires that the minister understand the conditions under which wholesome personality develops, and also the forces that frustrate such development; that he have some real understanding of the passions and desires that drive and motivate persons, the inner conflicts and environmental conditions that defeat them, and the factors that facilitate release and bring enrichment. And, above all, he needs a profound appreciation of the resources available in religious faith and practice to promote personal fulfilment and adjustment.

OPPORTUNITIES AND RESOURCES OF THE CHURCH

Pastors and churches, very generally, are awakening to a new sense of responsibility for a greatly improved service in their ministry to individuals,[3] and the opportunities and resources of the churches are many. We may briefly point out some of them:

First, the church is in active contact with the people. Approximately 50 per cent of the population of America holds membership in its various churches, and the Protestant churches have their full share of this total. In addition are many non-church members who readily indicate their "preference" when asked, and attend church regularly or occasionally. Moreover, the church's fellowship is an inclusive one. It is not, like lodges or clubs, limited for the most part to men or women; it includes children, youths, and adults. It embraces the family. And it limits itself to no social class; rich and poor, high and low, the privileged and the underprivileged all belong. Its services are available to all.

In the second place, the church provides a sustaining fellowship. A primary need for personality development—as, also, for personality rehabilitation if some disaster has been suffered—is identification with a group. Wholesome personality development requires

[3] The various significant experiments now being made by churches in all parts of the country to apply the insights and techniques derived from the psychological and social sciences to aid disturbed and frustrated individuals to achieve adequate adjustment and self-realization ought to be carefully studied by all churches. Life-adjustment clinics, co-operative programs with physicians, psychiatrists, mental hygienists, social case-workers, etc., as well as the efforts of individual pastors to utilize the findings of other specialists in their counseling work, point to a new awareness of rich resources which may prove to be of untold value to the pastor in aiding persons to achieve a satisfying adjustment. We would encourage pastors and experimentally minded churches to explore the possibilities in this direction and to share their findings with other churches (*Findings of the Interdenominational Conference on the City and the Church in the Present Crisis Held in Chicago, Ill., November 29–December 2, 1932*).

that one be an accepted and participating member of a group, sharing the group's interests and purposes, saturated by its spirit, and enjoying its love and respect. Nothing is more damaging to personality than isolation—to be left out, shunned, unloved. Probably the most prolific source of personality disorder is to be found in unsatisfactory social adjustment in childhood—a conflict in the home, or unhappy relationships in school or with the neighborhood group. Adequate socialization is essential to satisfactory personality development, and the adult needs such sustaining relationships as truly as does the child.

And the church is pre-eminently a fellowship. Here fellowship is provided about a wide range of vital interests, in worship, study, recreation, and service. There is the fellowship of the total group, bound about a common purpose, somewhat vaguely conceived perhaps, but viewed as the highest good. And there are the more intimate smaller groups—classes, clubs, societies—in which one becomes known and knows others, and in the shared life and activities of which one may have a significant part. The fact that the church is primarily a fellowship is a matter of paramount importance for the church in its work with individuals.

Third, the church is organized about the loftiest ideals. Of course it does not fully realize and embody its ideals; no institution does or can. But it probably approximates its ideals as fully as does any institution on earth. And it may say, with Browning:

What I aspired to be
And was not, comforts me.

What is of importance for the influence of the institution upon the individual is the direction in which it is moving, the values it cherishes, and the earnestness with which it seeks its goals. If the personality of the individual is to be organized upon high levels of ethical achievement, the institution which provides him a sustaining fellowship must cherish and seek the attainment of noble ideals. And this the church does. It stands for reverent regard for personal values, the cultivation of happy family life, wholesome community conditions, and integrity and good will in all social relationships. Its central ideals are those of faith, loyalty, hope, and love. The church is a rallying center for the higher unifying loyalties.

Fourth, the church is the institution of religion. It is by virtue of its specific task as a religious institution that the church is able to render its most distinctive service to individuals.[4] Religion touches resources of motivation and releases power for daily living unequaled by other factors. Nothing could have a more deadening effect upon efforts for personal fulfilment or for the achievement of lofty values than a belief that such efforts have no relevance in the total scheme of things. To believe that our little lives are but flashes lost in the

[4] While gratefully appropriating for pastoral counsel such insights and methods developed by specialists in other fields as are suitable, the pastor should not fail to recognize that his major resource is religion. Religion has always been the most significant of all agencies in aiding man to adjust himself to his world and to the problems of his life. Satisfying personality adjustment requires the integration of personality about some large commanding social purpose to which the individual can give himself with unqualified devotion. The Christian religion, with its apprehension of the purpose of God in Christ, challenges men with the very loftiest expression of such an integrating purpose (*ibid.*).

darkness, and that our noblest endeavors after good are but quixotic illusions with no lasting significance, is to cut the nerve of moral endeavor and to rob human life of dignity. Religion gives personal living the place of highest value in the whole hierarchy of values. And it sees human life, not as a mere process of mechanical adjustment in a material universe, but as the achievement and enrichment of personal values in the widest possible range of social relationships. It interprets the universe, and our experience in it, in such terms. It sets human life in a system of personal relationships on a cosmic scale; it interprets our best human purposes as not merely ours, but as a sharing of the will and purpose of the Eternal. Religion, thus, far more than any other factor in our experience, gives dignity and value to human life. It is the greatest and most powerful of all available resources in administering the cure of souls.

Fifth and last, the availability of the pastor provides an unrivaled opportunity for the church in its work with individuals. No leader of any other institution is, by tradition and present practice, so intimately and affectionately bound to the members of his group as is the pastor to his people. The good pastor shares with his people the whole range of their interests, and is brought particularly close in times of crisis. In the personal confidences which he receives the pastor's only rival is the physician. He shares the joy of the family when a child is born; through family visitation, as well as through the church and church school, he keeps in touch with the development of the child from babyhood through adolescence into adult life; he marries the young people of the congregation, buries the dead, and brings comfort and courage in times of grief. If people come to believe in his wisdom and sound judgment, his counsel is sought in all kinds of perplexities. There is no one available whose integrity and disinterestedness is more unquestioned. And if he has taken pains to acquire real skill in personal guidance (certainly a major responsibility of the pastor), there is no one who stands in quite as strategic a place to render a service of paramount importance.

It is, of course, true that churches generally fall far short of utilizing to the full their resources for ministry to individual needs. But, as has been said, there is a new awareness of opportunity and responsibility for better work. And all over the country interesting and even daring experiments in work with individuals are being made. Very briefly a few typical illustrations, chosen out of a vastly larger number, may be given. These illustrations can give only a hint of the wide variety of approaches; they range all the way from the pastor working alone, but utilizing psychological insight and training, up to the highly elaborated clinic.

CHURCH A

In this church of about five hundred members three features characterize the program of work with individuals. First, the minister sets apart a good block of his time when he is available for conferences about any problems his people may bring to him. This he supplements with a great deal of home visitation. While he is well trained in psychology, he makes clear that he is not conducting a psychological clinic but is seeking to render pastoral service. A religious atmosphere is carefully cultivated. Second, he has organized a board of consultants, consisting of a nutrition expert, a social case-worker, a child-guidance expert, a psychiatrist, and a doctor, to whom he can turn for counsel or to whom he can refer cases requiring special care. And, third, in addition to the regular religious services, certain organizations, such as the Home and Mothers' Club, the Adult and Child Health Guilds, and the Unemployment Meeting, are utilized as agencies for group therapy.

CHURCH B

This is a large and famous church in an eastern state. Specialized attention to individuals began in the church school, where the question arose as to what should be done about certain problem children who disturbed classes, stole articles, and manifested other forms of undesirable behavior. Should these children be dismissed in the interest of discipline or had the church a responsibility to help them? It was decided to accept the responsibility, and a consulting psychologist was added to the staff on part time. Counseling has been conducted with the children concerned, their parents, teachers, club leaders, and others, with a view to removing handicaps and providing stimuli to the achievement of the "abundant life." The church school has deliberately set itself a program which seeks not only to prevent undesirable behavior on the part of boys and girls but also to cultivate and promote desirable interests and activities. Many community resources have been utilized and the program is meeting gratifying success.

CHURCH C

This church, like Church B, began its counseling program in the church school. All church-school teachers are paid and are professionally competent. Each of the eight hundred children in the church school is given a psychological and personality test by a competent psychologist, and a personality evaluation on a prescribed form is obtained for each child from church- and public-school teachers. From this beginning an elaborate program has developed which reaches throughout the entire church fellowship. Counseling involves the child, parents, teachers, and others whose lives influence the child. Adult as well as child problems come into the foreground. It is evident that little can be accomplished with children who have been emotionally conditioned by parental attitudes and reactions until the home situation has been satisfactorily dealt with. Thus a very important counseling relationship is at once established with parents and possibly other relatives and friends, and very frequently the treatment of the child's problem involves a reformation of family relationships and home environment. In addition to the personal counseling the church has enriched its educational program with classes in child guidance and parent education, and with a series of lectures which run throughout the winter dealing with psychology as applied to everyday life. The church conceives its program in dealing with individuals as one of preventive education and therapeutic re-education.

CHURCH D

This is a church which has available in its membership and community very unusual personal and institutional resources. It conceives of personal counseling as a process which should permeate the entire program of the church, supplementing the various group activities, so that all sorts of difficulties of personal adjustment, whether suffered by a child, adolescent, or adult, may be recognized in their incipiency, if possible, and an adequate program developed to meet the needs of each case. The church has organized a Counseling Committee, composed of the pastors, representatives of the church school and other subsidiary organizations, and experts in the fields of vocational, educational, marital, and psychological counseling. The effort is being made to sensitize the entire leadership of the church and its many organizations to the need and opportunity for skilled guidance of individuals as part of the total program of the church, so as both to develop to the full the latent capacities of the members of the church fellowship and to prevent the development of serious maladjustments. Lectures and talks are given by competent persons to different groups, as, for example, addresses by physicians, educators, etc., to the college age young people's organization on premarital, vocational, and similar problems; and resource people, expert in their various fields, have been made available for personal conferences.

CHURCH E

Here a clinic, initiated by a church and still maintained in the church building, has developed into a "Life Adjustment Center" which is the Adult Department of the Mental Hygiene Association of the city, and is financed by the Community Chest. The Center has a small salaried and a large volunteer staff. The salaried staff consists of the director, who is also a psychiatric social worker, and a secretary. The volunteer staff includes psychiatrists, neurologists, psychoanalysts, psychologists, psychiatric social workers, physicians, lawyers, a dietitian, spiritual advisers, hostesses, special employment workers, and stenographers. The office of the Center is open daily from 9:00 A.M. to 5:00 P.M., and the clinic is held regularly each Monday evening from 7:30–11:00. Special appointments are made for those who cannot come at the regular hours. The quarters consist of an office, waiting-room, and eight private consulting rooms provided free by the church. The budget is about $3,000 annually, and no charge is made to the clients for services.

These are, necessarily, only thumbnail sketches of the work done by the churches mentioned, but they serve to indicate something of the wide range of practice from a very simple to a highly elaborated procedure. The main purpose in making this presentation has been to indicate some of the forms of response on the part of the church to the new awareness of the need for an improved practice in dealing with individuals.

NEWER APPROACHES TO WORK WITH INDIVIDUALS

As has been said, the pastor in his ministry today for the cure of souls does not see the task as quite so simple a matter as did his predecessor. It will not do to ascribe all the incorrigibilities and failures of men to an inherited depravity which is to be remedied by repentance and faith, important as these attitudes are. The minister asks: What is the nature and what are the conditioning factors of this individual's difficulty, shortcoming, or need, in all its stark discreteness, and what can be done to aid him meet and overcome it? And the resulting study of individual problems by pastors and others who have faced the task of personal guidance has led to the recognition of certain well-defined needs which call for a program of individual counseling. Among them may be listed the following as of special concern to the minister of religion.

1. *The guidance of children into healthy mental habits and good character.*—The utter dependence of the child upon factors which operate in his social environment for the mental and emotional patterns of his behavior must be evident to all. The church is interested in the child's realizing himself on the highest levels which his potentialities and his environment afford—that is, in his achieving the "abundant life." But the child can hope thus to realize himself only as forces that threaten to frustrate and defeat him are overcome, and stimulations and opportunities are provided that promote such development. The church can do something through its own institutional practices—its worship, its fellowship, its organized activities, and other phases of its program. But other influences, of family, neighborhood, school, and play group, are so insistent and powerful that unless a method of co-operation with these agencies is developed the church probably will play an insignificant part in the child's development. Leaders in the field of religious education need particularly to address themselves to this problem.

2. *The education of youth in dealing with the problems of daily life, such as relationships in the home, relationships between the sexes, and the choice of a vocation.*— Young people must emancipate themselves from adult control and assume self-direction. Yet they are faced with the necessity of making decisions upon matters of vital importance, both for themselves and for society,

with a minimum of experience and when impulse and passion are strongest. The development of a program of education in such matters, which shall not be autocratic, but in which young people shall be led to face these issues deliberately, with the aid of wise and experienced counselors, and in the light of life's highest values, is a matter of great concern. Such a program cannot be carried through entirely by group procedures. Personal guidance and counsel will be needed.

3. *Counsel on marital and premarital problems.*—Of all social relationships the marriage relationship is the one in which persons find their richest self-fulfilment or their most damaging and degrading frustration. And yet multitudes of people enter into marriage woefully ignorant of the physiological and psychological factors involved in achieving a happy adjustment. Many pastors are finding this the most challenging and rewarding area of counseling. It is not enough, they find, to preach cleanness of mind and body in general terms; it is necessary to guide young people into an understanding and proper direction of impulse. Certain studies that have been made reveal that most pastors fail to deal in anything but the most superficial manner with this problem; yet it is precisely at this point that the spiritual life is at stake for many. Most of the denominations and the Federal Council of the Churches of Christ in America[5] now have commissions studying this matter and are ready to provide guidance for the pastor who desires to undertake such a counseling ministry.

[5] Commission on Marriage and the Home, Federal Council of the Churches of Christ in America, 105 E. Twenty-second St., New York N.Y.

4. *Parental education.*—The "parental instinct," viewed as a native endowment which equips one to rear children wisely, has been regarded far too optimistically. It is all too evident that most parents need education in the care and guidance of children. Certain studies that have been made reveal that one of the chief areas of difficulty for young people concerns their conflicts with their parents. And it is not only conflicts between parents and children that prove damaging to the growing child or adolescent, but the conflicts which sometimes obtain between the parents themselves are scarcely less injurious. The child is exceedingly sensitive to the emotional tone of the home, and when conflict prevails, the reverberations of that conflict sound in his own soul. The sense of security, so essential to wholesome development, is undermined. The child is almost certain to suffer defects of personality as a consequence. Feelings of inferiority develop, and compensatory behavior in the form of tantrums, delinquency, and other undesirable conduct are likely to appear. These forms of behavior, if carried on into adult life, present serious problems. An understanding of these matters is of great importance to the pastor who would serve as a helpful counselor in preventing or remedying such calamities.

5. *The healing of "divided" personalities.*—William James once described religious conversion as "the process, gradual or sudden, by which a self hitherto divided, and consciously wrong, inferior and unhappy, becomes unified and consciously right, superior and happy, in consequence of its firmer hold upon religious realities."[6]

[6] *Varieties of Religious Experience*, p. 244.

The Christian religion has notably succeeded in healing those tragic conflicts within the soul, so well described by the apostle Paul, "The good that I would, I do not; but the evil that I would not, that I do."[7] And the method of religion has been essentially that which psychology describes as "sublimation." It presents a cause so fascinating and compelling, a leader and Savior so inspiring, resources of motivation so dynamic, that the forces of one's personality rally about that cause and leader and the better self is enabled to break through and take control. Whether this process of personality unification on high levels be gradual or sudden, it is the responsibility of the pastor as counselor to promote it. Religion has power to heal this sore division in the hearts of men who are in tragic conflict with themselves.

6. *Religious perplexities.*—Many people are confused and troubled by religious problems. Some are worried, fear-stricken, or in black despair because of disaster which has overwhelmed them. Others have found the religious convictions upon which the very structure of their lives seemed to be reared rendered untenable by new knowledge. Such problems call for skilled and sympathetic personal counseling. Not that the pastor can be expected to answer all questions, or provide easy solutions for all problems. Life is too complex for that. But it is his responsibility, in his ministry for the cure of souls, to guide his people through their religious perplexities, to bring to them, by his words and by the contagion of his own faith, new assurance and courage, and to mediate to them new power for daily living.

[7] Rom. 7:19.

7. *Bringing courage and peace to the discouraged, afflicted, sick, and dying.*—In such areas of need pastoral work has long had its largest expression and its greatest success. Religion has notably inspired men to face tragic circumstances with fortitude and inner serenity; it has strengthened the morale of the sick; it has transformed the utter loneliness and defeat of death into a thing of beauty and triumph; and it has brought comfort and solace to those sorely bereaved. And pastors, very generally, have mediated these resources of religion with a high degree of sympathy and effectiveness. But even here many pastors need to increase their skill. While fully recognizing that the factors of chief importance are genuine sympathy and brotherly concern, it still remains true that many cases will call for a better understanding of human nature and a more secure and adequate philosophy of life than some ministers possess. The pious platitudes frequently uttered in the face of stark tragedy bring little comfort or help to many modern men.

Valuable insights and techniques which have been developed by specialists in many agencies which practice "the art of helping people out of trouble" are available to the pastor, and should be carefully studied by him. The extent to which these insights and techniques are being utilized by pastors and churches has already been indicated by reference to specific church programs now in operation. Among the most significant of these approaches for the pastor which might be mentioned are those of social case work and mental hygiene.

The social case-worker's method of dealing with an

individual or family in distress offers, perhaps, the very best available corrective for the weaknesses of the conventional religious approach. The social case-worker has no revealed "plan of salvation" to prescribe for human ill, nor any ready-made assumptions to explain it. Her business is rather the much more commonplace but, nevertheless, exacting task of diagnosis and treatment. It is for her to find out, by a thorough exploration of her client's past experience and present situation, exactly what is the nature and what are the causes of the present disability, and to aid the development of a program of service designed to remove the causes, if possible, and, in any case, to assist the rehabilitation of the unfortunate individual. Medicine, psychology, mental hygiene, economics, sociology, religion, or any one of many other resources may lend assistance in understanding the problem and prescribing treatment. Each case is a special problem to be understood and appropriately dealt with, calling for exhaustive study to discover the conditioning factors of the trouble, and, in co-operation with the client, the formulation of a program designed to effect the client's reclamation and permanent rehabilitation. Such a realistic approach by the pastor to his task will greatly increase the efficiency of his work. And the social case-worker has devised methods of investigation and treatment which offer the pastor significant opportunities for rewarding study.

The goals sought in mental hygiene so closely approximate many of the most important goals of religion that the minister will do well to keep in touch with this developing science. Indeed, the major goal of both might be said to be "abundant life." In her recent valuable book Miss Clara Bassett speaks of mental hygiene as

that growing body of knowledge and techniques which has for its purpose the understanding of the evolution of human personality; the promotion of mental health as the expression of the highest development and integration possible . . . . of the physical, emotional and mental powers of personality; the study, treatment and prevention of emotional and behavior disorders which preclude the happy and effective functioning of personality . . . . ; the efficient organization and operation of community facilities which may be necessary for the achievement of these aims; and the progressive modification of social institutions and agencies which vitally affect the mental health of large groups.[8]

Reverence for personality is a central characteristic of the Christian faith. To bring personality to its richest fulfilment in the widest possible social relationships is the professed goal of the Christian religion; that is, indeed, "the Kingdom of God." Whatever understanding, therefore, mental hygiene is able to give of the conditions that frustrate such personal development, that issue in disintegrating inner conflicts, fears and worries, feelings of inferiority, isolation, and guilt, and whatever it can contribute toward the liberation, enrichment, and integration of personality in satisfying social relationships, is of the greatest importance to the pastor. And mental hygiene, as a science and as an art, has much indeed to contribute.

Of all the resources available to the pastor, however, in that phase of his ministry which seeks to promote the richest possible self-realization of his parishioners, the most powerful are those inherent in religious faith and practice. Love, faith, and hope—the virtues which re-

[8] *Mental Hygiene in the Community*, p. 3.

ligion sponsors—are integrating and socializing in both personal and communal living. The pastor, utilizing the opportunities presented by the church's fellowship and worship, as well as those opportunities which are provided him for intimate personal counseling, can stimulate and release these positive, constructive forces.

The resources available in the church's fellowship cannot be overstressed. God's love and care can be made real to the distressed individual by the love and care displayed by God's people; God's forgiveness and reconciliation can be mediated by their welcome; the sense of isolation can be cured by the sustaining fellowship of the Christian brotherhood; and the drives of the individual's life may be given direction and worthy occupation by participation in the church's program of work.

The pastor and church have at hand, then, the most mighty of all means of help to the distressed individual, as well as the most powerful dynamic to promote the growth of individuals in the good life. And if the minister and the church do not utilize them it does not appear who will be able to do so.

SELECTED BIBLIOGRAPHY

ADLER, ALFRED. *Understanding Human Nature.* New York: Greenberg, 1927.

An application of the principles of "individual psychology" to the organization of one's personal life.

BASSETT, CLARA. *Mental Hygiene in the Community.* New York: Macmillan, 1934.

A comprehensive picture of the relation of mental hygiene to urgent problems of community life. A chapter on "Mental Hygiene, the Church and Theological Training," of especial value to clergymen.

BOWER, W. C. *Character through Creative Experience.* Chicago: University of Chicago Press, 1930.

A study of the development of personality and character, with special attention to the significance of religion for character development.

CONKLIN, EDMUND S. *The Psychology of Religious Adjustment.* New York: Macmillan, 1929.

The function of religion in facilitating personality adjustment.

GROVES, E. R., and BLANCHARD, P. *Introduction to Mental Hygiene.* New York: Holt, 1930.

A useful introduction to the subject. Includes a chapter on the church and social hygiene.

HADFIELD, J. A. *Psychology and Morals.* New York: McBride, 1925.

An eminent psychotherapist's contribution to the study of personality development and adjustment, with emphasis upon the significance of ethical factors.

HOLMAN, CHARLES T. *The Cure of Souls.* Chicago: University of Chicago Press, 1932.

A practical treatment of pastoral counseling, with a consideration of the insights and techniques available to the pastor from the fields of social case work and psychiatry.

LICHLEITER, M. I. *The Healing of Souls.* New York: Abingdon, 1931.

A pastor's discussion of personal counseling in the light of recent psychological theories.

MACKENZIE, J. G. *Souls in the Making.* New York: Macmillan, 1929.

Psychological insight and religious faith as guides in pastoral counseling.

McNEILL, JOHN T. "Historical Types of Method in the Cure of Souls," *Crozer Quarterly*, July, 1934, pp. 323–34.

A scholarly review of the subject.

OLIVER, JOHN RATHBONE, *Pastoral Psychiatry and Mental Health.* New York: Scribner, 1932.

A psychiatrist who is also an Episcopal priest seeks to make psychiatric insight available to the pastor.

OVERSTREET, HARRY A. *About Ourselves.* New York: Norton, 1927.

A very helpful book on attitudes and habits favorable to mental health.

SCHWEINITZ, KARL DE. *The Art of Helping People out of Trouble.* New York: Houghton Mifflin, 1924.

A charmingly written book setting forth the principles of social case work with ample illustrations drawn from the author's rich experience.

SOARES, T. G. *Religious Education.* Chicago: University of Chicago Press, 1928.

The principles of religious education, based upon a sound social psychology.

STOLZ, KARL R. *Pastoral Psychology.* Nashville, Tenn: Cokesbury, 1932.

The application of psychological principles to pastoral counseling.

WEATHERHEAD, LESLIE. *Psychology in the Service of the Soul.* New York: Macmillan, 1930.

Special attention to the disguising of motives and emphasis upon the necessity of sincerity.

WOOD, L. FOSTER. *Six Tests of Marriage.* New York: Federal Council of the Churches of Christ in America, 1933.

An excellent booklet of premarital counsel. An examination of the elements that make a successful marriage.

WORCESTER, ELWOOD, and McCOMB, Samuel. *Body, Mind and Spirit.* Boston: Marshall Jones, 1931.

A valuable book growing out of the rich experience of the authors in the Emmanuel movement.

NOTE.—An excellent *Bibliography on Education in Family Life, Marriage, Parenthood, and Young People's Relationships* is published jointly by the International Council of Religious Education, 203 N. Wabash Ave., Chicago, and the Federal Council of the Churches of Christ in America, 105 E. Twenty-second St., New York, N.Y. It is annotated, and includes nearly everything of value in English.

CHAPTER VII

THE CHURCH AS A MISSIONARY AGENCY

CHRISTIANITY becomes especially creative when it crosses the frontiers of routine religious living and thinking and seeks to Christianize new areas of Christian experience. We of America have our own areas of dominant interest which arise out of our own peculiar environment. Consequently the churches are addressing themselves to such urgent questions as social reconstruction, economic justice, relations of church and state, and as they do so something new evolves, as is shown elsewhere in this volume.

However, the church has not been content to remain within the boundaries of its own culture region. It expands into non-Christian areas, and this expansion is known as "foreign missions." But once Christianity crosses culture boundaries, it does more than simply increase in numbers and geographical outreach. When the early church escaped from the confines of Palestine and entered the life of the great Mediterranean world, it came into contact with new needs which had to be met and new conditions which had to be faced. In wrestling with these newer issues of daily living the church entered upon three or four centuries of remarkable creativity, which were productive both of good and of evil according to our standards. A similar phenomenon is taking place today as Christianity comes into contact with the characteristic conditions and problems of foreign fields.

MOTIVATION

The impulse to expand is born from within. It springs up in the hearts of a few ardent souls—Paul and Barnabas among the early Christians, Zinzendorf and Carey at the beginning of modern missions, a few missionary enthusiasts within a local church. Only as missionary enthusiasm is kindled by a variety of appeals does this interest spread to increasing numbers within the total communion. The first practical task, therefore, which confronts the local pastor or the board secretary is to stir the fires of emotion and conviction until large numbers are moved to throw themselves heartily behind the cause.

The church has used a variety of appeals for arousing the emotional pressure which provides missionary motivation. One of these springs from the Christian's conception of God, and of his own relationship to such a God. When God is conceived of as sovereign will, participation in missions becomes essentially obedience to the command, "Go ye into all the world." Of late years God has been thought of rather as self-sacrificing love. This view finds expression, for example, in the sentiments of the Jerusalem meeting of the International Missionary Council. "Our true and compelling motive lies in the very nature of God, to whom we have given our hearts. Since He is love, His very nature is to share. Christ is the expression in time of the eternal self-giving of the Father."[1] Accordingly, the child of God strives to resemble his heavenly Father by sharing his choicest spiritual heritage with those who are afar off.

It was the distress of those who did not enjoy the blessings of Christianity which furnished the most powerful motive during the last century. The Christian pulpit pictured vividly the eternal suffering of unredeemed millions. Returned missionaries described in detail the sickness, poverty, and gross superstition of those who were without the advantages which we enjoy, and the Christian out of his fulness was moved to sacrifice on behalf of the needy. As a result of such benevolence during the more prosperous years from 1920 to 1925, Protestant societies the world over were supporting a total force of twenty-seven thousand foreign missionaries, and operating with a yearly income which reached the amazing total of sixty-nine million dollars.

But of recent years this benevolent appeal has been losing its force. The threat of eternal punishment no longer disturbs people as it once did. The portrayal of foreign conditions in their darkest colors is now recognized as bad form, and as giving a distorted picture of things as they really are. Signs of progress and elements of promise greet us from across the water. It is maintained that the time has come for the West to abandon its attitude of paternalism and grant to other peoples the right of working out their future as best they can. As a consequence, the old appeal to benevolence has lost some of its power, and must be supplemented by other

---

[1] *Jerusalem Meeting of the International Missionary Council*, I, 405.

motives, if the church is to continue to render its greatest service to the nations.

One of the newer motives springs from a growing appreciation of the solidarity of the race. We find ourselves huddled together on this planet like so many mariners in a little boat in which we must either sail the sea of life together or else go down to destruction through our joint folly. It becomes a matter of supreme concern, therefore, that all the parties involved learn to pull on the oars together and to keep the boat on an even keel, especially in stormy weather. At the present moment America is preoccupied with political, economic, and social reconstruction. But once one comes to see that these vital questions are not strictly local either in their origins or in their solutions and that one's fate is held largely in the hands of other peoples, the old motivation of benevolence is supplemented by the recognition of mutual dependence and by the discovery that we can help ourselves only as we help others. This raises self-interest to an ethical plane and frees benevolence from the objectionable implications of condescension and superiority. Not only am I my brother's keeper; my brother is also my keeper. Therefore, the character and condition of this brother becomes a matter of supreme concern, and any movement or activity which promises to make both him and me better brothers is well worth the effort.

For many years mission work has been divided into two great fields of activity, home missions and foreign missions. But a deeper insight reveals that whether in America or in Siam the human family is wrestling with the same great problems, and fighting the same great enemies. Therefore, the task of the church should not be divided in our thought along geographical lines. However, seeing that mission work is still organized under two departments and probably will be for some years to come, this chapter will be devoted to the consideration of foreign missions.

OBJECTIVES

What has the church been trying to accomplish through her missionary activities? This is an important question. Rarely do people give themselves to earnest endeavor unless they believe that the objectives are worthy of the efforts involved. Methods and techniques are dependent upon objectives. They must be such as will contribute to the ends in view. Three typical statements may be given which mirror the mind of the church at the present time.

According to a committee of prominent Christian leaders in America at the close of the war, the aim of missions should be to nationalize Christianity, to Christianize nationalism, to internationalize Christianity, and to Christianize internationalism.[2] This statement is significant in that it recognizes the object of missions to be the betterment of Christianity as well as the Christianization of the world.

The most representative pronouncement of recent years is that of the Jerusalem meeting of the International Missionary Council, held in 1928. The aim of Christian missions "is nothing less than the production

[2] *Missionary Outlook in the Light of the War*, chap. iv.

of Christ-like character in individuals and societies and nations, through faith in and fellowship with Christ the living Saviour, and through corporate sharing of life in a divine society."[3]

The Laymen's Commission of Inquiry expressed itself as follows:

The aim of Christian missions is to seek with people of other lands a true knowledge and love of God, expressing in life and word what we have learned through Jesus Christ, and endeavoring to give effect to his spirit in the life of the world.[4]

In these statements there will be noted a variety of interpretation concerning the objectives of missions and the methods by which they are to be realized. Is it by proclaiming a divine revelation and redemption which man accepts through faith? Is it by joining in a common quest along with other sincere people and by co-operating in a creative task? Or is it through some combination of the two? Such differences of opinion give rise to divergent types of work on the field and make it difficult for one missionary to have full confidence in the work of another. This much, however, all hold in common: Christian missions are the organized effort of the church to mediate to people of other religions and cultures what the Christian has found to be life's choicest treasures, and to unfold what he considers to be life's highest possibilities—a noble undertaking in any case.

ORGANIZATIONS AND METHODS

This leads to the consideration of the organizations and methods through which the church has sought to

[3] *Jerusalem Meeting of the International Missionary Council,* I, 407.
[4] *Re-thinking Missions,* p. 326.

carry out its missionary obligations as these have been understood from time to time. When the modern missionary enterprise was launched one hundred and fifty years ago, there were few precedents to follow. Consequently the church has been compelled to feel its way as best it could in the light of experience gained along the road.

The first societies were voluntary associations of missionary enthusiasts, in some cases restricted to one denomination and in others cutting across denominational lines. But in the course of a few decades, as the fervor of a few individuals grew and extended, the churches themselves were seized with a new sense of mission, and these early voluntary associations were transformed into denominational boards through which the whole communion as an organized body sought to discharge its obligations to God and the world. Thus these denominations which at first were expressions of doctrinal differences became transformed more and more into closely co-ordinated organizations for the purpose of carrying on missionary programs both at home and abroad. This served to strengthen sectarian ties. It also provided the cause of missions with the assured support of organized and loyal constituencies. But these gains were more than counterbalanced by the discovery that the denomination which has been the natural unit of Christian fellowship and activity at home is not an adequate agency for undertaking responsibilities which are worldwide in their ramifications. The task is too big and too complicated for any such body. Accordingly, an effort has been made to overcome these defects by the formation of interdenominational bodies, such as the Foreign Missions Conference and the International Missionary Council, through which mission boards and the churches abroad take counsel of one another and engage in a limited amount of concerted action. But even yet the prosecution of the work in foreign lands is handicapped by traditional forms of organization and procedure at home. One of the most urgent problems, therefore, is to increase the co-ordination, the resourcefulness, and the flexibility of these organizations so that they may be better fitted to the task in hand. In fact, much of the best idealism of the West is not being channeled through ecclesiastical organizations at all, but through such bodies as the Red Cross, peace foundations, and committees on the improvement of cultural relations between the races. The missionary movement must vindicate its claims and demonstrate its usefulness in comparison with such bodies if it is to command the support that it requires.

When missionaries found themselves face to face with the strange conditions which prevail in foreign lands, they did what anyone else would do under similar circumstances. They tried out in these new situations the organizations and methods with which they had become familiar in their own land. They banded themselves together into "missions" for the direction of the work. Preaching stations were opened up; schools were founded; hospitals and dispensaries were established; and some effort was made to improve the economic condition of the people. In due time converts were won and churches were organized.

During this period mission work was designed mostly on models transplanted from the West. But as the missionaries gained experience from the successes and failures of the passing years, and as indigenous leaders grew in wisdom and self-confidence, the movement began to emerge from the preliminary stage when the West served as the standard of what should be done in the East. It entered upon the present experimental period, in which more thought is given to a careful diagnosis of the definite situation in any locality, and all resources, both native and foreign, are mustered for the solution of the problems arising out of these situations. It is in the facing of these emergencies and in the successful solution of these problems that mission work really becomes creative.

A few of these problems may be mentioned as typical of the issues with which the church is wrestling, and upon the solution of which the future depends: (*a*) The transfer of jurisdiction from the mission to the native church and the awakening of a greater sense of responsibility and the development of a more effective leadership within these churches. (*b*) The application of Christian principles to the deplorable conditions prevailing in rural communities and also in the newly established industrial centers, where all the evils of Western industrialism are intensified. (*c*) How best to meet the keen competition of communism, fascism, and nationalism which offer their panaceas of speedy salvation to millions of people living in dire distress and insecurity. (*d*) As the government and other agencies proceed to take over some of the missionary activities of the past, such as education and medical work, what remains as the distinctive and permanent function of the Christian church? (e) The content and grounds of the Christian message. What claims can Christianity make, if any, to being a special and unique revelation from God? (f) In the face of theological differences and nationalistic ambitions, how can a world-wide Christian fellowship be built up and maintained?

It is evident that these and similar questions cannot be solved by mission boards in New York, and much less by the authoritative action of churches in Europe and America. Absentee landlordism is as disastrous in religion as it is in land tenure. These issues must be faced primarily by those who are living in the midst of them and are familiar with all the factors involved. But we of the West may bring to them the benefits of whatever wisdom or insight we may command, and assure them of our co-operation in working out the solution of these and other great issues of life, which in reality are not peculiar to any race. Only thus can a world-wide fellowship of Christians be built up in sufficient strength to bind the world together in a unity of mutual helpfulness.

THE PROCESS UNDERLYING MISSIONS

We now turn to the analysis of the process of cross-fertilization, resulting from the expansion of Christianity into other cultural regions. Only in so far as the Christian understands and controls this process will he succeed in realizing those world-ideals which he cherishes.

As a result of the labors of archaeologists, historians, and ethnologists there is gradually being pieced together the long story of the process by which history is written and civilizations rise and fall. Process implies the inter-action of certain units. The units in this case are people acting either as individuals, groups, classes, or great movements and stampedes. They are continually seek-ing satisfaction for certain biological urges and socially defined wishes through attaining objectives, values, and ideals which are held in high esteem. It is this tension between the urge or wish, on the one hand, and the satisfaction, on the other, which furnishes the dynamic to keep the process going. Abolish this tension and the process would give way to the quietism and inertia of Nirvana. This struggle for satisfaction goes on accord-ing to the method of trial and error, as units of people now in competition and now in co-operation interact with each other and with their total environment. It is out of the experience thus gained that different civiliza-tions have grown up, declined, and emerged again in the various culture regions of the world. As a general rule, the fortune of the individual rises and falls with the rise and fall of the society and the culture which surrounds him. The individual, the group, and culture constitute an interrelated whole.

By culture is meant something more than mere re-finement. A culture consists of the customary ways of thinking, feeling, and acting of a people. It provides them with a philosophy of life, objectives and values to be sought, and also with approved methods for achieving these. "Culture" is a comprehensive term including such things as art, politics, economics, science, social life, and religion—each of which is the outcome of human experience in the quest of certain kinds of satisfaction. Religion is a phase of culture. It is a particular way of thinking, feeling and acting by virtue of certain concepts held to be true with reference to the ultimate nature of reality, for the purpose of achieving what are judged to be the highest values of life. The religion of a people is the product of this long process of culture development, just as is the case with its art or its form of domestic life. It is also one factor which along with others has produced the past and the present, and is actually creating the future.

There are two lines along which this creative process of trial and error works. One is that of historical transmission, by means of which each generation falls heir to the culture heritage of its ancestors, reshapes it either for better or for worse in the daily struggle for existence, and then hands it on as a legacy to succeeding generations. The other line is that of the interpenetration of influences across culture boundaries, which goes on continuously once peoples come into contact with one another. The Hebrews, who lived at the crossroads of the Near East, felt the effects of this cross-fertilization, while they in turn exerted their own influence upon their neighbors. The Christian church has been caught a number of times in these cross-currents, which have facilitated the penetration of other civilizations by Christian influences, and encouraged the infiltration of extraneous influences into the Christian religion itself. Such resulting transformations as are approved are generally attributed to divine origin; innovations which are disapproved are traced to other sources.

The last two or three centuries have witnessed an amazing increase of communication between the continents, which seems bound to multiply rather than to diminish with the passing years. No tariff wall can permanently stop it. It is an inevitable part of the total process. So important is it that statesmen, business men, and interests of all kinds are seeking to control it for the furtherance of their own peculiar purposes. Foreign missions is the organized effort of the church to influence this exchange of culture elements in such a manner that it will result in the greatest good to mankind, which is supposed to be the supreme interest of the church.

As the Christian movement expands it plants mission stations, hospitals, schools, and churches in foreign lands. These serve as the local junction points where two streams of culture come together; one descending through the history of Christendom and more particularly through the life of the church; the other flowing down through the history of India, Asia, or Africa as the case may be. Each party makes its own contribution to the process of selection and rejection which ensues. Christian influences are presented to the Orient in the form of stimuli, as the Christian worker preaches his gospel, heals the sick, and lives his life as best he can. The indigenous people bring to this junction point their own characteristic response patterns, or traditional ways of belief and practice. They have been in the habit of curing smallpox by religious rites; the missionary says it is better to vaccinate. They have trusted the gods of their fathers for salvation; the missionary exhorts them to trust in his Savior, or to employ methods approved by science.

This impact of Western influence upon oriental thought forms and behavior patterns brings a variety of results. In some cases a conservative reaction sets in which defies change—at least for a period. But sooner or later the disruptive forces of disintegration begin their subtle work. Increasing numbers become interested in Western ideas and practices. The established ways of life begin to fall into disrepute. The customary groupings of society begin to go to pieces. Religious doubts arise and people find themselves wandering about like lost souls. In time the resulting confusion of counsel and frustration of effort become so intolerable that something must be done, and serious efforts are made to gain a new harmony and purpose in life. In some cases this new integration is sought by reform of traditional belief and practice, and on the surface it seems as though the old religion has taken on a new lease of life through the quickening of its own vitality. In other cases people are converted to Christianity, which on the surface appears to have been transplanted to foreign soil, without change. But a deeper study of what transpires reveals that in both cases there has been a fusion of East and West, only in different proportions. Mission work has been thought of as sowing the seed in foreign soil where it must produce after its own kind, if it flourishes at all. But in so far as a biological analogy is applicable to culture processes the figure needs to be followed still further. As soon as the seed takes root and the tender plant begins to flower, it is exposed to a cross-fertilization from indigenous sources, resulting in the production of a new seed or a new offspring; and, as is always the case, some of the offspring will resemble one parent and some the other, some will survive in changing forms through succeeding generations while the rest meet an early death.

These junction points where the Occident and the Orient come together are therefore among the great creative spots of geography and of history. The results of these new combinations may be either good or bad. In this sense the missionary may be thought of as a Burbank, working more particularly in the field of religion and ethics, and missions as a form of spiritual eugenics, practiced on a world-wide scale, in which the missionary by the preaching of his message, by the teaching of science, and by many other kinds of ministration is deliberately seeking to control this inevitable process of cross-fertilization so that it will be productive of nobler types of personality and higher forms of society.

TRENDS AND NEW DEVELOPMENTS

What, then, are some of the trends and new creations which are appearing, as Christianity along with other agencies seeks to control this interplay between the East and the West?

The most conspicuous and the most easily tabulated is the production of renewed men and women through the conversion and Christian nurture of individuals. In some cases the transformations wrought are so slight that grave doubt may exist as to whether the person should be called a Christian. In other cases the awakening has been so profound that there is every indication that the person has really become a new creature. Let a coolie or a peasant be inspired by the thought that it is possible for him, the victim of cruel fate and the object of human contempt, to become a child of God and an heir to the choicest blessings of life and he lifts up his head, becomes a new man, and takes a new interest in life. Little by little family life and social relationships are changed. When the number of Christians is sufficient, the whole village is made over and elevated to a higher standard of living. In like manner a limited number of the more highly educated who have abandoned the religion of their fathers find in certain interpretations of the Christian religion a satisfying philosophy according to which life gains a new meaning and purpose.

New varieties of Christianity are beginning to appear in these different culture regions. Wherever the missionary has gone he has carried with him his own brand of doctrine, ritual, and Christian institution. No more apology need be made for this than for the importation of tea or silk into the Western world. We of the West who have been patrons of missions are very much interested in just how far Christianity may be expected to breed true to type—our type—and to what extent it will be altered by foreign influences with the passing of time. Christianity tends to preserve its Western type in so far as the missionaries and national leaders believe that their own form of Christianity is built upon a divine model which must not be changed, and are able to inclose the small Christian community within a rigid quarantine where a strict discipline is exercised over the desires, thoughts, and actions of its members. Western Christianity will tend to preserve its type in so far as that type meets the needs and expresses the desires that are common both to Occidental and to Oriental. But the West has no monopoly on either truth, goodness, or wisdom. And in proportion as our Western forms of Christianity have partaken of qualities which are occidental rather than common to all mankind, and in proportion as distinctively oriental influences are allowed to make their presence felt, to that extent will the church in other parts of the world take on characteristics which are new and different, but not necessarily to be deplored. Although the modern missionary enterprise is not more than a hundred years old, anyone who is familiar with it can already detect in the churches of Japan, India, or Africa tendencies in diverse directions which are not unlike the local colorings which began to differentiate Alexandria from Asia Minor and Asia Minor from Rome in the early centuries of the Christian Era. There are being evolved before our eyes divergent types of Christianity which in time may be quite different from the mother-churches at home, and which will go far to determine the kind, or kinds, of Christianity which will prevail in the world five hundred years from now.

Furthermore, the missionary enterprise itself is being made over and reinterpreted while it is busily engaged in trying to remake the world. This subtle change is going on in spite of the inertia which seems to inhere in large and imposing institutions. There is a tendency to turn what was formerly a crusade of spiritual conquest into a co-operative and experimental undertaking on the part of sincere souls for the improvement of the lot of man. Christian activities and authority are being centered about the indigenous church instead of the mission. Our interpretation of the aims of mission work and of the methods by which these are to be realized is being revised. There is a growing tendency to rely upon scientific methods and principles. The Christian is inclined to modify his former claims with reference to the exclusive divine origin, power, and authority of his religion and to recognize some virtue in other faiths as well. These changes may be taken as signs of the decline of certain kinds of mission work and of the development of new approaches to the non-Christian world.

During the nineteenth century the foreign work of the churches was undergirded by one fairly uniform philosophy of missions. In the opening years of this century there has emerged a whole series of philosophies, ranging all the way from the most exaggerated supernaturalism, on the one hand, through a variety of mediating positions to an undisguised naturalistic interpretation, on the other. The Christian religion, as a continuing and expanding movement, has once again reached one of those periodical stages when the certainties and uniformities of former days pass through a transition of flux and upheaval, and no one knows what the final outcome will be. This is no reason for despair, nor should it tempt the church to sit down in inactivity and wait for the fog to clear. These rival philosophies are but tentative proposals made in the effort to understand better the inner nature and meaning of it all, and to indicate the directions of the greatest promise in the future. They constitute an indispensable stage in any movement which is not static. It is through the projection of alternate hypotheses and through the trying of these out in the fields of active labor and in the laboratories of human experimentation that in due time the fog will lift for a season and the way will be opened up for further advance.

These foreign contacts, missionary and otherwise, are also working changes within the church at home, so unobtrusive that they are likely to escape the attention of the superficial observer. One hundred years ago the most obstinate opposition to the new interest in missions arose from the orthodox doctrine of that day with reference to God and his plans for the world. Orthodoxy is not always right. It has been the missionary enterprise which has given to the church its current belief in a missionary God who is still interested in the welfare of all mankind, which strengthened denominational loyalties and perfected denominational machinery, and which now threatens to undermine this structure as the inadequacy of sectarian religion for the grander tasks becomes more and more apparent. It has added a new note of universalism to the concept of the Kingdom of God, and created a Christian fellowship which even now encircles the globe. Our ideas of right and wrong, of truth and error, are being molded constantly by their applicability to foreign conditions and by the beliefs and practices of other peoples. And now, within the last few years, the growing acquaintance with the virtues as well as the failures of other religions, coupled with the discovery that religions are the products of the age-long process of culture development, is providing Christian thinkers as never before with factual material—historical and scientific—which must be taken into account, and forcing them to face the crucial question as to just how far Christianity is warranted in claiming to be the uniquely divine revelation, and to what extent it likewise is the outgrowth of natural processes which have produced other religions. It is this issue which along with other forces will shape the Christian's thought concerning himself, his religion, and his God, and to that extent mold the theologies of the coming centuries. These, then, are some of the developments which indicate that the church, through the missionary enterprise, is in reality renewing its own perennial vitality and shaping into being the kind, or kinds, of Christianity which will prevail in the world one hundred or five hundred years from now.

While these changes have been taking place within the Christian movement as it expands throughout the world, equally important transformations are occurring within non-Christian religions and civilizations, partly as a result of missionary effort. Native clergy are aroused to greater concern for the welfare of their people. Gandhi launches his campaign for the emancipation of the untouchables. Some of the more objectionable practices and superstitions are condemned where formerly they were condoned. Definite reform movements are organized. While some pagan gods and religions are dying out, others are being moralized and spiritualized in order to make them more worthy of the devotion of their followers and the respect of others. There are two ways in which the spiritual welfare of a people may be improved: either by conversion to a better religion or else by bringing about sweeping reforms within the prevailing religion. This indirect effect of mission work is fully as important as proselytism, although much more difficult to tabulate and not so highly esteemed by the supporters of the work.

Thus as religion plays upon religion and civilization upon civilization we are witnessing the gradual recreation of this world of ours. Improved facilities of intercultural exchange permit the dissemination of evil as well as of good. The traffic in drugs or in vile motion pictures is organized on an international scale as well as the traffic in medicine and the world's best literature. All countries are finding it necessary to raise barriers against these dangerous inroads. In some cases there is a marked recrudescence of cultural pride and unrestrained nationalism, as people try to maintain their self-respect and their cultural identity as these are threatened by the incoming tide of foreign life. But in spite of the spread of evil, and underneath these divisive tendencies which may be trusted to safeguard the values inherent in diversity and individuality, there are being woven together the silken threads of common culture elements of which we would approve—a higher value placed upon personality, a growing desire for universal peace, the emancipation of womanhood from the domination of the male, the common fight against piracy, slavery, narcotics, and the white-slave traffic, a growing confidence in the scientific method rather than in magic, a demand for social and economic justice, an appreciation of our dependence upon one another, and the multiplication of international societies about various interests common to mankind. In time these common elements may succeed in binding the rival sections of the human race together into a new world-order, built upon some better principle of co-ordination than prevails at the present time. This, at least, is a goal sufficiently idealistic and feasible to merit our highest devotion.

APPRAISAL

How shall we evaluate this imposing movement through which the crusading spirit of the church expressed itself during the nineteenth century? It is losing the glamor of the earlier romanticism which gave a distorted picture of the missionary and his work. We are disillusioned with reference to the ill-founded utopianism which would evangelize the world in any one or two generations. The proposal of any one religion or people to set the rest of the world right is suspected of being a bit presumptuous, even although it is attempted in the name of God. It is not strange, then, that serious misgivings have arisen in the minds of many who formerly were supporters of the cause, and some feel that it may go the way of the crusades of the Middle Ages—a noble but misguided gesture.

This was the question to which the Laymen's Inquiry gave itself, and we cannot do better than take their judgment in this matter. Two years of painstaking investigation led them to the conclusion that to doubt the validity of the missionary enterprise in its better form is like asking whether good-will should continue or cease to express itself. . . . . At the center of the religious mission, though it takes

the special form of promoting one's own type of thought and practice, there is an always valid impulse of love to men. . . . . It is always reasonable to ask whether this good-will might take quite
different shape; but to ask whether it should cease to operate would
seem to suppose that the very substance of friendship among men
and races might somehow be mistaken. That these missions should
go on, with whatever changes, we regard therefore as beyond serious
question.

It is frankly acknowledged, however, that in their present
form some of the principles and policies of missions do
not measure up to the foregoing specifications and must
be revised before they are worthy of whole-hearted support. "In our judgement there is not alone room for
change, there is necessity for change . . . . and the ef-
fecting of such change should be the condition for any
further enlargement of the enterprise."[5]

In our opinion, then, if these missions are to continue
as the growing-points of the great Christian movement,
and to play their part in the creative processes of history,
they must be transformed in at least three important
respects. First of all, the missionary enterprise must be
made more flexible and resourceful, and speeded up
until it overtakes the rapidly changing conditions on the
foreign field; otherwise it will trail in the rear. In the
second place, it must be brought up to date in such a
way as to meet the convictions and capture the imagination of forward-looking young people and become the
channel through which their highest idealisms may find
an outlet. And, in the third place, before either of these
reforms can proceed very far, a change must be wrought

[5] *Re-thinking Missions*, pp. 4-5.

in the supporting churches at home, for in many cases the necessary reforms are delayed, and even vetoed, by pressure from conscientious church members, who rightly insist that they can support only what their consciences approve of, but who fail to educate their consciences so that these become reliable guides. The most urgent task today is to re-educate the mother-churches at home and the daughter-churches abroad, until they cease living in the nineteenth century, which is long since past, and become better fitted to minister to the twentieth-century world. And this re-education is primarily the work of the pastors of these churches.

There is no more reason to believe that the future prosperity of the church is assured by some divine decree than there is to hold that the progress of the world is assured by some eternal law of evolution. Both theories are equally dangerous in that they are likely to breed a false sense of security by minimizing the part which man himself must play in the working-out of that future. The past history of the church gives grounds both for misgivings and for hope and confidence. For nineteen hundred years the church has survived, sometimes contracting and sometimes expanding, sometimes destructive in its influence and sometimes creative, sometimes in world-conditions which were favorable and sometimes the reverse. It will continue to thrive as an expanding and creative community only as each generation of church members on both sides of the water addresses itself to each succeeding situation of human need and aspiration with all the intelligence, self-sacrifice, foresight, and sane idealism that it can command.

SELECTED BIBLIOGRAPHY

BAKER, ARCHIBALD G. *Christian Missions and a New World Culture.* Chicago: Willett, Clark, 1934.

Religion is interpreted as a phase of culture; foreign missions as one aspect of an inevitable process of intercultural exchange. This process is analyzed in an effort to gain a better understanding of the missionary enterprise.

PETTY, ORVILLE A. (ed.). *Laymen's Foreign Missions Inquiry: Regional Reports.* 7 vols. New York: Harper, 1933.

The most careful and comprehensive survey to date of mission work in India, Burma, China, and Japan, with a final volume on the home base.

Re-thinking Missions. New York: Harper, 1932.

Report of the Laymen's Inquiry giving appraisal of mission work and recommendations.

Report of the Jerusalem Meeting of the International Missionary Council, Vol. I: *The Christian Message.* New York: International Missionary Council, 1928.

An appraisal of the spiritual values of other religions, of the relation of Christianity to these, and of the essential ground and content of the Christocentric message, to which most of the mission boards have adhered for the last few years.

SAUNDERS, KENNETH. *The Ideals of East and West.* New York: Macmillan, 1934.

A brief interpretative statement of each religion is followed by a short anthology in which one may sample the choicest excerpts of the sacred writings of the East without wandering through a mass of detail.

SCHERMERHORN, WILLIAM D. *The Christian Mission in the Modern World.* New York: Abingdon, 1933.

For every missionary area there is presented an outline of history and of contemporary movements. With this as a background, the story of missions is told for each of these areas.

WARNSHUIS, A. L. (ed.). *The Christian Message for the World Today.* New York: Round Table, 1934.

The reply of nine representative American leaders to the question: What is the Christian message for the world today? A penetrating analysis of world-conditions and of the service which Christianity may render through proclaiming the Christocentric message.

CHAPTER VIII

THE CHURCH AND THE SOCIAL ORDER

THE word "church" has had a variety of definitions. It has been regarded as the visible body of Christ possessed of divine revelation through a channel of supernatural grace and with a clergy miraculously authorized to represent their Savior on the earth. On the other hand, the church has been regarded as a community of the regenerate assembled at a single place, possessed of a divine revelation but lacking the other elements of Catholicism. To those who hold such a view the church as an all-embracing institution is invisible, existing in heaven, and the local representative possesses no superhuman powers. Only metaphorically is it said to be the body of Christ.

These views have both been factors in history. Wholly apart from theological and ecclesiastical variations, both represent a common fact. Christianity, like every religion, has its social aspect, and bodies of Christians, whether local or world-wide, have been and are elements of various social orders. To discover what their relations are and may become it is necessary to recognize the fact that the church is one group among the many which constitute a social order. As such it affects and is affected by other groups although distinct from them by virtue of its function. As distinct from philanthropic, educational, and economic groups, its function is religious. And as distinct from other religions, its function is to inculcate and socialize the convictions and attitudes which have been derived from the teaching of Jesus and the significance given his person by Christians. In its authoritative teaching each orthodox Christian group has centered attention upon a salvation accomplished by a divine Savior who, by his death, has made it possible for God to forgive individuals who otherwise would be doomed to eternal suffering because of sin. The teaching of Jesus has not been ignored, but it has had slight influence upon the development of dogma and ecclesiastical practices. The Bible as a whole has been regarded as the source of infallible truth, and the teaching of Jesus has been no more authoritative than that contained in any canonical writing. Yet in the field of moral idealism and example Jesus has had his influence. His life has been an absolute ideal, and those who, like the monks, have given themselves, like him, to poverty as well as celibacy have been regarded as more spiritual than others.

The Christian movement is more extensive than the church. It has been in reality the religious aspect of Western civilization. A church, however, has implemented the religion and as an institution has been an agent of Christian influence. Without it the Christian movement might have been a philosophy or an esoteric religious cult.

A SOCIAL ORDER FURNISHES PATTERNS FOR ORGANIZATION AND DOCTRINES OF A CHURCH

As an organization the church started as a group of Jews who accepted Jesus as the expected Messiah.

Neither he nor they proposed an institution or a new cult. Thanks to the dispersion of Jews throughout the Roman Empire, there were large numbers of contacts between Judaism and the gentile world. In some cases this led to the addition of proselytes to the Jewish communities, but a considerable number, however, known as the God-fearers, without being full proselytes, accepted Hebrew monotheism, the observance of the Sabbath, the moral idealism of the synagogue, and the expectation of a new age. These communities of Jews and God-fearers became points of contact between the new hope of the disciples and the gentile world.

Because of the missionary activity of Paul and to a less extent of others, these communities became also points of contact between the Christian and the non-Jewish world, and the messianic quality of Jesus was restated in patterns derived from gentile rather than Jewish sources. As early as Paul the Christian faith was detached from any necessary relationship with Judaism and Jesus was worshiped as a divine heavenly being who had appeared in Palestine, had been killed as a fulfilment of ancient Hebrew prophecies, had been raised from the dead and ascended to heaven whence he would speedily return to set up the expected Golden Age and deliver his followers, whether living or dead, from the control of death. In this, by virtue of its new personnel, the churches were affected by current mystery religions and, later, by philosophical interests, within the Roman Empire. The Christian communities became reorganized. Their faith became a source of group solidarity, their practices grew into sacraments, their officials became priests, and the Christian communities were brought into provincial as well as local administrative units.

Roman imperialism as a pattern for Christianity.— When Christianity became a "licensed religion" in the Empire, and especially after Constantine's appropriation of its political possibilities, its development became increasingly an expression of the dominant forces within the Roman Empire. After the disintegration of the Empire it embodied in its formulas and practices successive social conditions and patterns. Of supreme significance was the separation of the Eastern and the Western halves of the Roman Empire at the end of the seventh century. Thereafter ecumenical Christianity which found expression in the Apostles', the Nicene, and the Chalcedonian creeds came under the influence of two social orders. In the East both the Empire and the church maintained the *status quo*. In the West the disintegration of the Roman Empire was succeeded by the period of slow reconstruction, which theoretically was dominated by the idea of a continuous imperialism, but was given direction by feudalism.

Within this period of reconstruction the representative of the imperial idea was the Roman church. European Christianity had preserved many of the administrative units of the Empire, and Rome increasingly made itself the head of the churches of the West. Both in its organization and in its theological assumptions and doctrines it preserved the ideal of imperial unity with the pope subject only to Christ. It developed a canon law substituting the Scriptures for that "law of nature" which lay beneath the Roman jurisprudence. Its power was undoubtedly furthered by the fact that bishops in many cases became officials and submission to orthodoxy came to possess much the same quality as loyalty to the Empire. Its dogmas were treated as laws and were given sanction not only by the control over *post-mortem* conditions believed to be exercised by the church but also by appeal to political authorities, who sometimes were ecclesiastical and at other times represented whatever type of state had emerged from the confusion of the early Middle Ages.

Feudalism as an ecclesiastical pattern.—This imperial conception of a Catholic church was not replaced but supplemented by the growth of feudalism. Many ecclesiastics became feudal lords. In the doctrine of the atonement set forth by Anselm and embodied in the doctrinal development of succeeding centuries, the Deity was conceived of as a transcendental emperor who possessed a feudal dignity which needed to be satisfied to justify his pardoning of those whom he selected from a race universally born liable to eternal punishment.

The influence of nationalism.—With the rise of nations there developed in the sixteenth century, first slowly and then violently, a struggle between the imperial and national forces that profoundly affected the church. Not only did the Holy Roman Empire as represented by emperors chosen by a small group of ecclesiastical and political electors find itself increasingly threatened with the rise of national units, but the struggle was intensified by the determination of political groups that had never been parts of the Roman Empire to control their own religious institutions. As a result of the Reformation there emerged in the non-Roman areas national churches which more or less formally substituted the authority of their political sovereign for that of the pope. The consequent conflict resulted in ecclesiastical differentiation varying along national lines. The Protestant state churches, however, did not abandon ecumenical Christian doctrines. They rejected such elements in the imperial Catholicism as seemed to be forbidden or not supported by current biblical interpretation. Protestantism was not committed to religious liberty but to the competency of the individuals to find justification in the approaching Day of Judgment through their faith in Jesus as expressed in the ecumenical Christology and to the right of government to decide what type of Christianity should be adopted by their subjects.

It was natural, therefore, that the patterns in which the Christian truth was organized in the confessions adopted by the various political units should have been drawn from the new monarchical nationalism. The most complete illustration of this is to be seen in Calvinism. The theological center of this movement, which became especially influential outside the areas of Lutheranism, was the absolute sovereignty of God. His relations to humanity were like those of the absolute monarch to his people. His rule was exercised through decrees and his human subjects possessed no rights. He would acquit those who had faith but only those whom he elected had faith. Theology became a transcendentalized politics.

The influence of democracy.—The various economic forces which combined to produce modern capitalism also gave rise to democracy. Those who paid the taxes believed that they had a right to decide as to how the taxes should be spent. On the continent of Europe the rise of the middle class was repressed until the period of revolutions, but in England the struggle between absolutism and constitutionalism not only resulted in progress toward a more completely constitutionalized monarchy, but it was accompanied also by movements toward democratic conceptions of the church. These non-Conformist movements were opposed by the representatives of the state church, and as a consequence there was a great migration of non-Conformist groups to the American colonies. Here they set up churches to their own liking and at the same time developed democratic government. On the American soil the church took on increasingly the patterns of democracy. Its theology was largely Calvinistic, but the liberty of thought and expression was sufficient to lead to considerable differentiation within orthodoxy, and the extension of population into the new territories west of the original settlers still further developed democratic tendencies within the Christian movement.

THE RELATION OF THE CHURCHES TO SOCIAL PROCESS

These facts make plain the intimate relationship of the churches as institutions with a social process. A church as a religious group in a social order has to a greater or less degree performed a twofold function. It has conserved religious values inherited from the past, and it has directly and indirectly affected economic and political trends.

The degree to which this influence has progressed has varied in different social orders, but is more obvious in nations in which there are free churches. Where the Roman Catholic church has been built into a national history, it has opposed the development of democracy both in politics and in religion. As one consequence of this policy on the continent of Europe the issue is sharply drawn between socialism and Catholicism without the intervention of democratic ideals and religious institutions such as have found expression in countries in which constitutional development has been conditioned by Protestantism. In Protestant countries in which a dictatorship has been accepted by the people the churches have been forced into a difficult position. While accepting the totalitarian state, they wish to maintain such independence as they possessed as state churches in a constitutional régime. The difficulties which the Protestant churches of Germany face are in no small measure due to the fact that they have emphasized theological conformity and pietism and have given comparatively little attention to the social significance of Christianity in organizing a group morality. Although the survivals of ecclesiastical conflicts still appear in a Protestant suspicion of political designs of the Roman Catholic church, a comparison of that church in democratic countries and in those in which democracy and Protestantism have never been successful makes it plain that it has responded to the influences from which democratic states have emerged.

In a general way denominationalism may be said to be a contribution of democracy to the Christian movement. The social forces accounting for its rise have already been mentioned.[1] It is needful now only to call attention to the intimate and indeed genetic relations that exist between the Christian movement as one element within a general social process. Absolutism has enforced conformity in religion as in all other aspects of a people's life, but American democracy has evolved social organization in the atmosphere of freedom. Individuals met in towns, and towns grew into colonial units; colonies became states, and states united in a federal government. The same process was true in the case of the churches. Despite the fear of overhead authority on the part of such early democratic church groups as the Baptists, the pressure of circumstances and the need of co-operation led to the growth of denominational organization, and these in turn became the exponents and guarantors of social conceptions which were held by their members. The Bible was used in different geographical areas to justify different social ends. With the exception of certain ethnic groups like the Moravians and the Dunkards, the churches were more subject to social influences than social control was subject to the churches. The extension of the various denominations into western territory was somewhat conditioned by the policies of their central organizations. Yet the churches were drawn into the struggle between the two rival economic orders of the South with, and the North without, slavery. The struggles between those who gave a loose and those who gave a strict construction to the Constitution reappeared in the ecclesiastical controver-

[1] See chap. iii.

sies, particularly among the Presbyterians, whose general structure clearly represents the federative process. But the churches have not been passive. They have contributed ideals and furnished direction for social change. Although they have initiated few if any changes in the social order, they have produced individuals and minorities who have been agents of social change. An illustration of the power of such ideals is to be seen in the innumerable declarations of the rights of man and the citizen which appeared both in America and in Europe during the latter part of the eighteenth century and the early part of the nineteenth century. Their origin has been shown to have been in the churches of the American colonies.

THE CHURCHES AND TODAY'S SOCIAL TRENDS

The close connection of the ecclesiastical development with social process enables us to understand the religious situation of our own day. The changes within the social order are not the same as those of the first half of the nineteenth century, but the Christian movement, now differentiated into churches and denominations, is none the less responding to social trends which are set by the new control over natural forces given by scientists and engineers. While any general statement is subject to exceptions, it would appear that economic trends constitute a situation by which the churches are affected, and to which they owe service. Protestant groups as a rule are composed of capitalist and non-wage-earning classes, although it would be a mistake to draw the line between them and Catholic churches exclusively along economic lines. Again speaking generally, the Protestant churches represent those who enjoy greater economic privilege. Such a statement is subject to important modifications wherever church life is conditioned by ethnic and political origins, as in the case of Lutheran churches which as yet hold the allegiance of those of the first and second generation of ethnic groups within different economic classes. The solidarity of these groups has not suffered as much as the non-ethnic denominations from the rural-urban conflict between the factory and the farm. The same is true of southern states, where the full results of new industrial development are only beginning to appear in church life. Throughout America industrial tensions affecting church life are complicated by the presence of a large negro population, as well as by the fact that the great masses of wage-earners are Jews or immigrants from lands where democracy and Protestantism have had little influence. For them religion is either a conventional loyalty to the religious groups with which they are acquainted or loyalty to labor organizations, socialism, or communism. Their indifference to Protestant churches springs in large measure from their sense of economic injustice which more or less correctly identifies the Protestant churches with capitalism, or from ecclesiastical enmities which have their basis in European rather than American history. The Protestant churches as representatives of the economically privileged classes are fortunately growing aware of these tensions, and are beginning to realize that they must educate their members in the morality of group as well as of individual relations.

As yet this extension of the Christian influences into the economic and social fields illustrates the inability of Christian churches to abandon inherited attitudes. Differentiation of Christian groups which has always appeared in moments of social tension is evident. On the one hand are those who are unwilling deliberately to affect the *status quo* and cling tenaciously to doctrines but condemn modern expression of that social idealism which marked certain early Protestant groups. On the other hand there is an increasing number of those who feel that loyalty to Christ and the essential values conserved in the Christian movement lead to an intelligent reorganization of economic relations within the social order. They believe that personal values rather than the acquisition of wealth should be paramount in a social order. Doubtless in large measure due to the absence of political creativeness, the outcome of this difference within Protestantism has not been the organization of new denominations but a gradual transformation of existing church life. When that is deemed unlikely, the church has been abandoned by the more socially minded who have transferred their loyalty to non-ecclesiastical institutions looking for human betterment. Such an attitude illustrates a tendency which has always characterized the Christian movement where there is no coerced ecclesiastical conformity. Individuals and minorities who have felt that an existing church life no longer met the actual needs set by new social conditions have thrown their influence into decreasingly ecclesiastical groups. Such social mutation is clearly seen in the emergence of state churches, free churches, Christian associations, the Salvation Army, social settlements, social service groups, and the organization of relief workers.

Thus the history of Christian churches as institutional expressions of the Christian movement makes it plain that both in their local and in their extended relations ·they are subject to general laws of group action and development. A social order is a group of groups, each possessing its own function and organized for action generally through some institution, but all mutually affecting each other through agreement or conflict. The Christian churches, considered both locally and collectively, constitute a composite group within these general groups. They cannot be treated as if they constituted a single body. In the differentiation of the Christian movement the different churches are not equally responsive to the changes of other groupings. Yet they are never free from such relations. Differences in the degree of their response to general trends depend very largely upon the variations in the structure and the personnel of local and collective churches. Yet in no case is the interplay between the church and the other groups which constitute its social environment altogether lacking. Through it, in accordance with the general laws of social process, the churches may exercise that moral influence which is essential to the performance of their functions as institutions of the Christian movement.

The social influences of a church within itself.—The methods by which churches have undertaken to fulfil their function as organized religious groups disclose the social significance of worship. In it the Christian group seeks contact with the supernatural powers, and finds sanction for certain social acts. Worship has, therefore, profound influence on the social life. Through its control of the approach to the Deity the church has often checked attempts at political or economic progress. This control, which is based on a church's claim to supernatural power, is not only through sacraments in the case of marriage, divorce, and, in consequence, the legitimacy of children, but it has been used to support relations of landowners to peasants, the subjection of women, education, and political institutions. While the data are lacking to establish a precise relationship between political change and supernatural claims of a church, recent history has given abundant evidence that the destruction of confidence in such power is essential for radical political change. In general, too, it may be said that social and political reorganizations are more rapid where the influence of a church does not depend upon its being regarded as possessed of supernatural powers. Inevitably such a church becomes the champion of the *status quo*.

But worship may have a more creative influence upon a social order. If it be centered upon the conception of the Deity as morally like Jesus, it can give divine sanction to intelligent attempts to make love a basis for action in all the fields of social life. The sacrifices which it can call upon the socially privileged to make in the interest of human welfare will be inspired by belief in the love of God. If worship lifts men into fellowship with a Deity of love and law as Christianity portrays him, it will make religion a leaven for social readjustment, for the giving of justice rather than the fight to acquire and maintain rights. Love will be seen to be a practicable basis for a social order.

In these particulars the church as a religious group has the unique function of serving as an instrument for the incoming of divine influences. Whatever view one may hold as to the relative merits of various ecclesiastical polities, the fact remains that as a social group a church furthers that adjustment between humanity and God which is implicit in any complete conception of life. It is this influence which as the incoming of the grace of God the church has emphasized for centuries. Whatever value may be given the sacraments, it is logically impossible to deny that they represent that which is essential in the religious conception of the world. The patterns in which man's relations to God have been expressed have always included those that recognize the manward action of God as truly as the Godward action of man. These doctrines have expressed a fact which could be equally well expressed in the pattern of a living organism in normal relationship with the environment which has contributed to its development. Religion is such a relationship between man and God, but is not one of atomistic individualism. Society is an element in the increase of social values of individuals. A church is a group through which divine influence can be expressed through a social agency. While no aspect of human life can be altogether divorced from the influences of its cosmic environment, those divine influences which make for the development of personal value not only require but are made more dynamic through a social medium whose function it is to assist that mediation. A religion that seeks only solitary religious experience lacks those divine impulses which are conditioned through groups. The church is more than an accidental element in the development of personal values. It is a social medium through which God operates in social process as well as individual experience.

The function of the church is not limited to worship of supernatural powers. It has always been a teacher of morality, avowedly devoted to the highest type of morality known to a given community—a sort of laboratory for experiments in shaping a better social order. True, the content of any moral code taught by the church is always relative to current social practices, but a Christian church has never stood for that which it regarded as evil. It may sometimes stand for that which the other groups in the social order regard as antisocial, and in such case the conflict of a more or less violent sort is inevitable. But in nations in which there is freedom of discussion and churches are not dependent upon the state, there is an increasing development within many religious groups of a sense of responsibility for the moral education of their members, and the extension of moral ideals both through them and directly to group action other than its own.

The possibility of such extension of moral ideals by a church into new social situations lies in its own function as the representative of Christian ideals. In Protestantism Christian experience itself is potentially social. Its ideal is not that of the withdrawal of the individual from the various activities of a social order, but rather the inculcating of ideals within that order. Love is a primary Christian virtue. Its expression is relative to the intelligence of a Christian group, but it constitutes a social attitude which, if embodied not only in the action of individuals and in the Christian group but in those other groups with which the church and its members come in contact, will furnish motives for social progress.

One of the first elements of such extension lies in the attempt of a church to develop among its members a discontent with unjust elements within society. The church has always demanded repentance from sin, but its conception of sin has not always been the same. As a Christian group has seen the evil effects of slavery, child labor, intemperance, usury, adultery, and sensuality, its moral education has included them in its call for repentance. It is only an extension of this call when individuals and minorities within a denomination or church call for discontent and repentance in the field of economics and politics.

Education in the social aspects of Christianity, with consequent discontent with certain elements in our social order, has been given direction by the so-called "Social Creed of the Churches" issued by the Federal Council of the Churches of Christ in America. Since its original form, drawn up by Frank Mason North in 1908, it has been subjected to several revisions. In its present form, adopted in 1932, it states that the churches stand for:

1. Practical application of the Christian principle of social well-being to the acquisition and use of wealth; subordination of

speculation and the profit motive to the creative and co-operative spirit.

2. Social planning and control in the credit and monetary systems and the economic process for the common good.

3. The right of all to the opportunity for self-maintenance; a wider and fairer distribution of wealth; a living wage, as a minimum, and above this a just share for the worker in the product of industry and agriculture.

4. Safeguarding of all workers, urban and rural, against harmful conditions of labor and occupational injury and disease.

5. Social insurance against sickness, accident, want in old age, and unemployment.

6. Reduction of hours of labor as the general productivity of industry increases; release from employment at least one day in seven, with a shorter working week in prospect.

7. Such special regulation of the conditions of work of women as shall safeguard their welfare and that of the family and the community.

8. The right of employees and employers alike to organize for collective bargaining and social action; protection of all in the exercise of this right; the obligation of all to work for the public good; encouragement of co-operatives and other organizations among farmers and other groups.

9. Abolition of child labor; adequate provision for the protection, education, spiritual nurture, and wholesome recreation of every child.

10. Protection of the family by the single standard of purity; educational preparation for marriage, home-making, and parenthood.

11. Economic justice for the farmer in legislation, financing of agriculture, transportation and the prices of farm products as compared with the cost of machinery and other commodities which he must buy.

12. Extension of the primary cultural opportunities and social services now enjoyed by urban populations to the farm family.

13. Protection of the individual and society from the social, economic, and moral waste of any traffic in intoxicants and habit-forming drugs.

14. Application of the Christian principle of redemption to the

treatment of offenders; reform of penal and correctional methods and institutions and of criminal court procedure.

15. Justice, opportunity, and equal rights for all; mutual goodwill
and co-operation among racial, economic, and religious groups.

16. Repudiation of war, drastic reduction of armaments, participation in international agencies for the peaceable settlement of
all controversies; the building of a co-operative world order.

17. Recognition and maintenance of the rights and responsibilities
of free speech, free assembly, and a free press; the encouragement of free communication of mind with mind, as essential to
the discovery of truth.

*The relation of Christian churches with other social
groups.*—The relation of a Christian group with other
social groups is varied, but in general it may be described
as a social ferment working within forces of social change
as Christian individuals and minorities participate in
such change, and in the second place by the formal
action of Christian bodies with reference to social evils
and proposed reform.

The interpenetration of the churches with other
groups is not always conscious but is usually traceable.
Perhaps as good an illustration of this would be the
attempt of Christian employers to develop the personal
welfare of the employee. The fact that in many cases
such interest seems more paternal than democratic
should not blind the observer to the fact that a church
can hardly be held responsible for a lack of sociological
and economic intelligence. So long as there is a difference of opinion as to how best to relieve economic and
social tensions, it is unwise to assume that one's own
program of reform is infallible. When, however, a proposed economic program or method is clearly in the
interest of the personal welfare of all the elements in a

situation, it should and generally does receive the support of Christian organizations. The evidence of this can be found in the encyclical letter of Pius XI, *Quadragesimo anno* (1931), in the resolutions of many church bodies like the Methodist General Conference, the Northern Baptist Convention, the United Church of Canada, and the actions taken by social service commissions of a large number of denominations. Probably as outstanding an illustration of the movement of churches into the field of group morality is to be seen in the recent establishment of the Congregational and Christian Council for Social Action. The General Convention of Congregational and Christian Church which established this new denominational agency also passed resolutions dealing with the social responsibilities of the churches. Among them was one calling for "the inauguration of genuinely co-operative social economy democratically planned to adjust production to consumption requirements and to modify or eliminate private ownership of the means of production or distribution wherever such ownership interferes with the social good." According to its public statement:

The Council for Social Action proposes a four-fold crusade: justice for the worker, fair play for the farmer, equal citizenship rights for the Negro, abolition of the war system.

It is committed to no social, economic or political formulae save those consonant with the progressive realization of the human well being. In the carrying forward of its crusades it seeks the widest wisdom of the church and the hearty co-operation of all varieties of opinion to which the church gives shelter.

The Council for Social Action conceives its procedure to be three-fold: research, education and action. It stresses the mood of exploration, and proposes to keep facts ahead of oratory. At each step in this three-fold process it seeks the sympathetic criticism and constructive suggestion of the entire constituency of churches. Preserving the historic right of the individual conscience, it proposes to advance the lines of human liberty and abundant life, so far as this can be concertedly achieved.

The influence of the church is also felt through the great number of radio programs which have been arranged either by the radio department of the Federal Council of the Churches of Christ in America or by the churches of different localities.[2]

The penetration of the Christian idea into business relations is distinctly furthered by various service clubs like the Rotary and Kiwanis. Through various local organizations the churches have been able to have influence in controversies and strikes. The Committee on Town and Country of the Home Missions Council and the Federal Council of the Churches of Christ in America have established a number of institutes in connection with various agricultural colleges, theological seminaries, and colleges.

The churches and the state.—The developing interest in social tensions has brought the church into the sphere of politics. That the future development of civilization and the contributing changes within the economic field will be increasingly political is clear. The nationalism which has so rapidly developed since the World War is largely concerned with economic problems and methods. It is one of the chief duties of Protestantism to see that the social readjustments discouraged by socially indifferent capitalists are accomplished without revolution. But

[2] The extent of such influence as well as that of literature is discussed in chap. x.

such responsibility will not be met if Protestant churches fail to educate their members to make such sacrifices as the giving of justice to the underprivileged may include, and also so to affect public opinion and national processes as to assure the appropriate governmental actions. Organized Christianity has never been altogether indifferent to the close relationship between the state and religion. The Holy Roman Empire which undertook to regard the church and the emperor and pope as joint regents of Christ was impracticable as an ultimate social theory, but expressed the belief that the state was to serve the church in stamping out heresy. The same general theory of the responsibility of the civil government for the crushing-out of false doctrine was held in Protestant state churches. It was inevitable that such relationship not only militated against religious liberty but added enmities of Catholics and Protestants to political rivalries. The evil effect of the entrance of the church as such into politics is beyond question. The need that Protestant churches of democracies should exert influence within the constitutional provisions which assure religious liberty does not justify the organization of a Christian political bloc. The dangers which lie within such a proposal must appall any person with historical intelligence. Theological controversies would immediately emerge in politics. Catholics, Jews, and Protestants would have their own political programs and rivalries. Human nature being what it is, such joining of political differences with religious differences and the utilization of religious antagonisms by politics would be disastrous. The experience of democracy indicates that the only way in which persons belonging to different ecclesiastical groups can co-operate will be in fields which are not formally religious. This fact must condition any wise attempt of Protestants to inspire politics with Christian principles. Those values which are common to the entire Christian movement rather than controversial theology and ecclesiastical rivalry must be brought to bear upon governmental action. Churches can train their members in the task of deliberately moralizing nationalism. Their members can be educated to constitute a moral reserve, superior to prejudice and devoted to legislation and administrative changes which clearly represent progress toward Christian ideals of personal value. In such procedure churches can become schools of group ethics. There are no theological issues for Protestants in the social creed of the churches. There may be differences of opinion as to the wisdom and practicability of proposed methods, but a common purpose will lead to common action.

We already see the churches united in the condemnation of war as a means of settling international disputes. Such general unanimity, however, should be extended to the support of those international relations which assure peace by removing grounds for war. Unintelligent pacifism might become as dangerous as unintelligent militarism. There will be no freedom from the dangers of war so long as Christian principles are not operative within those economic and interracial fields from which wars have sprung. It is the height of folly in a democracy to develop a negative attitude toward war while ignoring the moral obligation to participate as citizens in political activity. The danger in developing a Christian bloc must be avoided by the education of Christians in their obligations as citizens. We cannot expect national or local politics to express Christian ideals if Christians are indifferent to civic obligations.

The Christian individual and the social order.—These wider fields of influence should not divert the church from its task of producing Christian individuals. Personal relations, such as are found in the family, are, it is true, affected by public opinion, and the pressure of social groups, but the influence of the church in a group life will be particularly significant as individuals are affected by its teachings. All reforms would be easy if it were not for folk. In so far as the church produces persons who can recognize the worth of other personalities, it will make a much-needed contribution to social process. Reforms cannot be accomplished without both social and individual transformation.[3] A better social order will be impracticable until there are better men and women. If a person is to be regarded as a socialized individual, the Christian ideal of love will, if once put into operation, produce the sort of individuals who make social institutions better implements for forwarding human welfare.

SELECTED BIBLIOGRAPHY

BARRY, FRANK RUSSELL. *Christianity and the New World.* New York: Harper, 1932.

A well-balanced general discussion of its theme with special emphasis upon the social significance of Jesus.

[3] See chap. vi on "The Church's Work with Individuals."

COMMITTEE ON WAR AND THE RELIGIOUS OUTLOOK. *Church and the Industrial Reconstruction*. New York: Association Press, 1920.

INGE, WILLIAM RANDOLPH. *The Christian Ethic and Modern Problems*. New York: Putnam, 1930.

A historical account of the bearing of Christianity upon the development of modern life with special reference to the problems of England.

McCONNELL, FRANCIS JOHN. *Christian Ideals and Social Control*. Chicago: University of Chicago Press, 1932.

A temperate study of the appeal by Christians to political and other forms of coercion.

MATHEWS, SHAILER. *Christianity and the Social Process*. New York: Harper, 1934.

A historical study of Christianity as an impregnator of social change rather than an initiator of reform. It lays special emphasis upon the contributions of individuals and minorities.

———. *Jesus on Social Institutions*. New York: Macmillan, 1928.

A study of the social significance of the teachings of Jesus from the point of view of the recent New Testament studies of his eschatological teaching.

NIEBURH, REINHOLD. *Moral Man and Immoral Society*. New York: Scribner, 1932.

A contrast between individual and group ethics with reference to the necessity of organizing a Christian political bloc.

Reports of the Commission on Social Service of the Federal Council of the Churches of Christ in America.

VAN KIRK, WALTER W. *Religion Renounces War*. Chicago: Willett, Clark, 1934.

A comprehensive presentation of the actions of the larger religious bodies relative to international peace.

WARD, HARRY FREDERICK. *Our Economic Morality*. New York: Macmillan, 1929.

A frank criticism of existing economic order from the point of view of Christianity.

CHAPTER IX

THE TASK OF THE PREACHER

THE Protestant minister today is faced by an appalling diversity of tasks. On him rests the responsibility for leadership in the work of the church on every front presented in the several chapters of this volume.

VARIETY OF MINISTERIAL TASKS

The conduct of worship is one of the first duties of the minister. Its success will depend largely on his wisdom and skill in the use of music, liturgy, and other artistic aids to the awakening and stimulation of reverence, devotion, and religious idealism in the experience of the worshipers. He must also stand ready to act as personal adviser in moral and spiritual affairs to every individual and family belonging to his congregation, and to all others who come within the reach of his influence. Furthermore, he is called upon to supervise many differentiated forms of activity in which the church, in this age of specialization, finds itself engaged. The competent management of the institution requires that he give attention to numerous problems of administration, even when by the aid of efficient helpers he is spared a measure of the labor involved in the performance of details. As organized today, every church is a financial institution with whose business operations the minister must keep in close touch. It is also an educational establishment where the sermon alone can no longer furnish all the instruction needed for the healthful direction of the religious life and interests of the constituency. The task of formulating and conducting didactic programs suited to the needs of different ages and groups devolves ultimately upon the minister. Frequently the church is also a significant recreational center that demands the time and energy of the pastor. In a word, he has a care for every phase of the organization's activities; he is responsible for making its operations serviceable to the personnel severally and collectively; and he must be ever on the alert to maintain, renew, and increase the membership of the church.

The development of modern social interests has further enlarged the scope of the minister's work. While his primary obligation is to the members of his own church, he is impelled to direct his and their attention to the needs of the wider community, both Christian and non-Christian, extending from his immediate neighborhood to the farthest outpost on the mission field. In recent years a growing awareness of human solidarity has broken through the barriers that once permitted the minister, in all good conscience, to limit his efforts to his own flock and his particular denomination. Recognizing the fellowship of all churches, he welcomes the opportunity and the obligation to participate as far as possible in the co-operative enterprises of different denominations. Even the church and the world are no longer mutually exclusive categories in his thinking. His sensitivity to the brotherhood of all mankind awakens in him a feeling of responsibility for the well-being of society at large. While he may do his utmost to aid the world by bringing into the membership of the church as many communicants as he can, there still remains the more difficult and far-reaching endeavor to make Christian ideals prevail in human relations beyond the pale of the ecclesiastical group in those areas of living commonly termed "secular." The minister who has caught this vision will strive to make the church a power for righteousness in the city, the state, the nation, and the world, amid all the complex relations of mankind in the total social fabric.

From among the various duties to be discharged by a minister of the church today, his task as preacher has been singled out for specific treatment in this chapter.

PRESENT STATUS OF PREACHING

The status of preaching, as an effective instrument for advancing the work of the present-day church, is not at first sight perfectly clear. One is sometimes tempted to ask whether the usual sermon is not too often given a place in the church merely to perpetuate a sanctified habit rather than to serve an essential purpose. Often the minister finds himself so pressed by the necessity of maintaining efficiency in other fields of action that he has little time or zest left for the preparation of the one or two addresses usually delivered on Sunday.

When the Sunday services are conceived to be primarily assemblies for worship, the hortatory and instructive function of the sermon, as it has been cultivated by ministers of the less liturgically minded Protestant communions, is not well suited to the occasion. Under these circumstances the sermon needs to be more in the nature of an edifying homily that fits harmoniously into the other parts of the ritual and sustains, during the few moments alloted to the speaker, the spirit and rhythm of the service. If custom did not decree an address of the minister's own composition, often the desired effect might be more successfully realized if he were to read an appropriate poem, or a suitable piece of fine prose from the religious classics, or a sermon by some acknowledged master of the homilist's art.

Even in the non-liturgical communions, where the sermon has not as a rule been made subordinate to interest in worship, certain influences have been operative to detract from the prestige formerly attaching to the act of preaching. Today many ministers choose to emphasize some other form of activity that seems to them of greater significance in the professional leadership of the church. Sometimes by giving themselves more diligently to administrative and pastoral duties, they make their preaching a subsidiary interest. They believe that in this way they can most effectively serve the cause of Christianity. In recent decades, during which the educational activities of the church have made rapid advances, many ministerial students have been specializing in preparation for this type of work. Either they aim to labor in fields that support two pastors, where preaching and teaching can be developed as distinct interests, or, when the two have to be combined, the didactic ministry may remain primary. Others seek to render their service to religion by teaching in schools, colleges, or seminaries, where they believe they are able to make their largest contribution to the advancement of the church's welfare. Still others devote themselves to the social needs of the parish, or of the larger community, while not a few abandon the pulpit to act as executives in the administration of denominational or interdenominational affairs. With preaching as a definite enterprise these ministers of the church are not immediately concerned.

Amid the diversity of professional duties that have been imposed upon religious leaders by the expansion of the church's work in recent times, it is not strange that the sermon should have somewhat lost caste. In the competitive struggle of manifold interests for deserving attention, preaching is hard pressed to make good its once imperious claims to primacy over all other forms of ministerial activity. Occasionally one hears a busy pastor ask, in a moment of confidence, Why deliver so many sermons? Under present conditions it is inevitable that preaching should sometimes seem to be perfunctory, and should be attended by a sense of futility even for ministers who are sincerely desirous of advancing the best interests of the church and its constituency. They are caught in the confusion incident to a period of change from a situation in which the preaching function of the minister became definitely established in response to specific demands regarded in earlier times as the proper goal of endeavor. In the meantime the character and scope of the work of the church have altered and enlarged. If the preacher is to find his efficient place in the new situation he must rethink the significance of his task both in terms of its traditional heritages and in the light of its present necessities.

THE PREACHER'S HERITAGE

The Christian preacher today stands in a noble line of succession reaching back to the time of the great teaching prophets of Israel—Amos, Hosea, Isaiah, Jeremiah, and their followers. But in one important respect the modern clergyman differs from these ancient worthies. He is the recognized minister of an institution, while they were free-lances proclaiming a definitely personal message that often rendered them *personae non gratae* to the officially authorized leaders of religion. Israel's priests and legislators were entitled to "wear the cloth," so to speak, while the prophetic reformer was left to win recognition on the strength of his appeal to the conscience and spiritual idealism of his audiences. The same situation repeated itself in the case of John the Baptist, Jesus, and the missionary evangelists who first carried the Christian message to the Gentiles.

The institutional growth of the Christian movement gradually brought about a change of emphasis. The services of the Jewish synagogues in the Dispersion furnished the most immediate and useful model for the conduct of Christian worship. Following the Jewish pattern, the Christian assemblies met for prayer, psalm-singing, the reading and exposition of Scripture, and the personal testimony of individuals. To these activities Christians added the distinctive rite of eating together in memory of Jesus' last meal with his disciples. At first, spontaneity characterized all these performances.

But increases in membership and the multiplication of congregations soon necessitated a change of procedure, if all things were to be done decently and in order. The need for stricter supervision early became apparent, with the result that overseers (bishops) were selected, specific tasks were assigned to appropriate functionaries, forms of ritual were prescribed, enthusiastic personal utterances were suppressed, and the recognized spokesmen for the group became servants of the church as an organization. Unrestrained prophets and itinerant evangelists were displaced by bishops, presbyters, deacons, teachers, and other resident helpers duly authorized by the institution to perform their respective duties.

The task of the preacher shaped itself in accordance with the changed situation. The prophetic activity of the first heralds of the gospel gave way to episcopal supervision by ecclesiastical leaders and the didactic ministry of Christian scribes. With the growth of interest in sacramentalism, sacerdotal functions were exalted. Since sacerdotalism within Christianity did not come into prominence until after the destruction of the temple at Jerusalem in A.D. 70 and the consequent disappearance of priests among the Jews, priestly heritages from Judaism carried over only indirectly into the church. Christianity first cultivated this interest out of deference to the demands of gentile converts, but for its justification and interpretation the Christian minister drew heavily upon his Old Testament Scriptures. In the course of time the administration of the sacraments, the performance of the liturgy, and the management of the ecclesiastical machinery took precedence over preaching in the activities of the clergy. Sermons were still delivered, but they tended to become chiefly concerned with maintaining regularity in and fidelity to the church as a sacred institution. Its ceremonies were magnified, its doctrines were expounded, its rules for conduct were inculcated, and its claims to recognition were defended.

Frequently the preacher was a heroic figure throughout the centuries of Christianity's struggle for toleration in the Roman Empire. When our modern champions of the social gospel feel appalled at the vastness of their worthy undertaking, or grow discouraged in the attempt to make their cause prevail, they might well call to mind the burdens carried by their predecessors during the two centuries prior to Constantine. Quite naturally, the ancient preachers' notion about what constitutes a truly Christianized society was not that of the twentieth century, but the battle they waged on frontiers of crucial endeavor in their day called for a display of persistence and courage still highly worthy of emulation. The creative significance of their labors is seen more truly in the character of their attack upon the vital issues faced by them than in any surviving quantum of prescribed ritual, formulated dogma, or ecclesiastical legislation sponsored in their sermons.

Early in the fourth century Christianity was officially approved by the Roman government, and before the close of the century it was made the only legal religion of the Empire. The preacher had won in the long struggle, but only to find himself faced by new tasks. While imperial favor was a valuable asset to the Christian cause, it also proved to be a great liability. Latent hostility and open resistance had in reality been a stimulus rather than a deterrent to the ideals of moral excellence and spiritual vitality nourished by the early church, but when the fires of persecution were extinguished the preacher had to devise new means for separating the gold from the dross. Toleration and popularity increased his difficulties manifold. From within and without he faced fresh dangers. People who were disinclined or ill prepared to pursue the strenuous Christian way of life flocked into the imperially established religion, while rulers who distributed patronage assumed the right of dictatorship over the affairs of the church. This attainment of worldly prosperity contained a menace to Christianity that many of its spokesmen had neither the vision to perceive nor the courage to withstand. They, like Eusebius of Caesarea, seem to have been overwhelmed with a sense of gratitude to their regal benefactors. Yet there were conspicuous exceptions. Even imperial commands and repeated banishments could not restrain the doughty Athanasius from demanding rigid conformity to the beliefs that he held dear. One cannot fail to admire Ambrose for his valiant attempts to suppress pagan survivals and for his bold denunciations of an emperor's sins even with the powerful ruler, Theodosius, in the audience. And, most picturesque of all, is the zealous John Chrysostom, hurling his fiery oratorical darts of reproof at the very inmates of the imperial palace, although exile was the price to be paid for maintaining his moral integrity.

In the fifth and succeeding centuries Christendom in Western Europe participated in significant social changes involving preachers in many new problems. Emperors passed off the stage, leaving clerics to play the leading rôles. The period was so marked by the prolonged agonies of depression and civic collapse that one who now tries to live through it in historical imagination blushes at the displays of alarm, frustration, and self-pitying despair that moderns are sometimes wont to indulge in under much milder inconveniences. The preacher in that age, not unlike some of his successors today, often seemed to be groping about in the dark. He contented himself with blowing a horn in the fog, or he tramped old ecclesiastical trails that led to no hilltop whence vistas of a new future might break upon his vision. The altar was exalted and the pulpit neglected. Needy souls, sustained by emotional satisfactions derived from the observance of rituals, heard no ringing challenge from the preacher repeating in their ears the apostolic injunction to work out their own salvation with fear and trembling, in the belief that this is to be God's way of bringing his wishes to fulfilment in the world. Human efforts seemed too utterly futile to be of any essential significance for salvation. There were preachers, it is true, and some of them, like Augustine, Leo the Great, and Gregory the Great, are not without a measure of distinction. But their sermons were introspective, mystical, consolatory, and designed to confirm old values rather than to inspire new attainments. This being the service needed for that day, its mediators are to be given full credit for having discharged well their duty. They made the established ecclesiastical institution, with its creeds, its ritual, its officials, the guardian and authority for life in its totality. A religious imperialism took the place of the former political hegemony, while the high priest of the organization and his underlings eclipsed the prophet. There no longer seemed to be any place for the activity of aggressive and creative preachers.

As times changed preachers found new tasks. The smothering effects of ecclesiastical domination did not completely stifle the prophetic spirit even in the medieval age. Occasional and significant voices were raised in protest against contemporary evils in the church. Moreover, the rise to prominence of new national units in the population of Europe slowly augmented the trend toward initiative and independence. Religion was so inextricably bound up with the political, economic, and cultural life, and occupied so conspicuous a place in every European country, that leadership in this period of social transition quite naturally imposed itself upon ministers of the church. The distinction between sacred and secular, widely recognized today, was not the vogue five hundred years ago. Then all problems vital to human welfare were pre-eminently religious issues and were of primary concern to every churchman. Usually he offered ready-made solutions to all questions. But in the early sixteenth century there was a growing urge toward a new morality, a new learning, a new business activity, and a new political order; and those preachers who responded to this urge became the great leaders of the Protestant Reformation. As conceived by the Protestant preacher, his task was to restore the church's allegiance to the Bible as its ultimate authority and to renounce the supremacy of the established hierarchy with its unscriptural practices. But he did not propose a separation of church and state, nor did he believe that every Christian had the right to a private interpretation of Scripture. It was still the duty of the preacher to interpret religion to the government and to the individual, and to build up an ecclesiastical organization for implementing this ideal. Once the machine was perfected the Protestant preacher was as strictly obligated to his institution as was the Roman Catholic to his. Thus the prophetic spirit was again subjected to the will of the older prophets, who now appeared in the guise of legislators.

The age of democracy in religion, with its pitfalls and privileges, had not yet dawned. The process of ushering it in furnished preachers with another new task. The leaders of non-Conformity in England were its early heralds, and conventicles of Quakers, Congregationalists, and Baptists provided audiences for its champions. The Wesleyan revivalists lent it momentum, although they did not at the outset advocate the rigid separation of church and state that had originally constituted a fundamental principle for other separatists. The development of individualism and the complete severance of religion from politics were given further encouragement under the conditions of life prevailing in America. The result has been a rank growth of denominationalism, a wide variation in types of ministerial activity, a general acceptance of the notion that religious and secular concerns must be kept distinct, and an interpretation of the preacher's work that consigns him to a specific denomination and a local church. As the servant of the group by whom he is employed, he proclaims its creed, propagandizes for its interests, and seeks to glorify God and redeem man by persuading individuals to join its fellowship.

THE PREACHER AND HIS CONGREGATION

An assembled audience is the modern preacher's challenging opportunity. Without an understanding of its needs he will be quite incapable of defining for himself the fundamental elements in his task. It is very true that he and the members of his congregation bring to the occasion their respective personal heritage of thought, interest, and individuality, but unless they can find some common ground on which to meet, the sermon will be in vain. This necessity is one reason why effective preaching is so much more difficult to attain in these days than used to be the case. Diversity has become an eminent characteristic of our times. Rarely or never does the minister find before him on Sunday morning an assembly of people who are all on the same intellectual level, who represent the same social status, who have been engaged during the week in the same occupation, who entertain the same set of opinions on the vital issues of the day, or whose deepest personal experiences are shaped according to the same pattern. Uniformity is out of the question. The preacher must learn how to work effectively in the midst of diversity. The only other alternative is to limit his attention to a selected group of like-minded persons who dwell serenely within the sanctuary of a restricted creed or communion, while the larger world without moves heedlessly past the doors of the church.

Preachers are by nature idealists, prone to make generalizations, and they often attempt to solve the problem of diversity by devising a body of preachable "essentials" assumed to be palatable to every kind of audience on any occasion. Lecturers on homiletics who address seminary students on this subject often resort to striking epithets or trick phrases in their efforts to state the secret of success in a nutshell. One favorite phrasing popular a generation ago advises the novice to "preach about God and preach about twenty minutes." Another oft repeated slogan exhorts young ministers to "preach Christ." Still another sage injunction is to "preach *religion* rather than *about* religion." Even admonitions to "preach the truth" have been ventured. All are good prescriptions, provided the people in the congregation can be induced to take the medicine, and provided it happens to be the particular remedy that they need. The wise preacher, like the good physician, will precede prescriptions with careful diagnoses, and will be hesitant about claiming infallibility for any panacea. For, in the last analysis, the proof of the medicine is in its therapeutic efficacy, and ultimately the outcome will be determined by the capacities and condition of the patient. Success cannot be guaranteed to the preacher merely on the ground of his having something good to say. It will depend rather upon his ability to say what the people can understand, appreciate, and absorb.

The preacher who is sensitive to the diverse needs of his congregation, and at the same time conceives his task to be that of leadership, has discovered the elemental factors conditioning his success. He seeks to please without condoning the delinquencies of his hearers; he strives to lead them from where they are to where he thinks they ought to be, without forfeiting their confidence or offending their sensibilities. He tries to exemplify the proverbial wisdom of the serpent and harmlessness of the dove, and at the same time maintain intact his moral sincerity. He covets good will and enduring popularity, but he does not consent to purchase them at a ruinous price demanding the sacrifice of his self-respect, the nullifying of his duty to rebuke unrighteousness, or the blinding of his spiritual vision. Instead of "gaping after applauders," he desires, rather, like the old Stoic preacher Musonius Rufus, to have his audiences say of him: "He so hit upon what was done by us, and placed the faults of everyone before his eyes, that each of us who heard him supposed someone had accused us to him." To shallow flatterers who congratulated him on his sermonic performance Rufus used to reply: "If you have time to praise me I have spoken to no purpose." The kind of appreciation most appealing to the earnest preacher is one that attests itself by a display of willingness and zeal on the part of his people to realize in life and action the ideals depicted in the sermons of the minister.

When the preacher has learned the touring range, as it were, of his hearers' thinking and interests, and has established himself in their confidence, successful leadership depends chiefly upon his powers of vision and persuasion. His people will follow him out upon every frontier that he is prepared to explore. Some may be slow of motion, while others keep close upon his heels, according to their several abilities, but all will make progress in his direction if the rate of speed is properly gauged. And in the end he may be genuinely surprised to discover how large the number is who have pressed forward to peer over their once limited horizon into the possibilities that lie ahead. As a prophetic frontiersman of the church, the preacher shares a grave responsibility and an enviable opportunity.

THE PREACHER AND HIS SERMON

Sermons—good, bad, and indifferent—are legion. They may be heard on any Sunday delivered from a thousand pulpits or they may be read from the pages of multitudinous books. Why not declare a ten-year moratorium on sermonic production and advise the preachers of the present generation to repeat before their congregations the choicest masterpieces of the art? Were we to follow this course it would mean eliminating the emphasis on creative endeavor as the primary task of the minister facing the new responsibilities of the church in the present age. The result would be a calamitous devitalization of the preacher's essential function. It would make him a mere parrot-like imitator of the good things that have been, rather than a constructive force in the making of the better things that ought to be. The character of the preacher's sermons will determine his right to a place in the genuinely prophetic succession. They provide him the opportunity to harness moral force and spiritual power to intelligence and decision in dealing with the crucial issues of life.

One urgent need of the modern church is intellectual strength in its ministry. This does not mean that a good sermon must of necessity be generously besprinkled with dust from moldy tomes. Pedantry is offensive in the pulpit; that is not the place for a learned lecture. But it is no crime for a preacher to be interestingly informative. Indeed, if he is not he should have a guilty conscience, for cultural leadership is one of his fundamental duties. The day is passing when ignorance in the pulpit can be redeemed by any amount of emotional enthusiasm or any length of clerical broadcloth. Books, magazines, newspapers, and the radio disseminate information and opinion everywhere; schools, colleges, and universities all over the country are pouring forth yearly their thousands of graduates into every community. The preacher who does not exhibit in his sermons a readiness to keep himself abreast of the times cannot hope to command a respectful hearing from the public.

The problem of maintaining the intellectual respectability of the modern sermon is doubly difficult. Once upon a time it was generally conceded that in certain areas of thinking the preacher was, by virtue of his office, empowered to speak the final word of authority. His Bible, his creed, and his ethical standards were assumed to be authenticated by revelation. Thus a large part of the sermon, if not its entire content, dealt with matters lying outside the range of ordinary human wisdom. To-day educated people grant the preacher no such immunity. Secular learning has ruthlessly invaded the entire domain of religious ideas. Historical investigation unhesitatingly applies its methods and criteria to a study of the origins and growth of the sacred book, as well as to the evolution of the Hebrew and Christian religions whose story it records. Creeds no longer stand unshaken simply because they are official ecclesiastical pronouncements. Their every assertion about man, the world, and the Deity has to run the gauntlet of criticism from modern research in the fields of philosophy, psychology, and the natural sciences. And traditional codes of Christian ethics are subjected to the acid test of efficiency in the presence of stubborn facts brought to light by our extensively developed social sciences. Preaching that ignores or transgresses these disciplines will hardly win a hearing from cultured people.

When the minister tries to epitomize in his sermons modern scholarship's conclusions about the Bible, the creeds, or traditional ethical codes, immediately he runs into a second difficulty. Many persons in his audience— probably the great majority—will infer that he is endeavoring to dictate opinions in authoritarian fashion as though he had a new set of decrees to deliver from heaven. Those hearers who are still in any measure addicted to the long-standing habit of revering things ancient will resent the substitution of the new dictums for the old, and those who reject authoritarianism outright will remain unedified. For them the sermon is just so much static information, while for the others it may be only an unpleasant irritant. If the preacher is amazed to discover that his auditors fail to respond to the truth, then he needs to be reminded that truth is always more appealing when it is discovered in answer to a quest conducted by a diligent seeker than when it is handed out ready-made to a sedentary recipient. Even the most timid listener will enjoy provocative intelligence in a sermon, but no one can endure obtrusive and autocratic erudition.

It is not the business of the pulpit to exercise a dominating lordship over the minds of intelligent men in any area of modern knowledge, not even in that commonly termed "religious." The preacher and his congregation are engaged in a mutual quest for keener insights and larger vision in every field of observation and experience where religious interests are involved. Quite properly he desires to speak with authority, but if he is wise he will be hesitant about arrogating to himself the mandatory rights of a dictator. Rather, he is the leader in a co-operative enterprise in which the sincerity of his convictions and the sanity of his judgments must stand approved by the best that he can evoke in the minds and consciences of his audiences. They are not mere sand and rubble in which to entomb golden nuggets of sermonic wisdom, but are a promising soil for the germination of opinions and ideals implanted therein by the speaker's message.

Perhaps the strength of the sermon can best be judged by the reserves that it keeps more or less obscurely stationed in the background. Since its primary purpose is to make a significant contribution to the actual business of living by people who are daily involved in the intricacies of modern existence, it must ring true to reality as experienced by both the speaker and his hearers. If it is too doctrinaire it will fly wide of the mark. He will preach best who knows from personal contact with its problems the meaning that life has for him, and back of whose utterances lies a reserve of strength accumulated in the process of struggle. He will be able to give his congregation something to "chew upon," as the phrase goes, only when his own intellectual fiber has been tempered by diligent study and prolonged reflection upon the vital issues that are central in or contiguous to his theme. The message gains power from the fund of vital experiences by which it is flanked.

Sometimes there is a delightful freshness and familiarity about a sermon prepared casually while the minister was tinkering with his automobile on Saturday morning. Or snatches of wisdom gleaned at random from the latest books and periodicals, and reinforced by a few illustrative stories to point a moral, may give to a minister's discourse the semblance of modernity and timeliness. But the use of these devices will ultimately issue in futility unless they are buttressed by substantial and well co-ordinated intellectual reserves. One often suspects that the reason why some types of popular preaching so quickly grow stale, rendering a rapid turnover of pastorates desirable, lies in the fact that ministers have not been disposed to pursue, or have been unable to find time for, serious and continued study. They are interested in reading or hearing only what they hope will yield a sermon for next Sunday. This need is so pressing that they give little or no attention to strengthening the mental periphery, which constitutes in reality the very foundations necessary to support enduring sermonic superstructures. Frequently the members of the church by imposing numerous lesser concerns upon the time of the preacher, are more to blame than he is for the unhappy result.

Until it is delivered the sermon is only an assemblage of latent possibilities. When discharged, will it explode with power, or will it fall as a dud in the midst of a long-suffering audience accustomed to witness weekly the harmless flight of some of its predecessors? This is the question that trembles on the lips of many an earnest preacher when he enters his pulpit. He is to speak of things divine and sacred, but they are to be uttered by the mouth of a man. In this moment he is also especially conscious of his responsibility for the welfare of the people to whom he ministers. His ability to perform successfully the climactic act in his preaching task is once more to be put to the test.

The effective presentation of a sermon to the public involves consideration of structure, phrasing, and delivery—matters that often are given far too little studious attention. Perhaps the minister assumes that his seminary training in homiletics has amply provided for these needs. This inference is quite erroneous, however excellent that instruction may have been. Nothing but the rudimentary techniques of any art can be learned in a schoolroom. Only by diligent and persistent practices can these techniques be perfected, be revised and improved to meet specific conditions, and become naturally habituated to the pulpit. Everyone will concede that a sermon should be a closely integrated structure of parts arranged according to a well-planned outline. But sermon outlines, like other skeletons, had better be kept at home safely locked in the closet. Until the preacher learns how to clothe them with sermonic flesh and blood they should not be allowed to walk abroad. It used to be said of a certain distinguished teacher of homiletics, especially by some students who smarted under the sting of his incisive criticisms, that he knew so much about the proper construction of a sermon that he was totally unfit to preach one himself, for, when he did, the mechanics of his art screamed so loud that no one could hear the message of his sermon. The charge was not altogether just, but the danger it stressed is often a real one for the preacher. The skilful artisan is the master, not the slave, of his technique, and this mastery can be realized only by studied effort and diligent practice.

Sermons are composed of words as well as thoughts. A chaste diction and a pleasant utterance are valuable aids to the preacher even in these days when a display of oratory for oratory's sake is sure to provoke a smile, if not a less hospitable response. Language is the vehicle of thought, and beauty of phrase is quite in place when it does not divert attention from the occupant of the coach to the gaudy coloring of its wheels. But in this respect, again, efficiency can be acquired and maintained only by a constant process of self-education adjusted to the minister's capacities and aptitudes, and suited to the needs of his congregation. Unquestionably, every preacher will derive profit and inspiration from an acquaintance with good literature, and he will do well to lay under tribute the finest prose and poetry available.

But any urge he may feel to make his sermon a literary essay will be encouraged or restrained according to the specific ends to be served by his discourse. Similarly, whether he will preach from manuscript, memorize his composition, or speak extempore, will have to be decided on his own responsibility and in the light of carefully considered efforts to develop the highest degree of efficiency. In these, as in most other respects, the modern Protestant preacher is the shaper of his own destiny.

THE OUTLOOK FOR THE PREACHER

The outlook for the preacher today is inviting, or disheartening, according to one's point of view. When he surveys his task in the light of his traditional heritages, he discovers a constantly changing process in which the prophetic urge and institutional conservatism were frequently at war with each other. While the minister was content to remain the spokesman of the organization, he was usually serene and comfortable, but when he attempted to break through the shell of custom he commonly did so at his own peril. Thanks to his courage and leadership, Christianity in the past kept step, though sometimes tardily, with the varying demands of its changing environments. It has ever been the task of its most significant preachers to pioneer on shifting frontiers. One generation would establish what at the moment seemed to be a stable position and then leave to their successors the further task of readjustment to fresh problems emerging with the next revolution of the wheel of time. For the Roman Catholic clergy the course of development proved less disturbing, owing to the unity and surviving strength of their ecclesiastical institution. But the Protestant minister, especially in America with its multiplicity of denominations, found himself in a much more difficult situation.

Surveying his task today, the preacher within Protestantism finds individualism intruding itself prominently into the picture. Although as a rule he still ministers under the aegis of some organized Christian communion, his particular congregation and his personal sermonic efforts are in the main determinative for his future. He, rather than the institution, carries the chief burden of responsibility. This challenge, this freedom, this opportunity to test one's mettle, opens wide today the door of privilege for a preacher who is ready to undertake the venturesome task. The promise of institutional security may be even less reassuring than it was a generation or so ago. But the prospect for leading the church into new fields of endeavor, and for rendering service to a wider circle of mankind than formerly could be reached within the pale of the various communions as then constituted, has been greatly augmented. The task of the preacher in the work of the church in the modern world is one that cannot fail to appeal to men of genuinely prophetic temper.

SELECTED BIBLIOGRAPHY

BRASTOW, L. O. *The Work of the Preacher.* New York: Macmillan, 1914.
A study of homiletical principles and methods.

DARGAN, E. C. *A History of Preaching.* 2 vols. New York: Armstrong, 1905 and 1912.

Detailed description, with minor attention to appraisal and interpretation.

DAVIS, O. S. *Principles of Preaching*. Chicago: University of Chicago Press, 1924.

An inductive study based on sample sermons of Robertson, Bushnell, Brooks, Beecher, Chalmers, Spurgeon, Newman, and Ainsworth.

FOSDICK, H. E. *The Secret of Victorious Living*. New York: Harper, 1934

This is the latest volume of sermons by one who is today probably the most prominent preacher in America.

GARVIE, A. E. *The Christian Preacher*. New York: Scribner, 1921.

Includes "History of Preaching"; "Credentials, Qualifications and Functions of the Preacher"; "Preparation and Production of the Sermon."

HOYT, A. S. *The Work of Preaching*. New York: Macmillan, 1917.

A good handbook for beginning students.

JONES, E. DEW. *American Preachers of Today*. Indianapolis: Bobbs-Merrill, 1933.

Biographical appraisal of thirty-one contemporary preachers. A little inclined to "bunk" its heroes, but still good for human insights.

OXNAM, G. B. (ed.). *Creative Preaching*. New York: Abingdon, 1930.

A series of eighteen lectures given by different ministers at the Boston University School of Theology.

PATTERSON, T. H. *The History of Christian Preaching*. Philadelphia: American Baptist Publication Society, 1903.

A good general sketch.

POTEAT, E. McN., JR. *The Reverend John Doe, D.D.* New York: Harper, 1935.

Popular lectures on the place of the preacher in the modern world.

READ, R. H. (ed.). *The Younger Churchmen Look at the Church*. New York: Macmillan, 1935.

Essays on different aspects of ministerial leadership. See esp. chap. xiv: "What Is the Matter with Our Preaching?"; and chap. xv: "Does the World Still Need the Preacher?"

ROBERTS, R. *The Preacher as a Man of Letters*. London and Toronto: Dent, 1931.

Popular lectures on the minister's use of literature.

"The Harper Monthly Pulpit."

New volumes are being added regularly presenting sermons by modern American preachers.

"The Lyman Beecher Lectures on Preaching."

Delivered annually at Yale: includes many notable volumes. Among its classics are Phillips Brooks, *Lectures on Preaching* (New York: Dutton, 1880); John Watson, *The Cure of Souls* (New York: Dodd, Mead, 1896).

CHAPTER X

PRINT AND PROPAGANDA

IN ITS earlier centuries, the church's chief medium of communication, both within its own circle and between itself and the world, was the spoken word. There was also writing, of course; in the aggregate, a vast amount of it. For the preservation of the teaching and the records of the church and for their transmission from generation to generation, literature was indispensable. But the oral word was the principal means of instruction, exhortation, correction, and the propagation of the faith. The few read; the many heard. Even the most important documents, the Scriptures themselves, reached by far the greater part of their audience through oral delivery, and the relatively few written copies of apologetic and interpretative books had their influence multiplied a thousand times by the presentation of their message in living words to listening congregations. Hence the importance of the pulpit and the public services of the church. Later, the dramatic representation of religious themes gave instruction and edification to the non-literate masses.

The practice of spoken discourse for the promotion of religion has neither ceased nor diminished. But with the introduction of printing, with the increase of literacy and of the habit of reading as well as the ability to read, and with the rise of journalism to the place of primacy as the means of disseminating intelligence upon all kinds of subjects, the press has brought powerful reinforcement to the pulpit as an agency for the communication of religious knowledge. Within the past decade there has been added to this a new form of communication combining some of the qualities of journalism with the technique of oral discourse—the radio. These, then, are the modern instruments of propaganda and promotion: the press and the radio. They supplement, but do not supersede, face-to-face communication by the spoken word.

BEGINNINGS OF RELIGIOUS JOURNALISM

The modern church has always "inclined to publication." The phrase was first applied to the Congregationalists, but it is scarcely more true of that group than of others. Most American denominations have put themselves into print copiously. The rights of free speech and unlicensed printing had been won in an earlier phase of the struggle for liberty. Freedom of the press had been established before American Christianity felt the impulse to become journalistically articulate. That fact and the facile rise of new denominations representing varieties of conviction and practice that sprang up on the new soil have done much to determine the character of religious journalism in America during the nineteenth century. It is true that the principal denominational families in this country are due to importation and did not originate indigenously. The complex denominational structure of American Christianity, as compared, for example, with that of England or Germany, is primarily due to the coming of immigrants of varied national and religious origin. Europe in the seventeenth and eighteenth centuries had more varieties of religion than any one European country had then or has now; but America received settlers from all of them, and they brought their religions with them. To this imported diversity was added a proliferation of new sects due in part to the dispersion of population and the intellectual unrestraint of the frontier.

With few exceptions these denominations, both old and new, promptly began to avail themselves of the new instrument of journalism. It was a relatively new tool, not as young at the beginning of our federal period as radio is now, but much smaller for its age. There had been newpapers of a sort in England from the founding of the *Oxford Gazette* in 1665, in France from the *Mercure de France* in 1672, in the American colonies since the *Boston News-Letter* in 1704. But these periodicals and those that immediately followed them all operated under such difficulties—fewness of readers, high cost of paper, lack of news-gathering facilities, and in some cases governmental restrictions upon the free expression of opinion—that journalism had a long and feeble infancy. Its lusty growth in America began after the winning of national independence. It is estimated that there were about two hundred newspapers in the United States by 1800, and one thousand by 1830.

The first religious journal in America of which the writer can find evidence was an eight-page weekly called the *Christian History, Containing Accounts of the Propagation and Revival of Religion in Great Britain and*

America. Its issue for March 17, 1744, was "Number 55." It must therefore have begun early in 1743, and it continued for at least a year. As its title, contents, and date alike indicate, it was a product and a reflection of the evangelical revival in England and the Great Awakening in America.

Following the achievement of independence and the beginning of the westward march of civilization, came a new zeal for the propagation of the gospel both among the Indians and among the settlers. The *Connecticut Missionary Magazine* was founded in 1800 as the organ of the Connecticut Missionary Society, formed two years earlier "to Christianize the heathen in North America and to support and promote Christian knowledge in the new settlements within the United States." Its non-sectarian character was proclaimed in the Preface to its fourth volume, in the issue for July, 1803: "The magazine will be open to receive communications from all denominations of Christians who believe in the peculiar principles of Christianity; but if written on the distinguishing tenets of their respective sects, they will be excluded." But the limits of its theological tolerance were exhibited in an unsigned article in the issue for November of the same year entitled "The Serpent's Subtlety Detected," referring to "Universalists, Arminians, Socinians or something else which falls short of the truth as it is in Jesus." The Massachusetts Missionary Society and the *Massachusetts Missionary Magazine* were founded in 1799 and 1801, respectively.

Religious journalism, as an institution having an unbroken continuity to our own time, began with the *Her-*

ald of Gospel Liberty, established about 1804 by representatives of the New England movement known as
the Christian church. It had an uninterrupted course
under that name until 1931, when it was merged with
the *Congregationalist*, now *Advance*. The *Churchman's
Monthly* (Episcopalian) began in 1804, was temporarily
suspended during the War of 1812, and became the
Churchman (New York) in 1831, when the Civil War
caused another suspension. The present *Churchman*,
tracing its lineage from the *Calendar* (1845–65) and the
Connecticut Churchman (1866), took its present name in
1867. The advancing wave of Unitarianism led to the
founding of the *Panoplist* (Boston, 1805), for the defense
of orthodoxy.

Methodism began the practice of propaganda through
the printed page almost as soon as the denomination
began to exist. The Methodist Book Concern was
founded in 1789, and every preacher and presiding elder
was an agent for the sale of its literature. The first
Methodist journals were *Zion's Herald*, started in 1823
by "a society of the New England conference"; the
Wesleyan Journal, at Charleston (S.C.), in 1826; and the
Christian Advocate, established by the Book Concern at
New York in the same year. The Book Concern soon
bought the first two and consolidated them with the
third under the comprehensive title, the *Christian Advocate and Journal and Zion's Herald*. In 1828 the combined paper claimed fifteen thousand subscribers, "the
largest circulation then reached by any newspaper in
the world, the *London Times* not excepted." It was perhaps the first paper in the country, religious or secular,

to achieve what could be called a nation-wide circulation. The New England paper resumed publication two years later, and in 1833 it secured permission to resume its former name, *Zion's Herald*, under which it is still published as an independent Methodist paper. Eight other Methodist *Advocates* were started before the Civil War, all under the authority of the general conference. At the present time there are five *Advocates*, published at New York, Cincinnati, Chicago, Kansas City, and San Francisco.

Congregational journalism began with the *Boston Recorder* (1816), which, in spite of an honorable antiquity, seems to have doubtful claim to the honor of being "the pioneer of the American weekly religious press."[1] The *Congregationalist* was founded in 1849, and the two were merged in 1867.

Similarly, other denominations discovered the value of journalism for the dissemination of their teachings and the promotion of their work. The *Religious Remembrancer* began publication in Philadelphia in 1810, and the *Religious Intelligencer* in New Haven in 1816, both weeklies. The Unitarians had the *Christian Disciple* (Boston, 1813), which later became the *Christian Examiner*. The Baptists had the *Watchman* (Boston, 1819). The *Presbyterian* began publication in Philadelphia in 1827, and the *Reformed Church Messenger* in the same city in the same year. The *New York Evangelist* and the Dutch Reformed church's *Christian Intelligencer* were both founded in New York in 1829.

[1] Walker, *History of the Congregational Churches in the United States*, p. 386.

By 1828 there were thirty-seven religious newspapers in the United States.[2] By 1832 there were not less than fifty, besides about as many monthly and quarterly religious magazines.[3]

FUNCTION AND INFLUENCE OF PERIODICALS

When journalism began to grow, it grew rapidly, and nowhere so rapidly as upon the frontier where everything that happened at all happened rapidly. For example, Kentucky's first newspaper, John Bradford's the *Kentucke Gazette*, published at Lexington, was started in 1787. Eight other papers had begun publication in Kentucky before 1800, and thirty-two by 1810, of which about twenty still survived in the latter year.[4] Throughout the West generally there was a similar swift multiplication of newspapers. Many of them did not last long, but the net increase in the number both of papers and of readers was so great that by 1832 Mrs. Trollope, in her *Domestic Manners of the Americans*, could represent excessive addiction to newspaper-reading as a characteristic national vice. If not a vice, it was at least a habit. It developed into a "behavior pattern" which had both social and intellectual consequences by opening an avenue to leadership and by fixing the type of popular thinking.

Religion rode the crest of the wave of migration that carried population westward in the early years of the

[2] J. B. McMaster, *History of the People of the United States*, V, 274; W. W. Sweet, *Methodism in American History*, p. 182 n.

[3] Daniel Dorchester, *Christianity in the United States*, p. 425.

[4] R. L. Lusk, *The Literature of the Middle Western Frontier*, I, 132 ff.

nineteenth century. The men who planted new communities also planted churches. The pioneers were not all religious, but enough of them brought their religion with them over the mountains to give the church a development commensurate with that of the civil and secular institutions of the nascent society. As secular newspapers sprang up in the new communities to serve as channels for the communication of news, organs for the propagation of political opinion, instruments for the exercise of leadership, and, in general, agencies for the integration of settlers into a conscious and effective society, so religious papers came into existence for the exercise of analogous functions in relation to the church. Small papers, like small colleges on the frontier, were comparatively easy to start; it was not so easy to keep them going. In the journalistic as in the educational field, the rate of infant mortality was very high. Many of the papers never had more than a few hundred subscribers. Many were quite ephemeral. Mergers and changes of name and location were frequent.

But in spite of the weakness of many, even most, of the individual papers, the sum total of their contribution to the development of religious life and to the promotion of the churches and all their enterprises was very great. This was equally true, though for reasons not quite identical, in denominations having a strong connectional system of doctrinal and administrative control, such as the Methodists and the Presbyterians, and in those with little or no centralized authority, such as the Baptists and the Disciples. In the closely organized bodies the papers served as instruments for the promotion of the plans and the dissemination of the ideas officially sanctioned by the authorized leaders of the church, but generally with a considerable margin of liberty for the exercise of editorial independence. In those having no authoritative central organization, editorial independence covered the whole field, subject only to the limiting necessity of keeping the favor of a supporting constituency. Religious editors often became, in effect, bishops for denominations that had no bishops, not to say popes for those that had no pope. Among those groups which had neither legislative assemblies nor officials clothed with ecclesiastical authority it was the editors more than any others who directed the currents of religious thought, fixed the forms of religious practice, and, by their approval or disapproval, determined the success or failure of denominational enterprises.

As in the growth of all American institutions, so very definitely in the development of religious thought and practice as mirrored in and partly molded by religious journals there was an interplay of two factors: first, the inherited tradition, imported from overseas or from the relatively mature culture of the Atlantic seaboard; and, second, the influence of the local situation and of the frontier as long as there was a frontier. Important as the influence of the frontier has been in all the formative aspects of American history, it is possible to give it a disproportionate emphasis. Professor F. J. Turner's famous address and book on *The Frontier in American History*, a generation ago, marked the discovery of a neglected factor. But it is quite as important, for an understanding of the evolution of religion or of political and social institutions, to note what the pioneers took with them into the new country and what streams of influence thereafter flowed from the older to the newer civilization as it is to take adequate account of the repercussions of frontier thought and activity upon the development of the country as a whole.[5]

DENOMINATIONAL JOURNALISM IN ITS PRIME

The Golden Age of denominational journalism was the period from a few years before to about twenty years after the Civil War. In 1870 there were four hundred and seven religious papers in the United States. During the preceding two decades there had been more growth in numbers and in circulation of the religious than of the secular press in proportion to the total volume of each. With few exceptions, the religious papers were strictly denominational and their major interest, if one may judge by the allocation of space, was in the promotion of denominational work and the propagation of denominational ideas. It was a little later that a Baptist paper published in Kansas City was praised for being "thoroughly Baptistic in every line," but the sentiment and the type of journalism described were more characteristic of this period. Nevertheless, many of the denominational papers gave space to a wide range of cultural interests. Popular magazines and weeklies were neither so numerous nor so widely circulated as now, and the religious press was a large factor in adult education.

[5] For a discussion of this general topic and the presentation of a point of view in contrast with Turner's frontier emphasis see *Sources of Culture in the Middle West*, ed. D. R. Fox (New York, 1935).

Religious journalism, moreover, took an active part in the discussion of such social-political questions as temperance, prohibition, slavery, and reconstruction. In all these fields the religious press both expressed and helped to determine the attitude of the churches. The Christian conscience had become sensitive at all these points—with different results in different parts of the country, to be sure—and religious journals both mirrored the mind of the churches with reference to these matters of public policy and campaigned vigorously for specific programs of action.

Two great undenominational papers flourished in the latter part of this period—the *Independent*, edited successively by Beecher and Tilton, and the *Christian Union*, edited first by Beecher and then by Lyman Abbott. The *Independent* had originally been a Congregational paper, but in 1867 it became avowedly undenominational, as it had already become in fact. Through the Civil War years it was, in effect, Beecher's broadcasting station. This fact and its ardent defense of the union cause, with able editorship and a distinguished staff of contributors, brought it a large circulation and gave it wide influence. A large proportion of its space was devoted to political, social, and financial topics. In reconstruction years it was a vehement advocate of the program of the "Republican radicals," and there was scarcely a newspaper in the country which denounced President Johnson more violently, clamored for his impeachment more insistently, or demanded a "strong" policy toward the defeated South more urgently. In this respect it set the pattern which the religious papers and the churches of the North for the most part followed in those turbulent years. With changing editorship it became less definitely a religious paper and became a journal of opinion on the side of political and economic conservatism.

The *Christian Union*, founded by Beecher in 1870, was from the outset what its name indicated—an explicitly Christian paper owing allegiance to no denomination. Under the editorship of Lyman Abbott for nearly half a century, including the period after its name was changed to the *Outlook*, it represented scholarly and evangelical liberalism, a conception of Christianity which accepted evolution and biblical criticism, and a hospitable attitude toward the newer social interests which were beginning to stir the Christian conscience.

In addition to these two undenominational papers representing liberal theological tendencies and finding their constituencies largely among the intellectuals, there were others beginning only a little later and making a more popular appeal to the rank and file of church people. The *Christian Herald*, edited for a time by T. DeWitt Talmage—the perfect pattern of the "popular" preacher, with all the strength and all the limitations which the term suggests—was a family paper, warmly religious in tone, entertaining in contents and style, conservative enough in its underlying theology to be acceptable to those who opposed evolution and higher criticism as attacks upon the Christian faith, but avoiding theological controversy and controversial topics so far as possible. On this policy it has continued and flourished.

The *Sunday School Times* came into existence as an expression of the interdenominational religious interest embodied in the Sunday-school movement, especially after the organization of the International Sunday School Association and the initiation of the "Uniform Lessons." As a paper appealing to a constituency in all the churches, it necessarily stressed the common elements of their faith and teaching, to the exclusion of denominational differentia. Such papers, and indeed the whole Sunday-school movement, were an important factor in breaking down the sense of estrangement among denominations and in forming a body of doctrine and a type of thought which were conceived of as constituting the common body of Christian truth. As an influence toward unity of spirit and action, this had indisputable value. But the formulation of a body of teaching embodying the common Christian tradition, in terms acceptable to the majority in the evangelical denominations, necessarily excluded any restatement of religious truth in the light of modern scientific knowledge and the results of scholarly study of the Bible. It therefore tended to perpetuate traditional views of the Bible, its teaching and its place in Christianity, and to fortify and consolidate the conservative opposition to any critical examination of traditional views.

More recent organizations and publications devoted to religious education are animated by a quite different spirit and represent a different attitude. The International Council of Religious Education and its magazine, the *International Journal of Religious Education*, promote the preparation and use of a common body of intelligent and modern material. Interdenominational co-operation in this field has become the means of advancing a program of education that is thoroughly progressive with reference to subject matter, methods, and objectives.

Denominational papers may be classified as official and unofficial, according as they are owned and controlled by the denomination itself (either directly or through some agency having such a connection), or are owned privately and operated for profit. It might be supposed that those denominations which have centralized systems of ecclesiastical authority would have an official journalism subject to this authority, and that independent religious papers would be found only in those bodies that exhibit a high degree of individual and congregational independency. However, no correlation of journalistic with congregational independency exists, either positively or negatively. Roman Catholics, Episcopalians, and Christian Scientists are alike in having centralized and authoritative forms of organization. Yet the first two have never had, in this country, either an official publishing house or a periodical recognized as the official voice of the church, while the last have both and effectively prohibit private publication in the name of the church. On the other hand, the Baptists and Disciples recognize the legitimacy of no ecclesiastical authority above the local church, yet the Baptists have had at least one paper that was for several years the property of the Northern Baptist Convention, and the Disciples have a publishing house and a paper which, owned by a non-profit corporation governed by a self-perpetuating board of directors, are considered the property of the denomination and devote all profits to its missionary and other enterprises. Methodist organization is connectional, and Methodist journalism has for the most part been official, but *Zion's Herald* has been a conspicuous and important exception for more than a hundred years.

The distinction between official denominational papers and those privately owned is perhaps less significant, as determining the character of the papers, than one might expect it to be. The history of papers of both classes proves that it is possible for the influence of a constituency to determine the policies of a paper as definitely as the formal action of any ecclesiastical authority could, and, on the other hand, that a wide range of editorial liberty is sometimes consistent with technical and legal dependence upon the official representatives of a denomination.

RECENT TENDENCIES

Somewhat earlier than the beginning of the twentieth century it began to be observable that the Golden Age of denominational journalism was passing, and the symptoms of its decline have become more acute in recent years. One contributing cause of this tendency, though not the most important, was that the financial difficulties, always sufficiently embarrassing, were intensified by the falling-off of receipts from advertising. This, in turn, was the result of two causes: first, an increasing sensitiveness in regard to the kind of advertising that a religious paper should carry and the consequent elimination of most of the patent-medicine advertising that had been the most lucrative part of the business in this department; and, second, a change in the policy of the better class of national advertisers and the concentration of their copy in papers and magazines having larger circulation than any denominational paper could boast. Simultaneously with this loss of advertising revenue, the publication of Sunday-school literature, which had been a profitable sideline for many denominational concerns publishing weekly papers, also became less remunerative with the introduction of new forms of curriculums and new types of lesson material.

More deeply significant, and in the long run more decisive for the fortunes of the denominational press, was the general lessening of interest in denominational peculiarities, accompanied by a waning loyalty to the institutions of the group as such. Many papers which had been able to hold a sufficient constituency to support them found themselves unable to survive when reader-interest gradually took the place of inherited loyalty as the tie between the subscriber and the paper. For many years the concentration of attention by sectarian journals upon the propagation of the ideas of the sect and the promotion of its enterprises had matched the limited interests of the sectarian mind, and had therefore had survival value for scores of periodicals without other adequate reason for existence. The changing temper of the Christian mind in the present generation has tended to turn this asset into a liability. The inevitable and salutary consequence has been the disappearance of some papers and the broadening of the scope of others.

Such changes occur very slowly, and more noticeably in some areas than in others. There are denominational papers which continue to flourish with apparently undiminished vitality, as there are denominations which have maintained their morale without serious deterioration. Some of these have gained strength by the elimination of their weaker competitors. But the number of failures, discontinuances, and mergers in recent years has been very significant, especially in view of the venerable age and the importance of some of the papers that have disappeared.

Most of the denominational papers which show signs of continuing vigor reflect the attitude of the church as a whole by a less exclusive preoccupation with denominational interests and by a greater emphasis upon social questions. It is easy to exaggerate the absorption of the church and its press in sectarian concerns in the earlier years and to underestimate their part in the discussion of social issues. Neither the pulpit nor the religious press was silent on slavery, reconstruction, temperance, prohibition, the Spanish-American War, the responsibilities of imperialism, or the World War and the international questions that it raised. What is new is the note of social and economic liberalism. The removal of the causes of poverty has come to seem at least as important, and as religious, as charity to the poor, and the correction of social injustice does not rate below the salvaging of its victims as a Christian duty. There is less exclusive specialization upon combating the sins of the flesh and more stress upon curing the sickness of society and ending organized greed and legalized fraud. The church is less satisfied with being "patriotic," and more ready to challenge the position of the government itself on such questions as war, military expenditures and education, internationalism, the naturalization of pacifists, the treatment of "radicals," and the rights of labor. While the churches do not speak with united voices upon these controversial topics, their opinions have become articulate and the religious press—including the denominational press—has become a forum for discussion and a medium for utterance upon these undenominational themes. No catalogue of contemporary social forces would be complete without the names of such papers and editors as the *Churchman* (Shipler), the *Living Church* (Morehouse), *Unity* (Holmes and Reese), the *Christian Advocate* (Brummitt and others), and *Zion's Herald* (Hartman)—to mention only a few among many.

Undenominational papers, necessarily lacking the support of group loyalty, are more dependent upon the demand of a sufficient constituency for the service which they actually render from year to year and the response of individuals to the policy and the personality of their editors. They therefore do not have the institutional persistence of the stronger denominational organs. They compete in a wider field, and must either adjust to changing needs and conditions or disappear. The *Independent*, once the most influential religious paper in the country, perhaps in the world, became a secular monthly magazine and then suspended publication. The *Outlook*, heading the field of independent religious weeklies under Lyman Abbott and long maintaining its prestige though somewhat altering its character under the editorship of his son, registered its complete transformation by becoming the *New Outlook*, with Alfred E. Smith as editor. The *World Tomorrow*, outspokenly Christian and socialist, never became securely established. After a brief and brilliant career under Kirby Page, it merged with the *Christian Century*. The *Christian Herald* maintained its character as an evangelical, non-controversial, popular religious periodical for the family, but became a monthly magazine.

The *Christian Century* is at present the only undenominational religious weekly of national circulation. It is theologically liberal and devotes much attention to social and public questions. Originally an organ of the Disciples of Christ, of minor importance even within its own communion, it came into the hands of Charles Clayton Morrison, who promptly alienated most of the support which the paper had by championing causes unpopular in the denomination and gradually found a vastly larger constituency in the more progressive elements of all denominations.

Other important undenominational religious periodicals are of less than weekly frequency: the *Christian Community*, twice a month, succeeding the *Community Churchman* in January, 1935, the organ of the community church workers; *Church Management*, monthly, devoted to practical church administration; the *Journal of Religion*, a theological quarterly; *Religion in Life*, formerly the *Methodist Quarterly;* the *Christian Union Quarterly*, founded by Peter Ainslie as an organ of the Christian union movement, edited by him until his death in 1934, and now transformed (October, 1935) into a quarterly magazine of Christian scholarship and culture under the title *Christendom* and with the same management as the *Christian Century*.

It may be remarked that the project of establishing a Protestant religious daily paper, though often proposed, has never been seriously attempted. The Roman Catholic press in America includes 310 periodicals (as of 1932), of which 9 are daily, 113 weekly, 131 monthly. The National Catholic Welfare Conference maintains a news service which supplies news, editorials, feature articles, and pictures. The Catholic Press Association, a voluntary organization of Catholic papers and magazines, has a news-service bureau, a literature bureau, an advertising bureau, and committees dealing with other common interests.

THE CHURCH AND THE SECULAR PRESS

Most important daily papers have "religious editors," who are often clergymen, active or retired. The amount of religious news that they publish is, in the aggregate, very great; and, considering their immense circulation, the value of the publicity which they give to religious ideas and enterprises is inestimable. Ministers and earnest laymen do not always appreciate the extent or significance of this service, and they are often dissatisfied with the treatment of religious topics in the daily press. The secular press evaluates religious news as news, not as propaganda or promotional material. The minister wants to promote a cause, or to do good. The city editor wants to interest his readers, sell his paper, and avoid offending his advertisers. Protestants have no solidarity, as a bloc, to exercise pressure upon papers which offend them, as Roman Catholics and Christian Scientists can and do.

The secular journalist often has a distorted idea of what constitutes news, identifying it with sensation, but he is expert in knowing what the millions will read. Under these conditions the secular press can be utilized much more advantageously than at present for the promotion of religion and the dissemination of religious ideas if those who have contacts with the press on behalf of religious organizations or events will cultivate a sense of what is journalistic news, if they will prepare their news releases in such form that they can be used with the minimum of editing and re-writing, and if they will restrain the impulse to get free publicity for causes and to make propaganda under the guise of furnishing news. News itself has propaganda value and is a legitimate form of promotion, but city editors are properly wary of efforts to use their columns for the promotion of projects not of general interest to the mass of their readers.

Mention should be made of the conspicuous place occupied by articles on religious topics in the better magazines. This is a relatively recent phenomenon. A generation ago an article on religion in the *Atlantic Monthly*, *Scribner's*, *Harper's*, or the *Century* was a rarity. Today such articles are less infrequent than an issue of one of these magazines without one. In part, this results from a change of policy under which magazines once strictly "literary" have widened their scope to include the discussion of current social topics; but the inclusion of religion under this broader policy means a recognition that religion is no longer regarded as a peculiar and untouchable topic, but as a phase of the social problem which can be discussed without bated breath or a holy tone. Religion has been brought out into the open.

RELIGIOUS BOOKS

Statistics compiled annually by the *Publishers' Week-ly*, showing the number of books in each general field published during the preceding year, reveal a surprising number of titles classified under religion. As would be expected, fiction is always the most numerous class, but religion generally comes either second or third. Religion would perhaps rank lower in a quantitative analysis of current books if account were taken of the volume of sales rather than of the number of titles, but no figures are available indicating the circulation of religious books as compared with others. It is to be noted that not many religious books appear in the rental libraries which, according to a recent estimate, buy 40 per cent of the fiction that is sold and supply nine-tenths of the readers of fiction with the books they read. The place of religion in the nation's reading, so far as books are concerned, is proportionately smaller than the mere count of new titles would suggest.

But, on the other hand, it must be borne in mind that a religious factor is present in many novels and other books not technically religious. Furthermore, the enlarged modern conception of the scope of religion necessarily implies a broadening of the conception of what constitutes a religious book, in function and value if not in classification by the trade. It includes much that is classed as sociology, economics, history, biography, drama, poetry, political science, and philosophy. There is also a large and important body of specifically religious literature that is colored, and its character largely determined, by the inclusion of these interests.

Many of the standard publishers have religious departments. Others which, on principle, do not have separate departments, have men on their editorial staffs who are experts in religious literature and by their publishing policies illustrate the conviction that religious and secular subject matter cannot be segregated from each other.

Denominational publishing houses have an important function, and all the more so because they are generally not narrowly denominational in their publishing interests. In general, it may be said that, while the varieties of religious books have been vastly extended, one class has become so rare as to be almost extinct in Protestant literature—namely, books of sectarian polemic and propaganda. Even the more recent denominational histories have been written rather in the scientific spirit than with the motive of advancing denominational prestige and proving the superiority of one group to all others. There are religious books embodying the findings of scholarship and the results of modern thought. There is also an unfailing stream of books of the traditionally evangelical and pietistic type. But there are almost no definitely sectarian books bearing recent date.

RELIGIOUS BROADCASTING

The recent invention and rapid development of radio has made available to the church, as to every other organization with a message, an amazingly effective new means of communication. Any statements in regard to an institution which changes with such kaleidoscopic speed run the risk of being obsolete before they can be put into print. Radio can tell about books more safely than books can tell about radio. However, a few data may be given which were accurate when they were assembled.[6]

According to reports of 576 broadcasting stations to the Federal Radio Commission in 1932, the amount of time devoted to religious broadcasts was 8.37 per cent of the total radio time. The average was twenty-three fifteen-minute periods per week per station. Approximately one-fourth of this time was paid for, and three-fourths was donated by the stations. The time devoted to religious programs on Sundays is almost as much as on all week-days. The schedules show that the great majority of religious programs on week-days are at the hours which have least commercial value because listeners are fewest—that is, early morning and mid-afternoon. In each of the five radio zones some kind of religious program is within reach of practically every radio set in the early morning. Later in the morning and in the afternoon programs are within reach of many. At the popular noon hour and in the evening there are very few.

Religious programs originate with churches, with national religious organizations, with colleges and universi-

[6] The most complete study up to this time is by W. J. Dubourdieu, *Religious Broadcasting in the United States*, an unpublished dissertation for the degree of Doctor of Philosophy, Northwestern University, 1933.

ties, and with the stations themselves utilizing either members of their own staffs or individuals selected by them.

Audition and analysis of several hundred radio sermons and the classification of their materials according to the type of organization sponsoring them showed the following results: The programs put on the air by conventional Protestant bodies are chiefly ethical, devotional, and inspirational; they contain very little doctrine and less than 1 per cent of their time is devoted to presenting the merits or the peculiar tenets of the group represented; very seldom are they "organization-centered," in the sense of being apparently motived by a desire to gain advantage or adherents for the denomination. Twenty-five church federations have voted their agreement that "radio services should be interdenominational and broadly inclusive of all types of Protestantism."[7] The programs sponsored by the Federal Council of Churches have been of this character. Protestant fundamentalists and Roman Catholics present doctrine in at least half of their sermons; the doctrines presented are controversial in the sense that the great majority of them involve positions repudiated by at least 35 per cent of the ministers in Professor George H. Betts's *Beliefs of 700 Ministers*. Roman Catholics spend 31 per cent of their radio time in discussing the merits and claims of Catholicism. Those who may be called "irregular Protestants" —including the International Bible Students Associa-

---

[7] Frank C. Goodman, executive secretary of the Federal Council's radio department, in *Yearbook of American Churches for 1932*, ed. H. C. Weber, p. 96.

tion (Millennial Dawn), the Church of the Nazarene, Unity, the Assembly of God, and the Christian and Missionary Alliance—seldom offer a sermon which does not contain a large amount of doctrine, and they devote much time to presenting the merits of their peculiar views and attempting to win followers; they are in a high degree "organization-centered." The International Bible Students Association not only gives a large majority of the programs in this group but 50 per cent more than the Roman Catholics, who in turn occupy more radio time than any conventional Protestant body though less than all of them. Christian Science programs show a maximum of doctrinal and institutional preaching; they practically all deal with the special teachings and claims of Christian Science.

The resultant of all this is that liberal theological views, and even moderately conservative doctrines, are but slightly represented in religious broadcasts, while fundamentalist and Roman Catholic doctrines and the peculiar views of irregular and "unassimilable varieties" of Protestantism are expounded with great frequency and fervor. It should be added that the non-doctrinal and non-institutional sermons of conventional Protestantism, whether liberal or conservative, dealing largely with individual ethics and the inner life, have little to say about social and economic problems, and do not often deal with the Christianization of the social order.

The air is not always free, even to those who are willing to pay for it. Rev. Herman J. Hahn, Evangelical, was excluded from a Buffalo station because he was too socialistic. Rev. Robert P. Shuler (Methodist), of Los

Angeles, had his station closed by the Federal Radio Commission under such circumstances that the surest thing that can be said about it is that the alleged reasons were not the real ones. Father Coughlin (Catholic) had to organize his own chain.

Topics still requiring further study in connection with religious broadcasting include the establishment of a clearing house for information, general co-ordination of agencies, more satisfactory adjustment of hours, financial support, doctrinal balance, freedom from unreasonable censorship, type of address and of program most effective, more frequent and expert presentation of religious drama, the bringing of religious broadcasts into at least as much harmony with modern intelligence and scholarship and as much adjustment to the present needs of the world as religious literature now exhibits. The most modern instrument of communication cannot permanently remain the vehicle for disseminating the least modern religious thought.

SELECTED BIBLIOGRAPHY

W. J. DuBourdieu, *Religious Broadcasting in the United States.*

An unpublished dissertation for the degree of Doctor of Philosophy, Northwestern University, Evanston, Ill., 1933. The most thorough study so far of the religious use of radio.

The annual reports of the president of the National Broadcasting Company contain information on religious broadcasts. Additional data may be secured from M. J. O'Brien, chairman of the Committee on Religious Activities of the National Broadcasting Company, Radio City, New York City, and from Miss Mary Alice Jones, director of children's work, International Council of Religious Education, 203 N. Wabash Ave., Chicago.

W. E. Garrison, *The March of Faith.* New York: Harper, 1933.

A history of religion in America since 1865, including data in regard to religious journalism.

Rusk, Ralph Leslie. *The Literature of the Middle Western Frontier.* 2 vols. New York: Columbia University Press, 1925.

Gives an accurate, though incomplete, account of religious books and papers as part of a general literary history of the pioneer period in America.

Weber, Herman C. (ed.). *Yearbook of American Churches: A Record of Religious Activities in the United States, 1933 and 1934.* New York: Association Press, 1935.

Contains lists of religious periodicals, besides a vast amount of other data.

Note.—The various denominational histories may be consulted for information regarding the periodicals of the several bodies. The source materials for further study in this field are the files of the papers and magazines mentioned in the text.

CHAPTER XI

FACING THE FUTURE

THE CHURCH'S RESPONSE TO SOCIAL CHANGE

IT IS apparent from the foregoing chapters that the work of the Protestant churches in America is undergoing important modifications in the period of profound social change through which we are passing. In part it would appear that these modifications are a continuance of the unconscious accommodations which the historic church has characteristically made to the pressures of the cultural environment. In part they reflect a conscious and intentional attempt to meet in new ways the new demands of the present social situation.

In any case, the changes in viewpoint, methods of approach, and programs of work herein described are far from being characteristic of the entire Protestant movement. Minority groups have been sensitive to social change and quick to recognize the necessity of revising their beliefs to accord with the fresh discoveries of science, of adopting new methods of work, and of accommodating institutional arrangements to new conditions. It is to these minority groups that the church, like society, must look for progress. On the other hand, majority groups appear scarcely to be aware of the changes that are going on about them or of the significance of these changes. They continue to think in traditional thought forms, to employ religious techniques that grew up out of types of religious experience that are now outmoded, and uncritically to perpetuate institutional procedures that no longer fit altered conditions. Nevertheless, there are often evidences of slow movement in the mass. It is also characteristic that progressive movements evoke reaction on the part of other minority groups. Viewed in the mass, Protestantism exhibits a behavior that is rather thoroughly institutionalized and regimented by tradition and habit.

The Protestant churches, in so far as they can be regarded as a corporate movement, have for some time been in the second phase of the recurring cycle through which the church, like all other social movements, tends to pass. These movements have their origin in fresh insights and in an immediate and living experience of their contemporary world. In this stage they are vital, convincing, and often creative. But in time they tend to be overtaken by institutionalism. They lose contact with reality and become overlaid with the crusts of tradition and convention. They become routine, external, and authoritative. This second phase continues until the vital energies operative in the movement break through the crust of tradition and convention and re-establish fresh contact with realistic conditions. As a consequence of the Protestant churches being in the second phase of this cycle, they have, on the whole, lost their orientation to reality. They have ceased to be convincing to themselves or to society. They have to a large degree lost their sense of mission. The swift currents of modern life flow around and past them and are for the most part little influenced by them. Many, if not most, of the contemporary movements that are concerned with human and spiritual values have their origin and sphere of influence outside the churches. Only to a slight degree do these movements seriously take the church into account as an effective ally.

The Christian movement had its origin in the vital and immediate interaction of Jesus and his earliest followers with the world of reality. The Christian life was to them a vivid and self-authenticating experience. However, there are evidences in the New Testament itself that the second generation of Christians, who had not passed through the original experiences that gave rise to the movement, but to whom the convictions and attitudes of the Christian life had been in large part an inherited tradition, exhibited a different quality of devotion and a loss of creativeness. The Reformation out of which Protestantism grew was another such period of vital and immediate experience. But it, too, in course of time has been overcome by institutionalism. Without doubt the most imperative need of Protestantism which has ceased, on the whole, to be a movement and has become relatively static, is to re-establish fresh contact with reality as that reality appears in the experience of the modern world. That renewal will come not through any attempt to recapture the experience of the past but by breaking through the hardened shell of habit and convention to an unmediated experience of the real world of the living present. Neither will the tides of a new life set in from the church assuming a merely spectator or critical attitude toward the modern world, but from responsible participation in the actual processes that make for the fulfilment or frustration of the human values upon the achievement of which man's destiny as man depends.

This means that the church should be the first to discover the points at which human and social values are involved in the interplay of social forces and where and how these values are furthered or destroyed. Instead of allowing itself to continue to be a merely conservative influence in society because it is primarily concerned with the conservation of values, the church should become creative in its attitude toward any and every process that in any way affects the realization of values that in the changing stream of human experience are always in the process of coming into being. Just because religion is supremely concerned with these values, it, even more than science and technology, should not only be instant in its response to social change, but should play an important rôle in initiating change in the interest of human and social ends. A church that is sensitive to the operation of social forces and that is willing to make use of the insights of science should be able to discover the direction in which social experience is moving and to anticipate the effects of these movements upon human personality and upon society itself.

To this end the church needs to acquire an attitude of self-appraisal and a method of self-improvement. The church should not wait until it is forced tardily and reluctantly to modify its ideas and programs of work under the steady and irresistible pressures of social change. An aware and self-appraising church should be the first to detect the elements of strength and weakness in its program and to discover the specific points at which improvement could be made. In addition to acquiring an attitude of self-criticism, the church needs to discipline itself in the technique of self-improvement. The technique of improving a practical operation conforms to the pattern of empirical and experimental procedure. It begins by analyzing and appraising the results obtained by present practice. It then analyzes the process to discover, if possible, the factors that have been responsible for the present satisfactory or unsatisfactory results. It then reconstructs the process by eliminating certain factors or adding other factors with the intentional view of securing satisfactory ends. It again analyzes the results and then the process alternately until satisfactory results are achieved or the attempt is abandoned. This is the technique that has long been used by science and the technological arts and is chiefly responsible for the brilliant advances in those fields. But it is a technique which the church has yet almost entirely to learn.

From the use of this procedure it is obvious that the modification of the church's program is not a matter of wholesale or revolutionary change, but is to be accomplished through bringing about very specific improvements at the points where improvements can be made. Neither is it a matter of dealing undiscriminatingly with the whole operation *en masse*. It is, rather, a matter of scrutinizing specific aspects of the total result and of dealing with specific factors in a complex process that are responsible for particular items in

the total outcome. It must not be overlooked that the
church is a going concern. In seeking to improve its
efficiency the church should begin where it is in the
practical operation in which it is engaged. It should
modify its program with reference to the concrete conditions which it faces and with reference to specific
factors while at the same time preserving the continuity
of its work. Wholesale changes that break this continuity are likely to be radical and impermanent in their
results. In the most highly developed inventions the
distance between the earliest imperfect and the latest
relatively perfect models is filled up by very small, very
specific improvements on preceding models. The same is
true of the most genuinely and permanently progressive
social institutions. Moreover, the changes which the
church makes in its thought and programs of action
should themselves be continuous. Revolutionary and
spasmodic changes are inadequate to keep the church in
constant adjustment to a changing culture. Its adaptations need to be as continuous as the changes which call
for them. If the church is not able to achieve continuous
readjustment it must face the consequence of spasmodic
and radical changes.

SIGNIFICANT TRENDS

The points of view, methods of approach, and types of
activity described in the foregoing chapters clearly indicate certain trends that are of great significance and
promise as the church in our generation faces the future.
On the part of a considerable section of Protestantism
viewed in such corporateness as it presents, they are

indices of awareness, of sensitivity to social change and to its meaning, and of a self-appraisal of the effectiveness of the church in respect to the demands imposed upon it by social change. They offer grounds for hope that the church at work in the modern world may, through the use of its intelligence and its resources of historical experience, function creatively in its relation to the culture of our day.

A new conception of religion.—Perhaps the most fundamental of these trends, in the sense that it underlies and makes possible many of the others here recorded, is a new conception of the nature and function of religion in its relation to human experience. The church has inherited from its theological tradition a supernaturalistic and authoritative view of religion. According to this view, God was identified with those aspects of reality that are beyond the reach of man's understanding and control, while those aspects of reality that were understood and were amenable to human control were conceived as belonging to an entirely different order. In this way the world of man's experience was sharply divided into the realms of the "natural" and the "supernatural." In such a world a transcendent God, acting wholly on his own initiative and responsibility, invaded on occasion the "natural" world by acts of miraculous and supernatural grace, thus setting aside its normal processes. Divine truth was supernaturally revealed and therefore something given and immutable. Human nature, since it belonged to the realm of the natural, was corrupt and incapable of "any motion of goodness." Salvation was the work of supernatural grace made effective through redemption by a blood atonement.

To the modern religious mind this dichotomy in reality is no longer tenable. The world disclosed by science is a uniformity of many interacting forces. To the modern religious mind God is quite as much identified with the known and controlled operations of our world as he is with the as-yet-unknown and uncontrolled. Furthermore, the scientific study of religion has demonstrated that it has a natural history. It grows up and functions within man's normal and practical experience. It is an integral phase of his total culture. Religious concepts, practices, and organization emerge within the stream of man's experience and function in that experience by subjecting it to cross-criticism and redirection in terms of its fundamental, comprehending, and enduring values. From this point of view, religion is a potential quality of any and every phase of man's interaction with his objective world, rather than a unique and isolated type of experience. It is directly concerned with man's intellectual life, his research, his economic functions, his political activities, his industrial operations, his use of leisure time, and his art. In this enlarged view of a unified and continuous reality the traditional concepts of both the "natural" and the "supernatural" are no longer useful. They yield to a larger, more fundamental, and more comprehensive concept of reality in which God is identified with every behavior of the universe, including man, which makes for the creation and realization of those enduring and comprehensive values that lend dignity and worth to man's life in a moral world.

It will thus be seen that this newer concept of the nature and function of religion by no means eliminates God from the process. On the contrary, it greatly enlarges and enriches the concept of God. Perhaps the chief task of contemporary theology is to work out a formula for this central concept of Christianity that will accord with our scientific knowledge of the constitution of the universe. Certainly one of the most important undertakings of operative Christianity is to create, out of our experience of God in such a world, a more adequate symbol that will represent to the imagination God at work creatively in the normal processes of the world disclosed by man's experience.

The church a social institution.—A second trend, closely related to the first, is toward a conception of the church as the institutional embodiment of a social movement. Instead of a supernatural and authoritative organization whose fixed details were set forth in a divinely revealed pattern, the church appears as an association of like-minded persons who are drawn together by common beliefs and attitudes toward life and by cherished values which they hope to see prevail in the personal and associated life of their fellow-men. According to this view, the church is, in its deepest and truest nature, a supported and supporting fellowship. In it the experience of its members is set in a universal and ideal context. Within its associated life it has developed techniques for mutual self-appraisal, for release from the past and the possibility of making new beginnings, for self-discipline, and for laying hold upon those spiritual resources that reside in and beyond the group. These techniques include public assembly, group worship, preaching, public and private prayer, confession, the sacraments, and the celebration of the values cherished by the group through the impressive and vivid symbolism of architecture, liturgy, and ceremonial.

Moreover, the church is seen to sustain etiological relations with its community. Churches not only exert an influence upon the communities in which they are located, but their behavior is definitely conditioned by the social forces that operate in their communities. The objective observation of the behavior of churches shows that, in spite of inherited beliefs to the contrary, they follow no predetermined pattern, but assume endless varieties of types of activity and organization. Besides, each local community is influenced by the wider culture of a region, of the nation, and of Western civilization. The more remote influences of these larger cultural areas constantly impinge upon the thought, attitudes, and behaviors of the local community through the press, the radio, the theater, and the more intangible ethos of a folk.

Instead, therefore, of imposing a given and predetermined message and program upon its members and its community, the modern church seeks to build its message and its program upon a thoroughgoing analysis of the spiritual needs of the group and of the community in which it is located. Through preaching, religious education, work with individuals, and organization the church seeks to start with the group where it is in its experience of the concrete conditions which it faces. It seeks to help the group to interpret these experiences, to analyze and appraise them, and to explore their possibilities in the light of Christian ideals and purposes, with the utilization of every resource which historical Christian experience affords in the Bible, in symbols, and in the great achievements of the past. Above all, it seeks to develop loyalties around the great causes of human betterment.

A unified parish.—Unmistakably, the churches are moving in the direction of a more unified program representing the interaction of many different functions in a comprehensive program for the local church. Our generation has inherited a parish which presents a congeries of many more or less independent or isolated functions. This condition is readily understood when it is remembered that these functions, like those represented by the Sunday school, women's missionary organizations, Christian Endeavor, evangelism, and various types of social service, grew up around the older function of preaching in order to meet neglected needs in an expanding movement. As a consequence, each of these organizations worked out its objectives, methods, and programs of work without reference to what other organizations were doing. The result has been a more or less planless duplication of activities and personnel, serious omission of groups and interests, and conflict. This situation is not only ineffective; it is becoming more and more intolerable.

Many churches are experimenting with comprehensive programs which are built upon the carefully studied needs of the entire group. In this way what were once isolated and competing activities now tend to be absorbed into the total program of the church, each conditioning, and being conditioned by, every other function.

An appeal to a wider range of interests.—It would appear that if the church is to meet the spiritual needs of the various groups in the local church and community it will be necessary for it greatly to widen the range of interests to which its program appeals. As is pointed out in chapter viii, the Protestant church has for the most part included in its membership the capitalist and non-wage-earning classes. The intellectuals, on the one extreme, and the wage-earners and the dispossessed, on the other extreme, have to a considerable extent sought such spiritual satisfaction as they might find in non-ecclesiastical pursuits and organizations. As has frequently been pointed out, the behavior of some of these non-ecclesiastical groups displays many of the essential characteristics of religion. This is notably true of many of the groups of the underprivileged and the dispossessed whose members are actuated by ideals of social justice in which human values are involved and around which intense loyalties are built up. This selection of the more favored economic groups is evidence that the church is not in its present program meeting as wide a range of human interests and needs as it should.

This failure to meet a sufficiently inclusive range of spiritual needs is further evidenced by the rise of various cults, such as Christian Science, New Thought, Unity, Spiritualism, Russellism, Buchmanism, Theosophy, and

Bahaism, together with certain highly emotionalistic sects, such as the Nazarenes and the Holy Rollers. Within recent years a phenomenon of the same order has arisen within the more representative Protestant churches. There has been a marked tendency for certain elements in these "respectable" churches to drop away to the emotionalistic sects.

The rise of a new cult or the defection of members from the recognized Protestant churches into the emotionalistic sects is evidence that certain fundamental needs of the human spirit are not being met by the program of the churches. The preoccupation of the churches with metaphysical theology, formal ritualism, or institutional routine to the neglect of human values leads the dispossessed to seek satisfaction in devotion to a cause that stands for human rights against an acquisitive society. An undue emphasis upon a sterile intellectualism and a dilettante attitude toward the profound emotions have resulted in starved emotions that seek some adequate form of expression. To this result our entire American culture has contributed. Since emotional satisfaction cannot be found in normal and constructive channels around what should constitute the basic issues of life, it is sought in bizarre forms ranging from sentimentalism through sheer excitement to orgiastic seizures.

To undertake to meet these wider ranges of spiritual need presents the church with an exceedingly difficult task. Whether these needs can best be met by a differential program of interests and activities within an inclusive group or by programs for diversified groups can only be determined by competent analysis of the problem and by experimentation. But whether by a diversified program or by diversified groups, the church needs to assume responsibility for attempting to meet a wider range of interests and needs than it has met in the past.

Toward a greater corporateness.—The studies in this book unmistakably indicate a trend toward a greater corporateness among the Protestant churches. The issues which originally divided the Protestant churches, however vital at the time these divisions arose, are for the most part no longer living issues. The conditions which gave rise to them have changed. Other and more inclusive values have superseded those that evoked narrower and more intense loyalties. The Protestant church is becoming conscious of itself as one among many movements and institutions that in their interrelatedness constitute society. This has led to a greater sense of community of attitudes and purposes than of separateness. The conviction has grown that the inherited differences in Protestantism arose over relatively superficial phases of religion, such as theological definition, ecclesiastical polity, and political interests, whereas the enduring bonds of an essential fellowship rest upon the fundamentals of Christian conviction and purpose.

But even more significant has been a growing sense of the social responsibility of the church in the presence of social forces that in our complex modern life make for the enhancement of human values or for their destruction. The enterprises which such issues present are practical rather than theological or institutional. Doctrinaire attempts at co-operation upon a basis of agreement in regard to "minimal essentials" have generally ended in failure. But it was early discovered that Christian groups with wide differences of opinion regarding matters of faith and order could co-operate in espousing specific practical causes. This discovery has led to many forms of co-operation in which the essential unity of thought and purpose that characterizes Protestantism has found some form of corporate expression.

Even so, a widely felt desire for a greater and more effective degree of corporateness than co-operation can satisfy has been steadily growing. Groups within Protestantism, some of them of considerable size, as in Canada, have in recent years explored the possibilities of organic union. The social responsibility of the church and the difficulties presented by division on the mission fields have made vivid the sense of the incompetency of a sectarian church in the modern world. The experiments in this direction, both in America and in non-Christian lands, point to a development that is likely to grow in the future. Whether we may look forward to a united Protestant church comparable in its corporateness to the Roman Catholic church it is impossible as yet to conjecture.

Meantime, two considerations of great importance have contributed to the furtherance of the movement toward co-operation. One is the realignment of the constituencies of the churches according to new viewpoints, new sets of values, and new causes that cut directly across the traditional lines of demarcation between denominations. As a result there are greater distances between "fundamentalists" and "modernists" in most of the larger denominations than there are between the denominations themselves. In the presence of these more recent alignments the traditional denominational lines have, at least for their individual members, though perhaps not for the denominations themselves, become broken and blurred, and tend to disappear.

The other consideration is the emergence of a new theory of co-operation. This new philosophy of co-operation rests upon the idea that differences in experience, in thought, and in methods of work are assets of incalculable value rather than liabilities. These differences raise issues which supply the known conditions of reflective thought. They stimulate the suggestion of alternate courses of action. They greatly widen the range of the possibilities of any situation. They make for a greater degree of flexibility, for the supplementing of an otherwise limited fund of experience, and for inventiveness. Instead of avoiding differences, therefore, they are deliberately sought out and utilized as resources for an enriched and more productive fellowship.

The social outlook of the church.—A notable development within the Protestant churches in recent years has been their social outlook and a growing sense of responsibility for participating in the processes of social reconstruction. The view of religion which dominated the Protestant churches until the latter part of the nineteenth century was all but exclusively individualistic, other-worldly, and pietistic. At the same time, by virtue of its origin it became a factor in political life. The salvation which it proclaimed was from an evil world marked for early destruction to a future life whose amplitude of possibilities could be realized only after death. Its discipline was addressed to the inner life. But under the leadership of such social prophets as Walter Rauschenbusch the social implications of the teachings of the eighth-century prophets and of Jesus were rediscovered. In very recent years there has been a pronounced reaction from the gospel of the inner life to the social gospel. The relation of these two viewpoints constitutes a principal issue of contemporary Christianity.

Contributory to this reaction from the gospel of the inner life have been the rise of the social sciences, the progressive secularization of Western culture, and the rise of an indigenous philosophy of empiricism and experimentalism which finds the *locus* of reality in the present and evolving interaction of man with his world. The social sciences, finding that the self is to a large extent a social product, have demonstrated how impracticable is any program for the development of wholesome persons that neglects the social environment within which alone personality can normally develop. Even society as an association of persons, as distinguished from its structural aspects, shares with personality the dignity and importance of being an end in itself.

Nor can there be any doubt that the progressive secularization of American life has contributed to the social outlook of Christianity. Christianity itself has to a considerable degree undergone secularization. Viewed with alarm by those who hold to a supernatural and authoritative view of religion, this process has been hailed by liberal groups as bringing religion into a closer articulation with wider ranges of man's realistic and normal experience. By migrating from the cloister into the open spaces of man's natural and normal experience, religion finds itself more concerned with the practical issues of social living—research, industry, commerce, politics, letters, and art. This closer articulation of religion with the "secular" concerns of life has opened fruitful ways for it to become effective in spiritualizing these areas of experience. In order to function in the light of this secular drift, the chief problem of the church is to preserve such a degree of objectivity toward the surrounding culture that it will not lose its radical functions of criticism and reconstruction. It is the problem of preserving a proper balance between participation and detachment—a balance of great delicacy and one difficult to maintain.

There can be little doubt that the present reaction from the individual to the social gospel, like all reactions, presents an extreme view that to a considerable extent neglects the individual ends of religion. As a reaction it has already, together with other factors, contributed to a counterreaction in the supernaturalism of Karl Barth, with whom all initiative derives from a transcendent God conceived as the "totally other." Man is relieved of all responsibility for the practical course of social events, or such changes as man is able to effect are limited to the "natural" order in isolation from the "supernatural." It would appear that what is now needed is a new synthesis of the individual and the social gospel in a larger end and procedure in which the Christianization of the individual and of society takes place at the points where Christians interact creatively, and therefore reconstructively, with society. The salvation of the individual and of society are only different aspects of a total, undifferentiated process of interaction.

In its social outlook the church is definitely developing a will to be effective in social reconstruction, but as yet it does not possess the techniques of social reconstruction. With the best of purposes, its efforts have, on the whole, been more or less sterile of decisive results. Effectiveness in social reconstruction depends quite as much upon technical competency as it does upon intent. This technical knowledge and skill religious reformers do not for the most part as yet possess. As a consequence, they exhibit a genuinely prophetic purpose, but are amateurs in execution. The church faces the necessity of mastering through an analysis of the action of social forces and by patient experimentation the procedure of bringing critical and reconstructive influences to bear upon the relations and functions of social living at the points where Christians are involved in them.

The church's relation to other social institutions.—It is in connection with its social outlook that the church of the present encounters in quite new forms the problem of its relation to other social institutions. If the church is conceived as a supernatural institution with a predetermined program of action and as endowed with a divine prerogative, the problem is set in one way. But if the church, in keeping with the trends described in this book, is conceived of as a social institution functioning within a changing culture, the problem is set in a very different way. The church is one among many social institutions. Attention has been called in preceding chapters to the fact that the status and function of all these institutions are constantly undergoing modification. As was earlier pointed out, such fundamental institutions as the family, the church, and the local community are rapidly giving off functions at the present time while the state and industry are rapidly taking them on. This shift of functions, which is a matter of descriptive fact, raises sharply the problem of the relation of the church to these other institutions, especially to the state to which it is giving off its former functions in increasing measure.

This problem of the relation of the church to the state in American society is set in rather bold relief by the rise of the totalitarian state in other parts of the world, notably in Germany and Russia. While the reverberations of this conflict are still remote in American society, there are grounds for the surmise that, viewed on a world-scale, this may become one of the basic issues of Western culture.

At any rate, the problem is greatly accentuated by the entrance of the church into the field of social action. Under the conviction that the church should assume responsibility for social reconstruction, two points of view have developed within the church as to a basic philosophy and procedure regarding social action. On the one hand, there are those who, believing that the functions of the church and state should be kept separate, hold to the view that the church can best serve the ends of social reconstruction by maintaining its independence as a free critic of the ends and processes of all phases of our associated life, including politics. Those who hold this view believe that the church will be more effective by locating and defining issues where human values are involved, by helping Christians to become intelligent about these issues, and by creating attitudes and motives on the part of Christians to assume their functions as citizens in terms of Christian ideals and purposes. In this way Christianity becomes an impregnating influence in modifying the behavior of citizens as such functioning through the regularly constituted channels of political action. This is something which goes much farther than "converting" individuals or instilling an individualistic morality. It includes the orientation of Christian citizens in relation to their social and economic environments. On the other hand, there are those who hold that the church can become an effective agency of social reconstruction only through the organization of blocs of political power. This procedure would, of course, throw the church directly into the field of political action and therefore into conflict with the state. It is the conviction of the authors of this book that the first of these alternatives is the socially sounder and at the same time the more effective procedure.

A new emphasis upon work with individuals.—Simultaneously with the new emphasis upon social reconstruction has arisen a new emphasis upon work with individuals. The new emphasis, however, is very different from that of the former individualistic concept of salvation. It is based upon the findings of the supporting sciences in regard to what is known concerning the nature of personality and the processes by which it is developed. It proceeds from the point of view of the contribution which religion has to make to the adjustments which self-realizing persons are called upon to effect in relation to an extremely complex and difficult world. Satisfactory adjustments to such a complex world as modern life presents are difficult in any case. They are rendered much more difficult by the fact that at many points in the present social order human interests and needs are ruthlessly violated. While, therefore, the work of social reconstruction is going on, it is necessary that the church should give much more attention to helping individuals face their problems in the various areas of personal and social experience in such ways as to achieve through their solution the highest type of Christian personality. In this undertaking the church will use not only the special resources of the sustained and sustaining religious fellowship but all other resources available in such fields as that of mental hygiene.

A new attitude toward other religions.—One of the pronounced trends that appears in the foregoing chapters, and one which is closely related to the changing conception of religion and the church, is a changed attitude of the Protestant churches toward other religions. As long as a supernatural and authoritative view of religion prevailed, it was inevitable that the church should feel that it was in possession of divinely revealed truth. This drew a sharp line of "true" and "false" between Christianity and the other religions of the world. But with the growth of a functional view of religion it has become clear that a people's religion is a phase of their total culture, varying from group to group as the cultures of the groups vary, and changing from time to time within the same group as its culture develops. The line of division between the true and the false tends to disappear and to be replaced by a value judgment as to the greater or less contribution a religion has to make to the spiritual adjustment of a people to life. The perception that Christianity has developed historically within the medium of Western culture has led the church to discover that much that the missionary took to non-Christian peoples really amounted to the transplantation of certain aspects of Western culture.

This insight is leading the church to a new philosophy and method of missions. In its basic aspects missions assumes the form of an interpenetration of cultures. It is also leading to the conviction that if the values that lie at the heart of Christianity are to be vital they must become indigenous in the life of non-Christian peoples. The ends of the missionary enterprise will be brought about as the Founder of Christianity specifically suggested and so definitely embodied in his own method, not through the destruction or displacement of the religious life that is already under way, but through the fulfilment of those religious values that are already operative. In this the motive of missions is not destroyed; it is enhanced by the conviction that the church in the West is under obligation to share reciprocally with other peoples the spiritual values that it has found indispensable in the conduct of life.

Toward a more adequate symbolism.—With these developments of viewpoints and attitudes within the life of the Protestant churches, it is evident that there is great need that the church should create a new symbolism that will more adequately give expression to the new values that are taking form in current religious experience. If they are to be vital and effective, religious symbols, like all forms of art, must have their genesis in the experience of a people. They spring directly from the interaction of living human beings with their natural and social environment. With such an origin, symbols not only give expression to the values that are operative in experience, but they re-enter experience to enhance the sense of its meaning and worth.

Most of the symbols which the church is still using to body forth the values of the going experience of its members in imaginative form arose from intellectual concepts of religion and from types of religious behavior that no longer correspond to the realities of the modern world of thought and action. They express many attitudes toward God, the world, and man's own nature which the modern Christian no longer entertains. Such emotional response as they arouse in him is not infrequently at variance with his intellectual life. Modern life has moved away from many of the issues around which the appreciations that the traditional symbolism expressed grew up. The modern church has made only the slightest beginning in the celebration of life as it goes on in a scientific world, in the city, in the great movements of machines and workers in the industrial process, in the broad sweep of international relationships, through hymns, through prayers, and through ceremonials. In no aspect of its life does the church possess a more fertile field for the creative imagination than in the embodiment of its appreciations in appropriate symbols of architecture, ritual, and art that will set the religious quality of its personal and social experience in the modern scene in a frame of noble, imaginative expression.

THE CHURCH'S OPPORTUNITY AND RESPONSIBILITY

At no time in its history has the church faced a greater opportunity or a greater responsibility than it faces today. Neither have such exacting demands been made upon its resources of intelligence, resourcefulness, and adventurous courage. That the difficulties which it faces are unprecedented is attested by the complexity of life in the modern world and by the planetary scope which most of its problems assume. The possibilities that lie before the church arise out of the state of cultural development in our times when disillusioned men turn with wistful eyes from forms of life that are turning to ashes in our hands to the enduring values upon which the soul of man depends.

For one thing, the analysis of contemporary American culture in *Recent Social Trends* reveals the fact that our culture is not only uneven in its development, but that it is decidedly one-sided. The rapid advances of science and technology have supplied us with a vast amount of technical knowledge and an almost unbelievable equipment of techniques. Nothing can be clearer than that the superabundance of means at our disposal has for some time obscured the ends of living. In becoming technically efficient it may be said that we are in danger of defeating the life-process by losing the sense of convincing ends and of direction as determined by ends. Techniques are always relevant to the ends which they serve. Because life in the modern world has lost its hold upon the ends of living, it is losing its sense of reality and worth. A mood of futility and pessimism has overtaken modern man. The deeper yearnings for the abundant life, which cannot too long be denied, are at the present moment in the phase of frustration. This mood is the precursor of the affirmation of life that will seek to rediscover the ends of living and place them above techniques. Already there are signs that we have entered upon the early stages of a reaction from a culture that went out into the wilderness to hail Science as the Messiah of the West.

Within these larger outlines of contemporary culture, certain phases stand out that are of great significance for the church as it faces the future. One of these is the fact that science and technology have given us a mechanistic concept of the universe. It presents us with a concatenation of antecedents and consequents moving within a closed system. The now outmoded concept of cause and effect has been replaced by the little less ruthless statistical behavior of the natural world. This mechanistic view of the physical world has in more recent years been applied to man himself. According to this extreme behavioristic view, human behavior is a linkage of mechanical reflexes that render thought merely a concomitant of physiological reactions and purpose nothing more than an illusion. The machine which arose as a tool to serve man's needs has, for the time at least, grown to such proportions as to overtower the human spirit and to impose itself upon man's metaphysical thought. But values, which are the most priceless winnings of man from his experience of his world, find no home in an impersonal and purely mechanistic universe. But when values languish and die, life loses for man its meaning and worth.

A second phase of contemporary culture that springs from this same cultural drift is the rise of a materialistic view of life. The laboratory and the technological arts have focused attention upon things. The formulas of science have given man power over the processes of nature. The technological arts have made man aware of the vast stores of natural resources and have enabled him to exploit them. The techniques of production have increased wealth beyond the most utopian dreams of a preindustrial era. Enamored of the immediate and superficial satisfactions of material goods, modern man has come to think that his life consists in the abundance of the things which he possesses. But our techniques of production have outrun our techniques of distribution. America is now in the sixth year of a most intense and widespread economic depression which has brought frustration, black despair, and personal disintegration to millions of Americans who have the will to work without the opportunity. Surfeited by material goods, we are beginning to wonder whether in gaining so much of the world we have not come dangerously near losing our souls.

The third phase grows directly out of the second. The virus of acquisitiveness has entered our veins. The major operations of society are under the domination of the profit motive. This is but the most recent and acute form of a malady that is very old. Society has not yet found a way to integrate essential material goods and human values. So long as the profit motive is ascendant in an acquisitive society, human values will be ruthlessly violated. Unquestionably the most fundamental and difficult problem which man in his associated life faces is the problem of humanizing the processes of production and distribution in such a way that the production and possession of material wealth will further rather than defeat the more abundant life for all. This was the problem to which the eighth-century prophets addressed themselves with trenchant criticism. It was to this problem that Jesus, following in the line of the prophets, addressed much of his teaching.

It is clear that these trends in contemporary culture present the main issues that society must face in the period that is immediately before us if civilization is to regain some semblance of balance and consistency, and if it is to afford satisfaction to the whole range of man's needs. Unless civilization can again bring itself into a closer correspondence with the basic needs of human nature, it carries within itself the seeds of its own destruction.

To these considerations the church needs to add still another as it faces its future. The life of modern man has become atomistic. There are many reasons for this falling to pieces of the modern man's world about him. They are in part intellectual. They are in part social. They are in part technological. Even though science has given us a unified conception of the universe, its method of analysis has, on the whole, tended to the dismemberment of the world into fragments. When the units of man's associated life were smaller and more homogeneous, it was possible for him to have a vivid sense of the unity and wholeness of society. But modern life is no longer simple. Society is highly differentiated into geographical and interest groups. The individual person is, under the conditions of modern social organization, a member of many highly differentiated groups in which he assumes different rôles. At the same time that these groups have become differentiated, many of them have become world-wide in their scope, so that the units of association have outrun our social habits. So complex has modern social life become that it is all but impossible for even the most competent persons to visualize their world as a unit and in its comprehensiveness. To these factors of personal and social disintegration must be added the extreme degree of specialization in modern culture. Knowledge has increased so greatly that it is now necessary for scholars and researchers to specialize in very narrow fields. In the field of practical action technological processes have become so highly specialized that the operator is concerned for the most part with one very specific activity. Under the impact of these intellectual, social, and technological factors, the world of modern man has tended to fall in pieces about him. In view of the fact that personal integration can effectively take place only in an integrated world, the atomism of current culture presents a problem of the most far-reaching implications.

These matters, which constitute the basic defects of current culture in the light of human needs, are the very things with which religion is most concerned. Religion operates in the realm of ends. It is concerned with the fundamental and enduring values by which men live. It, together with philosophy and art, is one of the means which culture has developed out of the long and varied experience of the race for integrating man's experience at the point where he interacts with his objective world.

One of the greatest responsibilities of the church in its affirmation of human values and in its attempt to co-operate with other agencies in building a livable universe is not to allow itself to be drawn into a reaction from the results and the method of science, such as is at the present moment to be seen in several movements, including the Barthian movement, in which an empirical and experimental approach to the facts of life is repudiated. What is needed is not a reaction from science and technology, but the integration of both science and technology into a larger synthesis in which technical knowledge and processes shall be utilized for the achievement of human ends. We need not less, but more, science. Religion has an incomparable contribution to make to the culture of our time if it can help it to recover and reinstate the ends of the abundant life and to show the functional relation of the techniques of modern civilization to these ends.

There are those who believe that evidence is not wanting that we are at the beginning of a new period of synthesis in culture, comparable to those great historic periods in which life was intellectually seen and emotionally felt to constitute an essential unity. And there are those who believe that the new era into which we are moving will be essentially religious. This is the future which the church as a specialized institution for interpreting religion faces. Herein lies its creative task, not only in helping human beings to realize themselves as individuals, but in helping to build an associated life of persons that will constitute a divine-human society.

INDEX

Academies, 112, 119

Adaptations of churches in urban communities, 33–43

Advance, 240

Apartment-house areas, 40–41

Apostles' Creed, 63, 188

Art, 102

Atlantic Monthly, 256

Atomism, 291–92

Automobile, effect of, upon rural churches, 32

Bahaism, 276

Baptism, 88

Baptist World Alliance, 59

Baptist Young People's Union, 66

Barth, Karl, 281

Bible, 54, 80, 92–93, 109, 112, 120, 139, 140, 141, 186, 193, 274

Bible societies, 67

Book of Common Prayer, 84

Books, religious, 257–58

Boston News-Letter, 238

Boston Recorder, 241

Broadcasting, religious, 258–62

Buchmanism, 275

Calendar, 240

Catholic Press Association, 255

Century, 256

Ceremonials, religious: a celebration of life, 82, 83; grow out of social experience, 3, 82–83; and human nature, 86–88; of supernatural-ism, 83–86; and their symbolism, 80–105

Chalcedonian Creed, 188

Change: the basis of reconstruction, 12; and continuity, 1, 5–7; differential, 6; makes possible creativity, 6–7; offers opportunity for improvement, 6–7; present characterized by swift, 13–14

Child guidance, 150

Christendom, 255

Christian Advocate, 240, 241

Christian Advocate and Journal and Zions Herald, 240

Christian Century, 254, 255

Christian Community, 254

Christian Disciple, 241

Christian Endeavor, 65–66

Christian Examiner, 241

Christian Herald, 247, 254

Christian History, 238–39

Christian Intelligencer, 241

Christian Science, 275

Christian Union, 246

Christian Union Quarterly, 254

Christianity: an aspect of Western civilization, 53–65, 185; characterized by change, 5; a complex process, 5–6; conditioned by its past, 4–7; contemporary aspects of, 2–4; a continuing community, 1, 2, 3, 5, 8, 17; creative, 160, 174; creative function of, 15–17; a growing-point of a historic process, 4–17; a historic movement,

3-4; historical at one time contemporary, 9-10; an impregnating social influence, 203-5, 284; institutional growth of, 215-16; more extensive than the church, 186; needs to redefine functions, 16; new types arising, 175-76; a phase of culture, 171-74, 199; as process, 1; a quality of life, 2; social aspects of, 185-86, 201; a social movement, 1-5

Church: boards, 103; building, 89, 90; the community, 44-45; defined, 185, 272; as educator, 107-33; expansion of, into non-Christian cultures, 160-61; facing the future, 264-94; a fellowship, 142-43, 272; as a group, 19-21; an instrument of incoming grace, 199; as a missionary agency, 160-84; needs to acquire attitude and technique of improvement, 267-69; needs to redefine functions, 16-17, 264-65; one group among many, 197; opportunities and resources of, for work with individuals, 141-46; opportunity and responsibility of, 288-94; program of, 21-24; Protestant and Catholic conceptions of, 64; relations of, to community, 273-74; relations of, to other social institutions, 283-84; and the secular press, 255-57; a selective group in the community, 26-27; significant trends in, 269-88; social influence within a, 197-203; as a social institution, 272-74; and the social order, 185-209; and state, 57, 110, 283; task of meeting human needs, 23-24, 27; work with individuals, 134-59

Church college, the, 70, 119-27; administration of, 120; changes affecting, 121-23; earliest foundations in America, 119; financial support of, 120-21; function of, confused, 123; method of founding, 119-20; motives in founding, 120; period of rapid founding, 119; possible developments of, 123-25; and standardizing agencies, 123

Church federations, 68-69

Church foundations at state universities, 125-27

Church Management, 254

Church organ, the, 90, 94-95

Church Peace Union, 67-68

Churches: adaptations to communities, 27-44; in apartment-house areas, 40-41; capitalist and non-wage-earning classes, composed of, 194-95, 275 community, 37, 44-45, 68, 254; contrasting types of: rural, 31-33, and urban, 28-29; co-operation of, 45-47, 53-79; distribution of, 20-23; downtown, program of, 36; dying, 36; emphasize fellowship, 20; federating of, 36, 60, 68; in foreign lands, 172; function of, 200-201; group action, subject to laws of, 197; indigenous, 177; inner-city, 36-37; institutionalizing of, 36; and local culture, 24-27; minority groups in, 264; modification, undergoing, 264; moving of, 36; non-conformist, 57-58; organization varies with denominations and size, 21-23; and present social trends, 194-207; Protestant and Catholic differ in emphasis, 20-21; reactions of, to urban communities, major, 36-44; realignment of, 278-79; relation of, to other social groups,

203–5; relation of, to social processes, 191–94; response of, to social forces, degree of, 197; in rooming-house areas, 39–40; and the state, 57–58; in suburban areas, 41–42

Churchman, 240, 253

Churchman's Monthly, 240

Cities: concentric zones in, 33; cultural islands in, 34–44; local community in, 36; sectors in, 34

College: earliest founded by church, 119; junior, 112; period of development, 119

Colonies, American, 56–57

Columbia University, 119

Communication: expansion of, 172; oral, 236; through printing, 236–37

Communion service, 88

Community: Christianity a continuing, 1, 2, 5–7, 8, 11; churches, 37, 44–45; 68; 254; councils, 46–47; extended in space, 2; extended in time, 3; nature of, 26; needs, 47–50: education, 49–50; for cultivation of unity, 47; for definition of public issues, 47–48; family disorganization, 48; juvenile delinquency, 48–49; personal disorganization, 48; political corruption, 49; race and clan conflict, 49; recreation, 49; in urban areas, 34–44

Community Churchman, 254

Concepts: arise out of experience, 8–9, 11, 17, 271; enduring quality of, 8–9; instruments for expressing meaning, 2; as survivals, 8–9

Confession: effectiveness of Catholic, 136; private, 135–36, 138;

Protestant attitude toward, 136–38; public, 135, 138

Congregational and Christian Council for Social Action, 204–5

Congregationalist, 240, 241

Connecticut Churchman, 240

Connecticut Missionary Magazine, 239

Consumers' and producers' co-operatives, 31–32

Contemporary Christianity: can be understood only in the light of history, 4–5; conditioned by the past, 4–7; a differential process, 8–9; the growing-point of historical process, 1–18; interaction with objective world, result of, 5; necessary to understanding of historical, 9; practical, 9; reconstruction, 11–13; as the source of historical Christianity, 9; the source of ideas, techniques, and institutions, 11; unites change and continuity, 5

Continuity: and change, 1, 5–7; without change becomes static, 6–7

Co-operation: a conservation of religious heritage, 62; dangers of, 73; forced by common task, 77; growing spirit of, 61; of individuals, 65–68; through joint action, 63; among local churches, 68–69; of mission boards, 71–74; on mission fields, 72–73; need of, 60; new theory of, 279–80; through organic union, 63–64; paralleled by denominational loyalty, 61–62; in religious education, 69–71; rests upon common values, 62, 277; rests upon different conceptions of church, 64; Roman Catholic and Protestant views of, 62–63; types of proposal for 62–65; with welfare agencies, 99, 100

Council of Church Boards of Education, 70

Council of Women for Home Missions, 71, 72

Cults, rise of, 275–76

Culture: atomistic, 291–92; complex, 14 cross-fertilization of, 169–71; exchange of, 180; interpenetration of, 171–74, 180–81; materialistic, 290; mechanistic, 289–90; nature of, 170–71; rate of change in differential, 14–15; synthesis in, 293–94; trends in modern, 288–91; uneven development of, 288–91

Democracy: influence of, 190–94; in religion, 221

Denominations: allocation of responsibility, 72; a contribution of democracy, 192–93; giving way to co-operation, 61; grounds for, have disappeared, 60–61, 277; increase of, 58–59; outgrowth of American social conditions, 58–60; outgrowth of experienced needs, 60; and press, 237–38; social origins of, 54–59; waning interest in, 251

Divided personalities, 152–53

Domestic Manners of the Americans, 242

Downtown churches, 36–37

Drama and pageants, 101

Eastern Orthodox church, 54, 63, 136

Ecumenical Methodist Conference, 59

Education, public, 108, 109–13, 114, 116, 129–30

Educational work of the church, 107–33: capacity of church to adapt to social change, 130–31; changes in response to social change, 108, 129, 131, in colleges, 119–25; forms of, 108; in local church and community, 109–19; new interest in, 112–15; in state universities, 125–27; in theological seminary, 127–28

English religious life, 56

Epworth League, 66

Evangelical Alliance, 67, 74

Experience: religious, 80–83; the source of religious concepts, techniques, and institutions, 11–12

Facing the future, 264–94

Federal Council of the Churches of Christ in America, 71, 74–77; efficiency of, 76, 77; and public opinion, 77; and radio program, 205, 260; and social creeds, 201–3; its social creed, 77; organization of, 74, 75; purpose of, 74, 75

Federated churches, 68

Feudalism as an ecclesiastical pattern, 189

Finance, church, 103–4

Foreign-language groups, 33

Foreign missions, 72, 160, 163, 177

Foreign Missions Conference of North America, 72, 73, 167

Frontier: American, 58, 242–45; influence of, upon denominational development, 58; influence of, upon religious press, 242–45

God, 84, 86, 87, 139, 157, 161, 166, 186, 199, 270, 271, 272, 287

Harper, William Rainey, 114
Harper's, 256
Harvard University, 119, 124
Herald of Gospel Liberty, 239–40
Historical Christianity: continuous with contemporary, 4; necessary to understanding of contemporary, 4–5; subject to change through interaction with objective world, 5–6
History, function of, 9–11
Holy Rollers, 276
Holy Roman Empire, 55, 206
Home missions, 164–65
Home Missions Council, 71
Human nature: better understanding of, 141; and ceremonials, 86–88
Hymns, 93, 94

Immortality, 98, 99
Improvement: attitude of self-appraisal for, 267–68; gradual rather than revolutionary, 268–69; through specific items, 268–69; technique of, 267–68
Independent, 246
Individual co-operation, 65–66
Institute of Social and Religious Research, 70
Institutions, as social structures, 2
International: Congregational Council, 59; Council of Religious Education: origin and work of, 70, 115–16; Graded Lessons, 114; Journal of Religious Education, 248–49; Missionary Council, 73,

164, 167; Sunday School Association, 69, 115; Uniform Lessons, 114

Jerusalem Conference, 73
Jesus, 64, 75, 93, 107, 186, 190, 215, 266
Jews, 53, 54, 71, 186, 187, 206
Johns Hopkins University, 122
Journal of Religion, 254
Journalism, religious: beginning of, 237–42; function of, 242–45; in its prime, 245–50; recent tendencies in, 250–55
Judaism, 187

Kentucke Gazette, 242

Lag, cultural, 12–13, 26
Lambeth Conference, 59
Larger parish movement, 31
Lausanne Conference on Faith and Order, 62–63
Laymen's Inquiry, 165, 181–82
Living Church, 253
Local churches: adaptations of, 27–44; in apartment-house areas, 40–41; community, 44–45; and community agencies, 45–46; co-operation of, with other churches, 46–47; downtown, 36; in industrial suburbs, 42; inner-city, 36–37; and local culture, 24; location of, 20; nature of, 19–20; in nonindustrial suburbs, 41–42; organization of, 21–22; primary work of, 23–24; program of, 21; in relation to denomination, 23; in rural communities, 31–33; something apart from local community, 26–27; types of, 42–44; in urban communities, 33–43

London Times, 240
Lutheran World Conference, 60

Marital relations, 151
Massachusetts Missionary Magazine, 239
Materialism, 290
Mechanism, 289–90
Mental hygiene, 155–56
Mercure de France, 238
Methodist Quaterly, 254
Minority groups, sensitivity of, 264–65
Mission boards, co-operation of, 71–74
Missions: appraisal of, 181–83; changing view regarding, 177–78; or cross-fertilization of cultures, 169–71, 180, 286; effect of, upon American churches, 178–79; effect of, upon non-Christian religions, 179–80; growing-points in Christianity, 182; home and foreign, 163–64; motive of, 161–64; objectives of, 164–65; organization and methods, of, 165–69; phase of church's work, 160–84; problems of, 168–69; process underlying, 169–74; trends in, 174–180
Mohammedans, 54
Motives for missions: needy non-Christians, 162–63; solidarity of the race, 163; the will of God, 161–62
Mystery religions, 187

National Federation of Churches and Christian Workers, 74
Nationalism: in Europe, 55; influence of, upon pattern of Christianity, 189–90

Nazarenes, 276
New Outlook, 254
New Thought, 275
New York Evangelist, 241
Newspapers: effect of, upon rural churches, 33; religious, 236–63; secular, and the church, 255–57
Nicene Creed, 54, 62, 63, 188
Non-conformist churches in America, 57–58
Non-ecclesiastical institutions, 196, 275
Non-evangelical churches, 74
Non-liturgical activities, symbolism in, 99–105
Normal schools, 112, 121

Official boards, 103
Open and Institutional Church League, 74
Outlook, 247
Oxford Gazette, 238

Panopist, 240
Parental education, 152
Parish: larger, 31; meaning of, 19; social needs of, 214; unified, 274–75
Parochial schools, 109, 111
Participation in the divine, 104–5
Past, the: appears more definite than really was, 9–10; conditions the present, 3–7; lives in the present, 8–9; a resource, 7
Pastor: availability of, 145–46; and the care of souls, 134–59
Patterns of Christianity: democracy, 190–91; feudalism, 189; nationalism, 189–90; Roman imperialism, 188–89

Paul, 93, 187

Peace movements, 67–68, 167

Penance, 136, 137

Periodicals: function and influence of, 242–45; listed, 238–55; official and unofficial, 249–50; undenominational, 253–55

Personality: the end of education, 117; reverence for, 156

Population shifts, effects upon churches, 32

Practical, the: intellectual content of, 10; as related to historical, 9

Prayer, 95, 96

Preacher: and his congregation, 222–25; in the early church, 216–17; functions of, new, 213–14; his heritage, 215–22; in the medieval ages, 220–21; a minister of an institution, 215; in modern democracy, 221–22; in the nationalistic period, 220–21; outlook for, 232–33; in the Roman Empire, 217–19; and his sermon, 225–32; the tasks of, 210–35: shaped by changing situations, 220–22; variety of tasks, 210–12

Preaching, present status of, 212–16

Presbyterian, 241

Present: conditioned by past, 4–7; the *locus* of reality, 280; opens up possibilities, 7; past lives in, 8–9; result of interplay of antecedent and consequent, 4–5

Print and propaganda, 236–63

Problems of missionary procedures, 168–69

Profit motive, 290–91

Progress: not inherent in process, 6, 183; through minority groups, 264–65

Propaganda: and priest, 236–63; through printing, 236–37; through spoken word, 236

Protestantism: and capitalism, 194, 275; common task of, 77; contrasted with Catholicism, 62, 63, 64, 101, 102; institutionalized, 265–67; needs to re-establish fresh contact with reality, 266–67; and religious liberty, 190

Public school: elementary, 112; relation of religious education to, 108, 109–13, 114, 116, 129–30; and religious education, 129–30; state and city systems, 112; and total population, 112

Radio: effects of, upon churches, 32; Federal Commission on, 262; a medium of church influence, 205; religious broadcasting over, 258–62

Recent Social Trends, 14, 288

Reconstruction: caused by social change, 12; in contemporary Christianity, 11–13; creative function of, 15–17; lags behind change, 12–13

Red Cross, 167

Reform movements, 67

Reformation, the, 55–56, 190, 220, 266

Reformed Church Messenger, 241

Religion: arises and functions within man's practical experience, 271; and current culture, 293–94; a new conception of, 270–72; nature of, 80–83; a phase of culture, 171–74; a quality of experience, 271; scientific study of, 271; a social fact, 199

Religion in Life, 254

Religious assemblies, symbolism in, 88–89

Religious education: aims of, 117; co-operation in, 69–71; an integral part of the parish, 118; a laboratory of Christian living, 117–18; in the local church and community, 100–101, 109–19; the method of Jesus, 107; new interest in, 112–15; and public education, 114, 129–30; reconstruction of, 116–17

Religious Education Association, 114

Religious experience, need of a restatement of, 80–83

Religious Intelligencer, 241

Religious journalism: beginnings of, 237–42; passing of, 250–53; in its prime, 245–50; recent tendencies, 250–57

Religious liberty: and the press, 237–38; a product of ecclesiastical variety, 57–58; and Protestantism, 190

Religious Remembrances, 241

Rituals, means for establishing and making effective relations to objective world, 2

Rôle assumed by persons, 50

Roman Catholic church, 12, 55, 56, 61, 64, 67, 101, 136, 185, 188, 192, 194, 255, 278

Roman Empire, 55, 187, 188, 217

Roman imperialism as a pattern for Christianity, 188–89

Rooming-house areas, 39–40

Rural churches, 31–33

Russellism, 275

Sacraments, 199

Schools: earliest in America, 109; secularization of, 109–10

Scribner's, 256

Sectarianism, the outgrowth of cultural conditions, 53–60

Secular press, 255–58

Secularization: of culture, 280–81; of schools, 108, 109–10

Sermon: effective presentation of, 230–32; intellectual content needed in, 226–29; and intellectual reserves, 228–29; loss of prestige, 213–15; a part of church assemblies, 91–92; in relation to ritual, 213

Social action, 283–84

Social Creed of the Churches, 77, 201–3

Social gospel, 279–82

Social order: and the church, 184–209; furnishes patterns for organization and doctrines of church, 186–91; and individual Christians, 208

Social process, relation of churches to, 191–94

Social reconstruction: function of, 281–82; technique of, 282; and work with individuals, 285

Spiritual life, 82

Spiritualism, 275

State: and church, 57, 110, 200, 205–7, 283; totalitarian, 192, 283

State church, 57

State universities, 112, 121, 125–27

Stockholm Conference, 63

Student Volunteer Movement, 66

Suburban areas, 41–42

Sunday school, the, 69, 110–11; education in, 111–12; followed sectarian organization of churches, 112; origin of, 110

Sunday School Council of Evangelical Denomination, 69, 115

Sunday School Times, 248

Supernaturalism, 3; and attitude of, toward other religions, 285–86; ceremonials of, 83–86; and the church, 185; inherited, 270; in missionary philosophy, 177; and naturalism, 270–72, 281; and origin of church, 272; and political change, 198; and worship, 200

Symbols: a celebration of life, 287; grow up within experience, 3, 287; a means of participating in the divine, 104–5; need for new, 80–83, 286–89; in non-liturgical activities, 99–105; and recreation, 102–3; in religious assemblies, 88–99; and religious ceremonies, 80–105; as techniques, 2; in transition to new forms of experience, 80

Theological seminary, the, 70, 127–28

Theology, current reconstruction of, 11–13

Theosophy, 275

Time, illusory effects of, 9–10

Trends in contemporary Protestantism, 269–87; toward greater corporateness, 277–79; toward more adequate symbolism, 286–88; toward new attitudes toward other religions, 285–86; toward a new conception of religion, 270–72; toward regarding church as social institution, 272–74; toward relation with other social institutions, 282–84; toward social outlook, 279–82; toward a wider range of interests, 275–77; toward work with individuals, 284–85

Trends: in missions, 174–81; in modern culture, 288–91; in recent religious journalism, 250–57; relation of church to, 194–207; in religious education, 112–17

Uniform Lesson series, 69

Union, efforts toward, 59–62; and the disciples, 59; organic, 63–64; rests upon spirit of love, 64–65

Union ministers' meetings, 68

United Church of Canada, 204, 278

Unity, 275

Unity, 253

University of Chicago, 122

Urban churches, 33–44

Urban-rural conflict, 195

War and the church, 207

Watchman, 241

Week-day and vacation religious education, 113

Wesleyan Journal, 240

Work with individuals, the church's, 134–59: an ancient function, 134; child guidance, 150; the confessional, 135–38; counsel on marital relations, 151; divided personalities, 152–53; education of youth, 150–51; historical development of, 134–41; and mental hygiene, 155–56; in the Middle Ages, 135–36; ministering to the afflicted, 154; in the New Testament, 134–35; newer approaches to, 149–55; opportunities and resources for,

141–46; religious perplexities, 153; theological assumptions of, 138–41; trend toward, 284–85; types of, 146–49

World Alliance for International Friendship, 68

World Alliance of the Reform Churches, 59

World Missionary Conference, 73

World Sunday School Association, 69–70, 113

World Tomorrow, 254

World War, 60

Yale University, 119, 124

Young Men's Christian Association, 65–66, 120, 126

Young Women's Christian Association, 65–66, 120, 126

Youth movements, 66–67

Zion's Herald, 240, 241